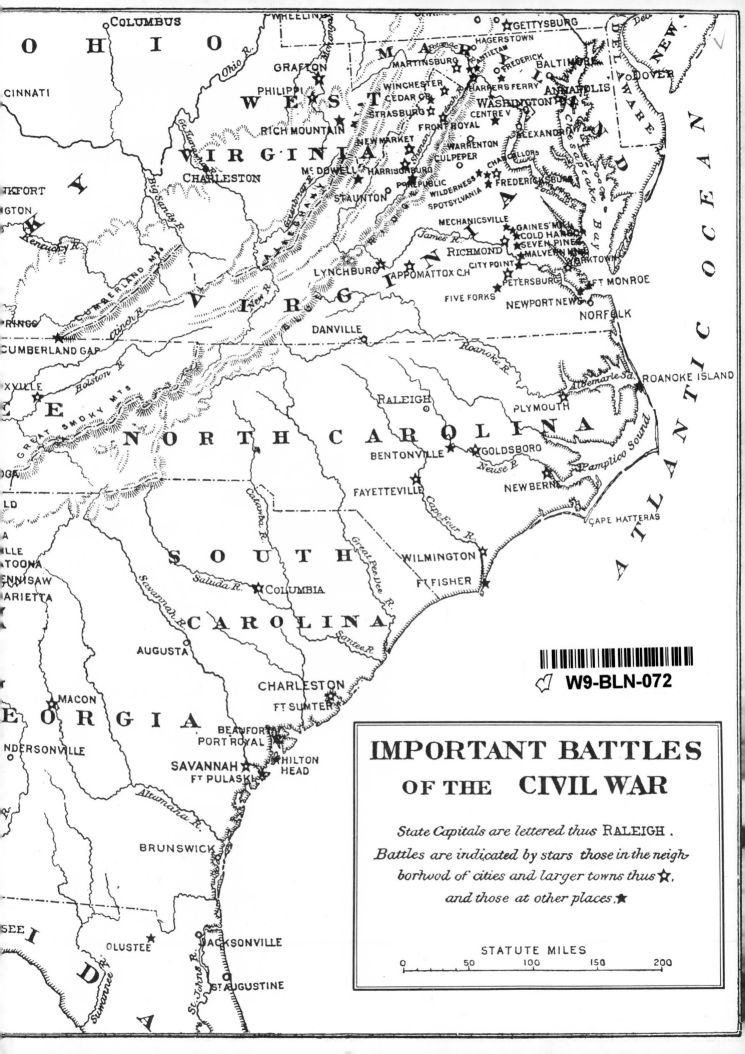

W9-BLN-072

IMPORTANT BATTLES
OF THE CIVIL WAR

State Capitals are lettered thus RALEIGH.

Battles are indicated by stars those in the neighborhood of cities and larger towns thus ☆,
and those at other places ★.

STATUTE MILES

0   50   100   150   200

BATTLE CHRONICLES OF THE CIVIL WAR 1864

JAMES M. McPHERSON, Editor

Princeton University

RICHARD GOTTLIEB, Managing Editor

Grey Castle Press

MACMILLAN PUBLISHING COMPANY
New York

COLLIER MACMILLAN PUBLISHERS
London

Text © 1989. *Civil War Times Illustrated*, a division of Cowles Magazines, Inc., Box 8200, Harrisburg, PA 17105.

Introduction, Transitions, Index and Format © 1989. Grey Castle Press, Inc., Lakeville, CT 06039.

Published by Macmillan Publishing Company
866 Third Avenue, New York, NY 10022

ILLUSTRATION CREDITS—Some sources are abbreviated as follows: Battles and Leaders, B&L (*Battles and Leaders of the Civil War*); CWTI Collection (*Civil War Times Illustrated* Collection); FL (*Frank Leslie's Illustrated Newspaper*); HW (*Harper's Weekly*); KA (Kean Archives); LC (Library of Congress); NA (National Archives); SCW (*The Soldier in Our Civil War*). Illustrations without credits are part of the *Civil War Times Illustrated* Collection.

Library of Congress Cataloging-in-Publication Data

Battle Chronicles of the Civil War.

    Includes bibliographies and indexes.
    Contents: 1. 1861—2.1862—3. 1863— [etc.]
    1. United States—History—Civil War, 1861–1865—
Campaigns.   I. McPherson, James M.
E470.B29   1989   973.7'3   89-8316
ISBN 0-02-920661-8 (set)

Printed in the USA

Contents

1864—AN OVERVIEW

In the East . . .

The war assumed a more terrible character in 1864. On March 9, General U.S. Grant came east to take command of all Federal armies. Grant's strategy was brutally simple: The North would henceforth wage total war. All Federal forces would plow ahead in an unrelenting drive to apply pressure at all points of the Confederacy. Battle casualties, war weariness, and Federal occupation of large chunks of Southern territory had reduced Confederate arms appreciably. Grant reasoned that the South's depleted armies could not successfully defend every sector. Nor could it recoup losses in the face of seemingly unlimited Northern manpower. A war of attrition, Grant called it; sledgehammer tactics, his critics would charge.

In May, Grant's strategy burst upon Virginia. Three separate offensives began almost simultaneously. Some 6,000 troops under Franz Sigel moved into the Shenandoah Valley; Benjamin F. Butler and 36,000 men in the Army of the James started up the Peninsula from Fort Monroe; and Grant, traveling with the 118,700 Federals in the Army of the Potomac, crossed the Rapidan to interpose himself between Lee's 60,000 Confederates and Richmond.

The main Union drive quickly became entangled in the Wilderness, an area of thick forests and dense undergrowth west of Fredericksburg. On May 5, the hosts of Lee and Grant came to grips in the wooded darkness. Neither cavalry nor artillery could take any part because of the tangled forests. Infantry were left alone to grope blindly after unseen enemies. Organization disintegrated as the two armies attacked and counterattacked. Flames roaring through the underbrush cremated scores of wounded men. For two days the inferno of battle raged.

On May 7, having suffered 17,666 losses, Grant broke off the conflict and sidestepped to the east in an effort to turn Lee's right. The Army of Northern Virginia had suffered 11,400 casualties in The Wilderness, but it won the race to Spotsylvania Court House and was waiting entrenched when Grant's forces arrived. Eleven days (May 10-21) of intermittent but heavy fighting ensued. The climax of this action came in fourteen hours of battle on May 12, when Federals temporarily overran a sector of Lee's lines now known as the "Bloody Angle." The Spotsylvania stalemate cost Lee untold casualties and Grant about 18,000. Especially painful to Lee was the death of the dashing "Jeb" Stuart, mortally wounded on May 11 in a cavalry fight at Yellow Tavern.

Grant continued his southeastward movements. "I propose to fight it out on this line," he vowed, "if it takes all summer." Early in June his army reached Cold Harbor, a strategic crossroads not far from Richmond. But again Lee's men blocked the advance. Grant lost his patience and ordered three corps to make direct frontal attacks on the strong Confederate works. The result was the June 3 battle of Cold Harbor, which many consider a massacre. Federal troops made no fewer than fourteen assaults on Lee's lines. Not one succeeded. In the opening stages of the conflict, over 7,200 Federals fell dead or maimed in a half hour's action. A broiling sun intensified the suffering of the wounded, hundreds of whom lay unattended on the field for more than a day.

Council of war: Ulysses S. Grant and staff at Bethesda Church on May 21, 1864. (Battles and Leaders of the Civil War)

In less than a month, the Army of the Potomac was reeling from 55,000 losses—close to the strength of Lee's army at the outset of the campaign. Yet Grant was unswayed. Knowing that Lee had incurred proportionately higher casualties than the North seemed to Grant to make the sacrifices worthwhile. After Cold Harbor, however, Grant altered his strategy. He secretly began shifting his army across the James on the night of June 12. Columns of men filed across a pontoon bridge more than 2,500 feet long and headed for Petersburg, a vital rail junction twenty-five miles south of Richmond. Seizing Petersburg and its railroads would force Lee to come out of his works and meet the Federal army in open combat.

The Federal transfer caught Lee by surprise and almost outflanked the Confederate army from Richmond. Grant's new movement might easily have succeeded had Butler's Army of the James not fallen victim to its commander's ineptitude. Butler had started westward from Fort Monroe as Grant had thrust into The Wilderness. Yet the slowness of Butler's advance enabled General P. G. T. Beauregard at Petersburg to assemble hastily an "army" of 18,000 soldiers, militia, and shopkeepers. The appearance of this heterogeneous force so unnerved Butler that he withdrew his army to Bermuda Hundred and a thin stretch of land lying between the James and Appomattox Rivers. Beauregard promptly entrenched his men across the narrow opening to that peninsula. Grant observed disgustedly that Butler's force was "as completely shut off from further operations . . . as if it had been in a bottle strongly corked."

Beauregard pulled back at Grant's approach. The Southern general's indomitable defense of Petersburg during four days of attack (June 15-18) by the lead elements of Grant's army saved the city—and probably prolonged the war—while inflicting several thousand casualties on the Federal army. The arrival of Lee and the Army of Northern Virginia convinced Grant to switch to the siege operations that proved so successful at Vicksburg. Federal troops began constructing an elaborate network of trenches and earthworks on the eastern front of Petersburg.

Lee countered desperately by trying to divert Grant's attention to the Shenandoah Valley, where things had not gone well for the Union.

Franz Sigel's advance into that region in May got only as far as New Market. Confederate General John C. Breckinridge put together a hodgepodge force of 4,500, including a contingent of cadets from the Virginia Military Institute, and moved

Fort Sedgwick ("Fort Hell"), a strongpoint in the Union lines surrounding Petersburg, Virginia. (National Archives)

down the Valley to confront Sigel. On the afternoon of May 15, the out-numbered Confederates launched a heavy assault. Southern losses mounted swiftly and forced Breckinridge to call on the VMI cadets in reserve. The 247 youths made a bold charge across the rain-swept field and helped break Sigel's line, precipitating a rout of the Federal army. Sigel lost 831 men. Listed among the 577 Confederates casualties were ten VMI cadets killed and forty-seven wounded.

Grant replaced Sigel with stern David Hunter, who wasted no time in stabbing again at the Valley. On June 6, Hunter struck a skeleton army of Confederates at Piedmont, south of Harrisonburg. Federals overwhelmed the small force, killed its commander, General William E. "Grumble" Jones, and seized 1,000 prisoners. Hunter burned his way to Lexington, then cut eastward across the mountains to Lynchburg.

Lee had just won his last victory—Cold Harbor—when this occurred. He detached General Jubal A. Early and Jackson's old corps to block Hunter. Early's men rushed to Lynchburg and nipped at Hunter's heels as the Federals fled to West Virginia. The Valley was momentarily clear of Federal invaders.

With Lee anxious to break Grant's hold in front of Petersburg, Early then started down the Valley and into Maryland to threaten Washington from the north. The Confederates were so delayed by a battle at Monocacy, Maryland, on July 9 that by the time Early reached the outskirts of the Northern Capital, reinforcements from Grant's army were manning the city's defenses. While Early demonstrated briefly against the works, Lincoln rode to the front and watched part of the action from atop a Federal parapet—thus becoming the only President ever to come under enemy fire. Early soon concluded that the Washington defenses were too strong for his meager forces. His Confederates withdrew to Virginia in disappointment.

Grant now ordered Hunter to move back into the Valley "to eat out Virginia clear and clean as far as they go, so that crows flying over it for the balance of the season will have to carry their provender with them."

Hunter's hesitancy in tangling again with Early caused Grant to replace him with General Philip H. Sheridan. This pint-sized cavalryman promptly mustered 40,000 men and moved directly on Early's 16,000 troops at Winchester. Sheridan struck the Confederates first at Opequon Creek (September 19) and then at Fisher's Hill (September 22). Early lost 5,500 men in the two bitterly fought engagements. The Southerners retreated up the Valley with Sheridan's army—also dented by 5,500 casualties—in slow pursuit.

The Federal army encamped at Cedar Creek, near Strasburg, while Sheridan journeyed to Washington for a military conference. Early received enough reinforcements from Lee to bring his army back to 18,000 men. On October 19 the Confeder-

In the Shenandoah Valley: Union troops chase exhausted Confederates through the town of Strasburg, Virginia, on October 9, 1864. Drawing by Alfred R. Waud. (Library of Congress)

ates delivered a surprise attack at Cedar Creek that sent the major portion of the Federals fleeing in panic from the field. But Sheridan made a now-famous ride from Winchester, rallied his broken columns, and hurled a full-scale counterassault that routed Early's meager forces. Early lost 2,910 men, 25 cannon, all of his ammunition wagons, and most of his baggage and forage wagons.

Sheridan now controlled the Shenandoah. His men completed a systematic devastation of the area; the "breadbasket of the Confederacy" was reduced to crumbs.

At Petersburg, meanwhile, Grant had completely immobilized Lee's dwindling army. Both Lee and Grant realized that if the Confederates left their trenches, Petersburg and Richmond would quickly fall. Lee therefore had no alternative but to maintain his position.

Grant was not idle during this time. He steadily advanced his siege lines to the southwest, a move that threatened the last two railroads leading to Richmond and, at the same time, stretched Lee's already thin defenses ever farther. In addition, Grant made periodic stabs at the Confederate lines in attempts at a breakthrough.

The most famous of these attacks was the July 30 "Battle of the Crater." Coal miners in the 48th Pennsylvania Infantry volunteered to dig a tunnel to a point beneath the Confederate works southeast of Petersburg. A large charge of explosives would be detonated at the end of the shaft. In the ensuing smoke, confusion, and death, heavy Federal columns would drive through the breach and widen the gap in Lee's lines. Grant saw distinct possibilities in the extraordinary proposal and granted approval.

The tunnel, when completed, stretched 511 feet from the Federal lines to beneath a Confederate artillery emplacement. Early on the morning of July 30 about 8,000 pounds of gunpowder exploded and blasted a hole 170 feet long, over 60 feet wide, and 30 feet deep. Federal troops easily occupied the area around the crater, but the important second wave of Federals broke down from incompetent leadership and lack of aggressiveness. Confederates recaptured the sector late in the afternoon after some of the most vicious fighting of the war. The episode, which Grant characterized as a "stupendous failure," cost 4,000 Federal casualties. Confederate losses were about 1,200, including 278 men killed in the blast.

Grant returned to more orthodox siege tactics. With naval vessels running supplies regularly up the James to the main supply base at City Point (now Hopewell), Grant's forces became increasingly stronger. Time was now on the Union side; and as the siege continued month after month, hunger and exposure took a heavy toll of Lee's dwindling army.

Terminus of the Union military railroad at City Point, Virginia. This hamlet at the junction of the James and Appomattox Rivers was only eight miles from Petersburg. (CWTI Collection)

In the West . . .

Observers invariably commented on the "half-wild expression" of his eyes, his "terrible cerebral excitement," his incessant smoking, and complete disregard for food and sleep. Many war correspondents considered him dangerously mad. Most of the Confederacy came to that opinion in 1864, when General William Tecumseh Sherman made his name anathema in the South.

With Grant's promotion to General in Chief, Sherman became supreme commander of the Federal armies in the West. "Cump" Sherman was a man who wasted neither thought nor time. He regarded the Confederacy as an arch enemy that had to be brought to its knees as rapidly as possible. To accomplish this, Sherman devised the first major use of psychological warfare. Whereas Grant's strategy was to hammer away at an opposing army, Sherman thought more in geographical terms. He would strike at enemy cities, fields, and facilities; he would break the Confederacy's will to resist by slashing through the very heart of the South.

By early May, Sherman was poised east of Chattanooga with three armies, totaling about 112,000 veteran soldiers. The ill-equipped Confederate army, now under defensive genius Joseph E. Johnston, numbered approximately 60,000 men. Johnston's position was at Dalton, Georgia, astride the Atlanta-Chattanooga railroad. Sherman's plan was to move down that line toward Atlanta and to extend the Federal right beyond Johnston's power to resist. Thus caught in the vise of attack from north and west, the small Confederate army would be shattered. The valuable railroad and industrial center of Atlanta would then surrender, and the Deep South would be at Sherman's mercy.

Combating Sherman's offensive, while on the short end of 2 to 1 odds, required all of Johnston's defensive skill. He fell back to Resaca in the face of Sherman's two-pronged advance. During May 13-16, Johnston held fast at Resaca against several Federal assaults. The two armies suffered about 5,500 losses each before a Federal flanking movement again forced the Confederates into retreat through the mountain passes to the west.

Heavy skirmishing followed at Adairsville, Kingston, and Cassville. Johnston continued to wage delaying actions until Federal flanking columns threatened his rear. Then he would make an orderly retirement—always destroying bridges and railroads as he went. A series of heavy clashes at Dallas (May 25-28) delayed but did not deter

Sherman makes a futile assault on Johnston's impregnable position on Kennesaw Mountain. Painting by Thure de Thulstrup.

Sherman's advance. On June 27, Sherman abandoned a flank maneuver and sent three divisions in a headlong, direct assault against Johnston on the slopes of Kennesaw Mountain. Entrenched, determined Confederates were more than a match for Union courage: Sherman suffered nearly 3,000 casualties to Johnston's 500-700. The Federal commander resorted again to turning movements and, early in July, drove Johnston into the trenches of Atlanta.

Confederate officials in Richmond were unimpressed with Johnston's skillful use of inferior numbers. They saw only that Sherman was now at Atlanta's doorstep. So Johnston on July 17 was removed from command and replaced by General John B. Hood.

Sherman had good reason to be "pleased at this change." Hood's valor (he had lost a leg and the use of an arm in earlier battles) overshadowed a lack of skill and caution. These defects Hood quickly demonstrated by launching a July 20 attack on Sherman at Peachtree Creek that accomplished nothing but the loss of 2,500-3,000 irreplaceable Southern troops. Two days later, Hood attacked anew east of Atlanta. Again he was repulsed, this time with 8,500 casualties. Sherman then extended the Federal lines slowly around Atlanta.

By the end of August the Federals were on the verge of cutting the last rail link to the city. Hood attacked desperately at Jonesboro but was easily beaten back. The Confederates evacuated Atlanta on September 1, and Sherman's army marched triumphantly into the city the following day.

The effects of the fall of Atlanta can hardly be exaggerated. For the Confederacy, it meant the loss of the Deep South's most important rail center; and it foretold intense destructions yet to come. Conversely, the seizure of Atlanta was a tremendous boost to Northern morale sagging from "Grant's butchery" and setbacks elsewhere. It assured the re-election of Lincoln and Republicans dedicated to carrying the war to a successful conclusion.

Confederate successes in the West paled appreciably when compared to the loss of Atlanta. In the spring of 1864, Confederates in the Trans-Mississippi theater dealt General Nathanial P. Banks his worst—and final—defeat. Indeed, Banks' last campaign, known as the Red River Expedition, was one of the costliest fiascos of the war. Two factors prompted the campaign: Federal desire to seize large quantities of cotton so valuable to Northern and European mills, and the need to strengthen the Union's control over Louisiana and east Texas by securing Shreveport, Louisiana, and the adjacent countryside.

The Federal effort was a joint land-and-water operation under Banks and Admiral David D. Porter. The armada included 30,000 troops, 20 warships, and double that number of transport vessels. Only 15,000 scattered Confederates offered any obstacle. The campaign began March 12 and ended May 21; in every respect for the North, it was an utter failure. Southerners burned $ 60,000,000 worth of cotton to prevent its capture; Banks suffered inglorious defeats at Sabine Cross Roads and Pleasant Hill;

Banks' costly expedition: Confederate troops fire on Federal gunboats on the Red River, Louisiana. (Naval History Division)

the fleet floundered for miles in the turbid Red River, constantly under harassment from sharpshooters; bitter quarrels erupted among the officers as morale in the ranks melted.

Total Federal losses were 8,162 men, nine ships (including three gunboats), 57 guns, and 822 wagons loaded with supplies. The campaign deprived Sherman's army of additional manpower, delayed the capture of Mobile by ten months, and enabled Kirby Smith's Confederates in the Trans-Mississippi to hold out for another year. Banks was speedily removed from command.

That spring, too, the Confederate "Wizard of the Saddle" was active. Nathan Bedford Forrest was an uneducated cavalry leader who nevertheless exhibited an intuitive genius that made him one of the leading captains in the Civil War. On April 12, Forrest's men stormed the Federal garrison at Fort Pillow, Tennessee. The alleged "massacre" that followed remains one of the most controversial incidents of the 1860's. The Federal push into Georgia a month later sent "Old Bedford" on a rampage through Tennessee and northern Mississippi. Sherman then dispatched a heavy force under boastful Samuel D. Sturgis to take care of Forrest once and for all. Sturgis' command numbered 8,300 men, 22 guns, and 250 wagons. Forrest had at his disposal less than half that strength.

Nine days after leaving Memphis, on June 10th, the Federal expedition met Forrest—and disaster—at Brice's Cross Roads. The Confederate attacks were so sudden and severe, Sturgis reported, that "order gave way to confusion, and confusion to panic." What was left of the Federal command made the return trip to Memphis in two and a half days. Sturgis lost 2,240 men, 16 guns, 176 wagons, 1,500 small arms, and 300,000 rounds of ammunition.

The fall of Atlanta in September was but an intermediate step in Sherman's strategy. Not until the Confederacy was viciously cut in half would he consider his campaign successful. "You cannot glorify war in harsher terms than I will," Sherman warned. "War is cruelty, and you cannot refine it."

When Hood's skeleton regiments moved from Atlanta to Tennessee to threaten Sherman's rear bases of supply, the Federal general refused to take the bait. He sent part of his army under George H. Thomas to check the Confederate threat. With the remainder of his force—60,000 soldiers—Sherman cut his traces, marched away from Hood, and struck for the sea. On November 16, leaving Atlanta in flames, Sherman's army headed eastward in two columns toward the ocean.

Sherman purposefully kept his wings spread wide. No Confederate forces of any size stood in his path. Hence, his troops could—and did—cut a swath of destruction forty to sixty miles wide. Union forces easily occupied the state capital of Milledgeville and held a mock session of the Georgia legislature. In the course of the march, plundering occurred with an alarming thoroughness; anything that would prove beneficial to the Confederate cause was taken or destroyed. Sherman himself esti-

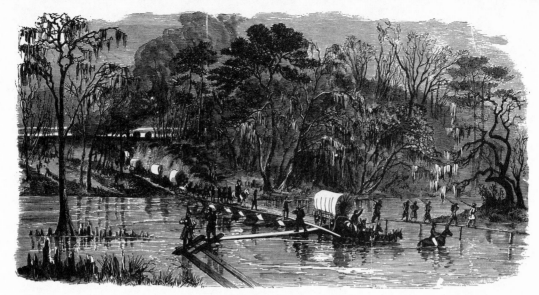

Sherman's troops cross the Edisto River during their march to the sea. Though brutal, the march achieved its objective: the end of the South's determined resistance. (CWTI Collection)

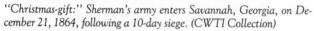

"Christmas-gift:" Sherman's army enters Savannah, Georgia, on December 21, 1864, following a 10-day siege. (CWTI Collection)

mated the total damage at $100,000,000. The "March to the Sea" became one of the most brutal episodes of the entire war. Yet it achieved its purpose. When Sherman on December 22 reached his destination and presented Savannah to Lincoln as a "Christmas-gift," morale and determined resistance in the Deep South were dead.

By then the same plight had befallen the once-proud Army of Tennessee. Hood's forces drove into Tennessee and, on November 30, encountered part of Thomas' command at Franklin. The aggressive Hood was convinced that the Army of Tennessee under Johnston had forgotten how to attack. He rashly ordered his troops to charge across mile-wide open fields without artillery support. The result was a slaughter: over 6,000 Confederates killed or wounded, among whom were five generals killed and one mortally wounded, and more than fifty regimental colonels. Still Hood stubbornly persevered. He moved to Nashville and made a weak siege of that city, giving Thomas the time to collect his full army. On December 15-16, Thomas delivered a series of heavy assaults on the Southern positions. Hood's lines snapped as Union forces gained "one of the most smashing victories of the war." The 6,000 Southern casualties represented half of Hood's army. Those Confederates who survived trudged southward in defeat, singing with wry humor of how "The gallant Hood of Texas played hell in Tennessee."

—James I. Robertson, Jr.

WILDERNESS AND SPOTSYLVANIA

Battle of the Wilderness by Joseph P. Cullen

Battle of Spotsylvania by Joseph P. Cullen

Detour on the Road to Richmond by Joseph P. Cullen

Battle of the Wilderness
by Joseph P. Cullen

SHORTLY after midnight the morning of May 4, 1864 the Army of the Potomac, over 100,000 strong, was put in motion from its winter camp around Culpeper, Virginia, heading once again for the Rapidan River. On old maps of Virginia the river appeared as "Rapid Ann" but no one knew for sure whether it was because the unknown woman had a fast gait or simply a reputation for being somewhat skittish. To the veterans in the ranks it didn't really matter, but that river had played an important part in the history of the army. Now many of them wondered how long it would be before they saw it again. Although none of them could know it, they would now cross it for the last time as an army.

The Army of the Potomac had a new leader again, Lieutenant General Ulysses S. Grant. In March President Lincoln had appointed him commander in chief of all the armies of the United States, over one half million men. His headquarters, however, would be in the field with General George Meade's Army of the Potomac, which in effect put Grant in immediate command.

Fresh from his recent dramatic victories in the West, Grant had an excellent working relationship with Lincoln, which was something none of the previous commanders enjoyed. "He doesn't ask me to do impossibilities for him," Lincoln is reported to have said, "and he's the first general I've had that didn't." And before the campaign started he wrote Grant: "The particulars of your plans I neither know nor seek to know. You are vigilant and self-reliant; and, pleased with this, I wish not to obtrude any constraints or restraints upon you. . . . And now with a brave army, and a just cause, may God sustain you." To which Grant replied in part: "And since the promotion which placed me in command of all the armies, and in view of the great responsibility and the importance of success, I have been astonished at the readiness with which everything asked for has been yielded, without even an explanation being asked. Should my success be less than I desire and expect, the least I can say is, the fault is not with you."

ALTHOUGH new to the East, Grant was fully aware of what had happened in that theater of war. As he stated:

The Battle of The Wilderness, May 5-6, 1864. (Coll. of LC)

Federal corps commanders at the Wilderness and Spotsylvania. Left to right: Generals Winfield S. Hancock, Gouverneur K. Warren, Ambrose E. Burnside, and John Sedgwick. (National Archives)

"Before this time these various armies had acted separately and independently of each other, giving the enemy an opportunity, often, of depleting one command, not pressed, to reinforce another more actively engaged. I determined to stop this. . . . My general plan now was to concentrate all the force possible against the Confederate armies in the field."

His immediate objective in the East, however, was General Robert E. Lee's Army of Northern Virginia which had spent the winter encamped in the Mine Run area of the Rapidan, just across the river from Culpeper. "To get possession of Lee's army was the first great object," Grant wrote. "With the capture of his army Richmond would necessarily follow." But he had no intention of attacking Lee behind the strong Confederate entrenchments at Mine Run. Instead, he planned to flank the Confederate position by crossing the Rapidan lower down at Germanna and Ely's Fords, thus forcing Lee to come out in the open and fight. Or, failing that, he hoped to get the Army of the Potomac between Lee and Richmond. To do this, however, he would have to risk battle in an area known as the Wilderness, a dense forest of second-growth pine and scrub oak, with numerous creeks, gullies, swamps, heavy tanglefoot underbrush, few farms or open spaces, and most of the roads mere winding trails. Here his preponderance of forces, particularly the cavalry and artillery, could not be used to best advantage. Grant was willing to take that risk. However, as General A. A. Humphreys, Meade's chief of staff, explained, it was hoped "that by setting the whole army in motion at midnight, with its reserve artillery and great trains of over four thousand wagons, it might move so far beyond the Rapidan the first day that it would be able to pass out of the Wilderness and turn, or partially turn, the right flank of Lee before a general engagement took place."

AND so as dawn broke that morning long lines of blue-clad soldiers could be seen once again crossing the Rapidan in the start of a campaign that would not end until the war was over, almost a year later. Before dawn the cavalry had driven the Confederate pickets away from the crossings and by 6 a.m. the pontoons were ready for the infantry and artillery to cross. Gouverneur Warren's V Corps, preceded by James H. Wilson's cavalry division, crossed at Germanna Ford, about eight miles below Lee's position at Mine Run. John Sedgwick's VI Corps followed Warren, while Winfield S. Hancock's II Corps crossed at Ely's Ford, about six miles below Germanna, preceded by David M. Gregg's cavalry division and followed by the artillery, commanded by General Henry J. Hunt. A. T. A. Torbert's cavalry division remained north of the river to prevent the Confederates from crossing and possibly getting in the rear of the Federal army among the wagon trains. The commander of the cavalry was General "Phil" Sheridan. Grant had still another corps at his disposal, Ambrose Burnside's IX, which was left back in the Warrenton area to protect the Orange & Alexandria Railroad from Manassas Junction to Rappahannock Station in case the crossing of the Rapidan should be delayed. He was alerted, however, to be ready to march at a moment's notice once the crossing had been accomplished.

By nine o'clock that morning Lee had been informed of the Federal crossing by the Confederate signal station atop Clarke's Mountain. Although he had anticipated Grant's crossing at the fords, he decided not to contest the crossing for several reasons. One was the powerful Federal artillery, and another was the position of the Army of Northern Virginia. R. S. Ewell's corps was on the Rapidan above Mine Run, with A.P. Hill on his left even farther up the river, while James Longstreet's corps was encamped around Gordonsville, about ten miles south of

Hill. Lee apparently believed that he would not have time to bring up a sufficient force to contest the crossing. And he was also concerned about the physical condition of his army. The arms and other equipment were generally satisfactory, but food and clothing had been in scant supply all winter. As General Evander Law wrote later, "A new pair of shoes or an overcoat was a luxury, and full rations would have astonished the stomachs of Lee's ragged Confederates." Not knowing which way Grant might proceed once he was south of the river, Lee nevertheless now ordered Ewell to march east on the Orange Turnpike, while Hill moved parallel with him on the Orange Plank Road. Longstreet was ordered to march for the general area of Todd's Tavern in order to come up on Hill's right. When all arrived Lee would have something over 60,000 troops.

SHORTLY after noon Grant crossed the river at Germanna Ford. Almost immediately he was handed a message from a signal station, which had intercepted a Confederate dispatch, that Ewell was moving forward. Grant immediately ordered Burnside to join the Army of the Potomac, marching by way of Germanna Ford. "Make forced marches until you reach this place. Start your troops now in the rear the moment they can be got off, and require them to make a night march." By mid-afternoon the II Corps was encamped around strategic Chancellorsville, while the V and VI Corps were on a line running generally north and south just west of the Wilderness Tavern area. To be sure, the Army of the Potomac was not out of the Wilderness, although the II Corps was actually on the eastern edge of it, but it did have control of all the strategic roads in the area. At Chancellorsville the Ely's Ford Road met the Orange Turnpike which ran east and west from Fredericksburg

to Orange. A few miles west of Chancellorsville at Wilderness Church the Orange Plank Road took off to the south from the Turnpike and then ran generally parallel to the Orange Turnpike until it rejoined it again just west of Mine Run. At the Wilderness Tavern the Germanna Ford Road leading south crossed the Turnpike. South of the Turnpike, but before it met the Orange Plank Road, the continuation of the Germanna Road crossed Brock Road which led south and then southeast to Spotsylvania Court House.

Major General George Gordon Meade took command of the Army of the Potomac three days before the Battle of Gettysburg (above). (Battles and Leaders of the Civil War) Confederate corps commanders at the Wilderness and Spotsylvania (below). Left to right: Generals James Longstreet, A. P. Hill, and Richard S. Ewell. (National Archives)

Union artillery crossing the Rapidan at Germanna Ford, May 5, 1864, to start the Wilderness Campaign. (*Library of Congress*)

In effect, then, the whole Army of the Potomac had ground to a halt early in the afternoon and while still in the Wilderness. Nevertheless Grant was not dissatisfied with the progress made. The halt had been made in order that the army not become separated from its long wagon trains, which if spread out in single file would stretch from the Rapidan to Richmond. If Lee's infantry captured or destroyed a large part of the trains by getting between them and the Federal army, Grant would be forced to retreat back across the Rapidan to be re-supplied, and that above all he did not want to do. Also, most of the army had been on the march since midnight and many of the men, particularly the recruits, were more than ready to call it a day.

SOME of the veterans remembered later that a sad silence seemed to settle over the army that night in bivouac. The haunting cry of the whippoorwill echoed through the deep shadows. Occasionally someone stumbled over the bones of the unburied dead from the Chancellorsville battle just over a year before, sapping the morale of the new men in the blue ranks. Around the campfires in the stillness of the woods the veterans were unusually quiet, haunted by memories or premonitions.

One recalled that they all seemed to have "a sense of ominous dread which many of us found almost impossible to shake off." Later in the night the pickets near the Wilderness Tavern heard a rumbling off to the west and guessed that the Confederates were moving somewhere in the night to meet them.

They guessed right, of course. Ewell and Hill were on the move. At 8 o'clock that night Colonel Walter S. Taylor of Lee's staff sent the following message to Ewell: "If the enemy moves down the river, he wishes you to push on after him. If he comes this way, we will take our old line. The general's desire is to bring him to battle as soon as possible." At that point Lee apparently believed that Grant would either go down river to Fredericksburg or up river to attack him directly. If he moved down river, the movement would of necessity be slow and a large rearguard would be required to protect the wagon trains. Ewell could attack that rearguard until Hill and Longstreet came up, in which case Lee might be able to swing them around to hit Grant in flank, as he had done to Hooker at Chancellorsville. If, on the other hand, Grant came up river then Ewell could fight a delaying action until Lee got behind his entrenchments at Mine Run. It was not until about midnight, when he received reports from his cavalry commander "Jeb" Stuart, that Lee realized Grant was not going to do either. It appeared now that he was going to march south through the heart of the Wilderness. Lee apparently was pleased at this opportunity to strike Grant in flank on the march in an area where Northern numerical superiority would be of small advantage, despite the fact that it would be at least another twenty-four hours before Longstreet could get up, leaving Lee with only two corps for the contemplated attack.

AT the first gray streaks of dawn the next morning, May 5, the vast Federal camp was astir. Hancock marched south from Chancellorsville and then angled slightly west in expectation of uniting his right with Warren, who then moved south from Wilderness Tavern, to be followed by Sedgwick. Warren wisely took the precaution of leaving Charles Griffin's division on the Turnpike facing west to protect his right flank while he started his other

divisions south. By now the head of Burnside's corps was approaching Germanna Ford after an all-night march.

Shortly after daylight Griffin reported a strong Confederate force in his front, apparently getting ready to attack. Meade informed Grant at 7:30 a.m.: "The enemy have appeared in force on the Orange Pike, and are now reported forming line of battle in front of Griffin's division, Fifth Corps. I have directed General Warren to attack them at once with his whole force. Until this movement of the enemy is developed, the march of the corps must be suspended. I have, therefore, sent word to Hancock not to advance beyond Todd's Tavern for the present." Grant replied: "If any opportunity presents itself for pitching into a part of Lee's army, do so without giving time for disposition."

Warren's other divisions were now ordered into line south of the Turnpike on Griffin's left and Sedgwick's corps north of the road on Warren's right. But in the dense

WARREN'S V CORPS ATTACKS EWELL'S RIGHT AND CENTER
Showing the situation at about 1 p.m., May 5. Johnson and Rodes have deployed to meet Griffin's and Wadsworth's attack, while Heth has ordered a deployment on the line established by Cooke's brigade. Birney and Gibbon are moving north to reinforce the line established by Getty, while Wright is marching to extend Griffin's right.

The maps used in this article are reproduced from Edward Steere's The Wilderness *through courtesy of the publisher, the Stackpole Company.*

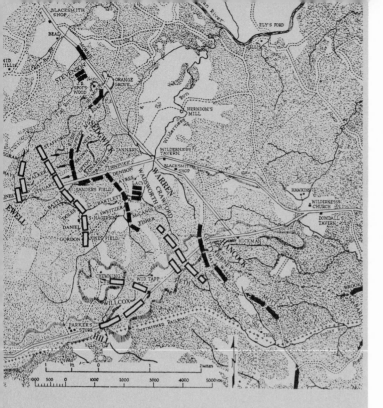

SEDGWICK CARRIES THE ATTACK TO EWELL'S LEFT
This shows Wright's advance to the attack at about 3 p.m., May 5. Warren's division has been pulled back, and Ricketts is marching down the Germanna Plank Road, off the map to the north.

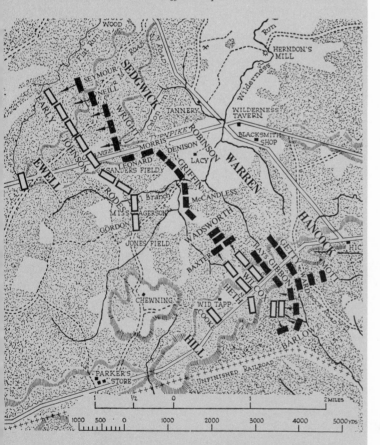

HANCOCK'S DOUBLE ENVELOPMENT CLOSES ON HILL
Showing the situation at about 7:30 p.m., May 5. The two flank attacks close on Heth as Wilcox goes to the latter's relief. On the north the fighting continues. Seymour's attempted envelopment of Ewell's left flank is frustrated by the arrival of Hays and Pegram. Thus Lee wins the race of local reserves. The fighting between Sedgwick and Ewell continues until dark.
The trains of the Army of the Potomac have closed up at Dowdall's Tavern. Johnston's brigade of Rodes' division is still enroute from Hanover Junction; it arrives on the battlefield the morning of May 6.

"As for the fighting, it was simply bushwhacking on a grand scale in brush where all formation beyond that of regiments or companies was soon lost, and where such a thing as a consistent line of battle on either side was impossible." A veteran of the 5th Texas Regiment when captured and asked what he thought of the battle replied: "Battle be —! It ain't no battle! It's a worse riot than Chickamauga was. You Yanks don't call this a battle, do you? At Chickamauga there was at least a rear, but here there ain't neither front nor rear. It's all a — mess! And our two armies ain't nothing but howlin' mobs!"

DESPITE the impossible conditions, Hancock's advantage in numbers began to tell as Hill's men were slowly driven back down the Plank Road in complete confusion. In the hot, still air the musketry smoke clung to the ground before lifting, and through it the guns flashed and crackled as men fired blindly. The noise roared to a crescendo that left them dazed. Regimental and company commanders lost communication and control in the dense forest, amid the underbrush, swamps, creeks, smoke and noise. In some places even companies had to retreat in single file, not knowing who or what was on their left or right. Fortunately for Lee, darkness ended the fighting just as Hill was about to suffer an outright defeat.

Tragic as the fierce fighting had been all day, now a new horror developed as the tinder-dry forest caught fire in several places. "Flames sprang up in the woods in our front," wrote a soldier in the 2d Massachusetts Artillery, "where the fight of the morning had taken place. With crackling roar, like an army of fire, it came down upon the Union line. The wind drove the blinding smoke and suffocating heat into our faces. This, added to the oppressive heat of the weather, was almost unendurable. It soon became terrible. The line of fire, with resistless march, swept the thickets before its advance, then reaching out its tongue of flame, ignited the breastworks composed of resinous logs, which soon roared and crackled along their entire length. . . . The fire was the most terrible enemy our men met that day, and few survivors will forget this attack of flames. . . ." Many of the wounded burned to death that night in the flaming Wilderness.

Despite the heavy fighting all day, the lines were still approximately the same when darkness finally put an end to it. Grant, realizing how close Hancock had come to breaking through that day, ordered him to attack again at 5 a.m. in an attempt to drive Hill back and roll up Lee's right flank before Longstreet's corps could arrive. Sedgwick and Warren were to keep pressure on Ewell to prevent Lee from shifting forces from left to right in order to help Hill. Burnside with two divisions was to fill the gap between Warren's left and Hancock's right and if he succeeded "in breaking the enemy's center, to swing around to the left and envelop the right of Lee's army." His other division was sent to support Hancock directly.

LEE was well aware of how close he had come to dis-

Rescuing the wounded from the burning woods of the Wilderness (above). Drawing by Alfred R. Waud. (Library of Congress) Distributing ammunition under fire to Warren's V Corps, May 6, 1864 (below). Engraved from a drawing by Alfred R. Waud. (Battles and Leaders of the Civil War)

Alfred R. Waud's note on his drawing (above) reads, "Genl. Wadsworth's division in action in the Wilderness, near the spot where the general was killed." (Library of Congress) Federal soldiers rest behind breastworks while their comrades clear a field of fire during a lull in the fighting (below). (Frank Leslie's Illustrated Newspaper)

tangled thickets and heavy undergrowth it took a long time for even couriers to carry messages, and hours to maneuver divisions into positions, so it would be afternoon before Warren would be ready to attack.

By late morning Grant was convinced that it was more than a Confederate reconnoitering force on his flank, so Hancock was now ordered back to protect the strategic Orange Plank and Brock crossroad, where only a thin line of cavalry patrolled it. It would be late afternoon, however, before Hancock's troops could possibly get there, which Grant realized, so George Getty's division of Sedgwick's corps was sent to hold the crossroad at any cost until Hancock could come up.

EWELL, meanwhile, came into line of battle across the Turnpike with Edward Johnson's division in the center, Robert Rodes's south of the road, and Jubal Early's to the north facing Sedgwick. When Ewell informed Lee, who was on the Orange Plank Road with Hill, of his position, he was told to base his movements on the head of Hill's column, whose position he could judge by the firing in its front, and not to bring on a general engagement until Longstreet was up, which would not be until the next morning. Ewell, however, was in no position to control events and there was no way for him to prevent the Federals from bringing on a general engagement.

About 1 p.m. as Griffin's men moved west along the Turnpike the air became still and sultry, the dry underbrush crackling beneath their feet. From beyond the trees in their front came the dull popping of the skirmishers' guns. Yellow slits of light began to blink along the regimental lines and little balls of smoke, gray and compact, floated slowly upward in the stifling air. The initial attack hit Johnson's division in Ewell's center and drove it back, but Johnson quickly counterattacked and stabilized his line. As the troops on both sides spread north and south of the road, they disappeared into the twilight gloom of the dense foliage among the gnarled and twisted tree trunks. Soon the woods echoed to the roar of cannon, the crack of musketry, the angry, confused shouts of men trying desperately to kill each other.

Over on the Confederate right Hill advanced along the Plank Road, quickly driving off the Federal cavalry patrolling the vital Brock crossroad, as Getty's division raced south along the Brock Road in a desperate effort to save it. Getty with his staff was already at the crossroad waiting impatiently for his troops to arrive. One of these officers described what happened next:

> Soon a few gray forms were discerned far up the narrow Plank Road moving cautiously forward, then a bullet went whistling overhead, and another and another, and then the leaden hail came faster and faster over and about the little group until its destruction seemed imminent and inevitable. But Getty would not budge. "We must hold this point at any risk," he exclaimed, "our men will soon be up." In a few minutes, which seemed like an age to the little squad, the leading regiment of Wheaton's brigade, the 1st, came running like greyhounds along the Brock Road until the first regiment

Brigadier General James S. Wadsworth died from wounds received during the fighting of May 6. (Battles and Leaders of the Civil War)

passed the Plank Road, and then, at the command "Halt!" "Front!" "Fire!", poured a volley into the woods and threw out skirmishers in almost less time than it takes to tell it. Dead and wounded rebel skirmishers were found within thirty yards of the crossroad, so nearly had they gained it, and from these wounded persons it was learned that Hill's corps, Heth's division in advance, supported by Wilcox's division, was the opposing force.

The Federals had saved the vital crossroad, just barely, but Getty's men were in for a few rough hours as Hill with two divisions (Richard H. Anderson's division was not yet up) attacked furiously. But by late afternoon Hancock's troops began to arrive, David Birney's and Gersham Mott's divisions in the lead, and Grant now ordered Getty and Hancock to attack before Anderson arrived. For the remainder of daylight the fighting continued at a furious pace, fighting such as these two armies had never seen before and would never see again. Troops could not maneuver in the wild country, battle lines broke into small fragments, nobody could see anything at all. Line officers guessed at the progress of the battle by the sound of the firing. Regiments, brigades, and even divisions inextricably mixed. As Confederate General Law wrote: "It was a desperate struggle between the infantry of the two armies, on a field whose physical aspects were as grim and forbidding as the struggle itself. It was a battle of brigades and regiments rather than of corps and divisions." A Federal soldier remembered that,

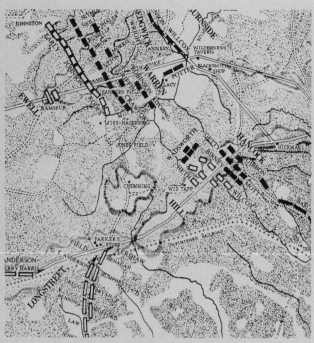

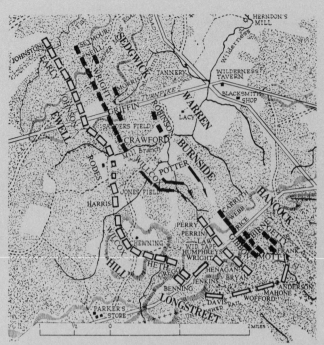

EWELL BEATS MEADE TO THE PUNCH

Hancock, Warren, and Sedgwick attack simultaneously at 5 a.m., May 6. However, Ewell anticipates this by attacking on his extreme left a half hour earlier. Burnside's corps is moving toward the gap between Hill and Ewell. Gibbon has been assigned to the command of a provisional corps of five brigades, posted to cover the Federal left flank.

Longstreet's corps and R. H. Anderson's division are arriving on the field. Johnston's brigade of Rodes' division has just arrived after its long march from Hanover Junction.

LONGSTREET STARTS AROUND THE FEDERAL SOUTH FLANK

The stalemate on the north flank continues. Burnside, ordered to move by the left flank and attack Longstreet, has begun this movement. Longstreet, after assembling an enveloping force, is moving the brigades in column against Hancock's left and rear.

The remnants of Wadsworth's force, including the heavy artillery brigade under Kitching, have been withdrawn in reserve near the Lacy house, but have been omitted from this map.

Grant whittling during the first day's fighting in the Wilderness. Drawing by Charles Reed. (Library of Congress)

aster that day on his right flank. Consequently, Longstreet was now ordered to make an all-night march in order to reach the field by daylight to relieve Hill's weary troops. Ewell was ordered to open a heavy fire at daylight in the hope that this might relieve the pressure on Hill, at least until Longstreet could get into position. Stuart with his cavalry was ordered to try to get on Hancock's left and rear to disrupt his supply line.

Promptly at 5 a.m. Hancock moved out on the attack and proceeded to drive Hill back. Hancock's men were relatively fresh compared to Harry Heth's and Cadmus Wilcox's, who were "thoroughly worn out," according to General Law. "Their lines were ragged and irregular, with wide intervals, and in some places fronting in different directions. In the expectation that they would be relieved during the night, no effort was made to rearrange and strengthen them to meet the storm that was brewing." Soon the whole line gave way and the Federals rushed forward, driving the Confederates west along the Orange Plank Road. About two miles west of the crossroad was a meager little clearing in the woods around the Widow Tapp farm. Here stood Lee himself among the guns of William Poague's artillery desperately trying to rally the men until Longstreet, expected momentarily, could arrive. Another mile west and the Federals would be

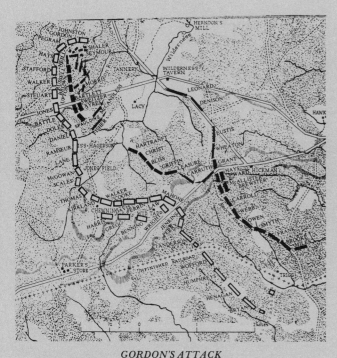

GORDON'S ATTACK

The situation at about 7:30 p.m., May 6. Gordon, supported by Pegram and Johnston, smashes Seymour and Shaler. VI Corps local reserves stop this attack. Crawford's division moves north to reinforce the Federal flank.

Lee now abandons his assault and commences to entrench along his front. On the Federal side, Burnside is also entrenching and connecting with Hancock's Brock Road line. The broken units of Wadsworth's division near the Lacy house have been omitted from this map.

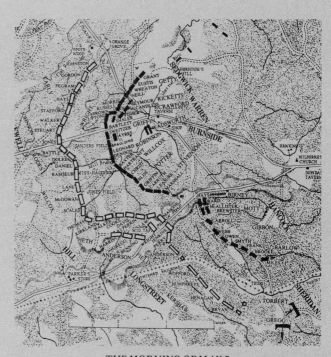

THE MORNING OF MAY 7

By morning of May 7 most brigades have rejoined their divisions, and the corps are again sorted out. Meade has refused his north flank, and both sides are continuing to entrench. Sheridan's cavalry has been relieved of its mission of guarding the trains, being replaced by Ferrero's division. Sheridan withdrew his cavalry, somewhat, after Hancock's reverse on the 6th, but later reoccupied his line covering the Federal south flank. Sheridan is now moving Torbert and Gregg to Todd's Tavern, and Wilson (off the map) is at Piney Branch Church. Only light skirmishing occurs on this day. The battle is over.

around his right flank and among his supply trains, and the Army of Northern Virginia would be in grave danger.

But as Hancock's men emerged from the woods into the Tapp clearing, the massed Confederate cannon blasted them back. In the confusion they paused to regroup and reorganize their lines for another attack. Hancock was jubilant. To an officer on Meade's staff he cried, "We are driving them, sir! Tell General Meade we are driving them most beautifully." In reality, however, things were not going as well as Hancock at first believed. Burnside, dilatory as usual, was not up and would not be in position to have any effect until the afternoon, and his division sent to support Hancock was just now arriving and would not be in line for several hours yet. "I knew it!" Hancock yelled. "Just what I expected! If he could attack *now*, we would smash A.P. Hill all to pieces!"

HANCOCK was probably right, but at that dramatic moment Longstreet's troops appeared on the field. Seeing the welcome reinforcements, Hill's troops rallied and moved to the left to close the gap between them and Ewell's right and thus were in position to block Burnside across the Chewning plateau. Longstreet advanced along the Orange Plank Road with Charles Field's division on the north and Joseph B. Kershaw's on the south, driving

the Federals back, the blow falling primarily on Birney's and Mott's divisions. Finding Hancock's left flank somewhat in the air, Longstreet now swung his brigades south of the road along an unfinished railroad and hit the Federals hard in flank driving them back to their entrenchments around the crossroad. It now seemed as if Lee had an opportunity to roll up Grant's left flank, but Longstreet's troops attacking to the north became mixed up with Hill's facing east and had to halt to straighten out the lines and regroup. During this process Longstreet was wounded, the command then falling to Anderson.

A temporary lull now settled over the field as both sides tried to organize for another attack. In mid afternoon Grant ordered Hancock and Burnside to attack, but Lee beat him to the punch. Personally taking command of Longstreet's corps, Lee hit Hancock again. But according to General Law, "When at 4 o'clock an attack was made upon the Federal line along the Brock Road, it was found strongly fortified and stubbornly defended. The log breastworks had taken fire during the battle, and at one point separated the combatants by a wall of fire and smoke which neither could pass. Part of Field's division captured the works in their front, but were forced to relinquish them for want of support. Meanwhile Burnside's corps, which had reinforced Hancock during the day, made a vigorous

Grant's troops cheer him in the Wilderness, May 7, 1864 (above). Drawing by Edwin Forbes. (Library of Congress) The Union army's night march to Spotsylvania (below). Engraving from a drawing by Edwin Forbes. (Thirty Years After: An Artist's Story of the Great War)

attack on the north of the Orange Plank Road. James Lane's (Alabama) and Edward Perry's (Florida) brigades were being forced back when, Heth's division coming to their assistance, they assumed the offensive, driving Burnside's troops beyond the extensive line of breastworks constructed previous to their advance."

THUS it continued for the remainder of the day, neither side able to gain any permanent advantage. Over on Hancock's far left and rear, the cavalry of both sides had fought a more or less separate battle during the day. When Grant learned that Stuart's cavalry was attempting to get in rear of Hancock he had sent Sheridan and the Federal cavalry over to stop him. Brisk skirmishes were fought at the intersection of the Furnace and Brock Roads and at Todd's Tavern, with neither side gaining a clear-cut victory. But Stuart was stopped and Hancock's rear protected. And just as darkness fell that night, Ewell ordered an attack on Sedgwick's right flank which was hanging in the air unprotected. A force under General John B. Gordon hit it hard in a surprise attack. Part of James Rickett's division gave way and two generals and a large part of a brigade were captured. But in the darkness and the woods the Confederates became disorganized and the attack fizzled. Gordon later claimed that if he had been supported he could have rolled up Grant's whole right flank, but Early maintained that if the Federals had realized how badly the Confederates were disorganized they could have inflicted serious damage on Ewell's corps. In any event, night closed the Battle of The Wilderness.

"More desperate fighting has not been witnessed on this continent than that of the 5th and 6th of May," wrote Grant. The Federals had lost over 15,000 in killed, wounded, and missing; the Confederates, probably about 11,400.

IT was now evident to both Lee and Grant that the two armies were entrenched so strongly that attack by either side would probably be suicidal. As Grant stated,". . . the moment arms were stacked the men entrenched themselves. For this purpose they would build up piles of logs or rails if they could be found in their front, and dig a ditch throwing the dirt forward on the timbers. Thus the digging they did counted in making a depression to stand in, and increased the elevation in front of them. It was wonderful how quickly they could in this way construct defenses of considerable strength." The same situation, of course, applied to the Confederates also. Consequently, early in the morning of May 7 Grant ordered Meade to "Make all preparations during the day for a night march to take position at Spotsylvania C. H. with one army corps, at Todd's Tavern with one, and another near the intersection of the Piney Branch and Spotsylvania road with the road from Alsop's to Old Court House."

In other words, instead of retreating to lick his wounds as other commanders of the Army of the Potomac had done, Grant again decided to move around Lee's right flank by sliding leftward and southward. And he reported to Washington: "At present we can claim no victory over the enemy, neither have they gained a single advantage." A very accurate and honest description of the situation.

The remains of the unburied dead several months after the Battle of the Wilderness. (Library of Congress)

Battle of Spotsylvania
by Joseph P. Cullen

SOUTH and slightly east of the Wilderness area was another strategic crossroad at the village of Spotsylvania Court House. The place itself was just a sleepy hamlet, a handful of houses scattered carelessly about a country crossroad, but Federal possession would seriously endanger the Confederate line of communication to Richmond. "My object in moving to Spotsylvania," Grant wrote, "was two-fold: first, I did not want Lee to get back to Richmond in time to attempt to crush Butler before I could get there; second, I wanted to get between his army and Richmond if possible; and, if not, to draw him into the open field."

Shortly after dark on May 7 Warren was ordered to pull out of line and proceed toward Spotsylvania Court House by way of Brock Road, passing behind Burnside's and Hancock's corps. Sedgwick would follow Warren by way of Chancellorsville and the Piney Branch Church Road to where it met the Brock Road. Burnside would march farther east and take the Fredericksburg-Spotsylvania Court House Road. When the rest of the army had moved out, Hancock would follow Warren on the Brock Road. Sheridan and the cavalry had been ordered to clear the way.

During the day the Confederates had been alert for any movement that Grant might make. Lee's scouts informed him that the bridges across the Rapidan had been removed and the area around Germanna Ford abandoned. Obviously, then, Grant was not going to retreat as Hooker had done just a year ago. But when the Federal wagon trains started to move they raised a huge cloud of dust, as the roads were powder dry. So Grant was moving somewhere. If he was just changing base, he could be going to Fredericksburg, but, if he was moving south, his next immediate objective would undoubtedly be Spotsylvania. In either event, Lee decided he had better move his army to Spotsylvania, so he ordered a clearing cut through the forest from the Orange Plank Road to the road running from Orange to Spotsylvania in the area of Shady Grove Church. That night Longstreet's corps, now commanded by Anderson, was ordered to take the route to Spotsylvania. Hill and Ewell would follow Anderson as soon as they could.

FOR an army to make an all-night march after two days of brutal combat and one day of nervous alert was no easy task, and much confusion existed that night. Warren reached Todd's Tavern on the Brock Road about 3

Attack at Spotsylvania Court House. *Engraved from a painting by Alonzo Chappell.* (*New York Public Library*)

Spotsylvania Court House, focal point of bloody fighting in the Wilderness Campaign. (Battles and Leaders of the Civil War)

a.m., but here he was halted as the road was blocked by Sheridan's cavalry, and a little farther on was Stuart's cavalry. It took several hours to drive the Confederate cavalry off and to clear the road, and as Warren approached Spotsylvania Court House it was becoming daylight. But he never did reach it. The delay had enabled Anderson to take up an entrenched position on a slight rise, about a mile and a half northwest of the vital crossroad. In his *Memoirs* Grant stated:

> But Lee, by accident, beat us to Spotsylvania. Our wagon trains had been ordered easterly of the roads the troops were to march upon before the movement commenced. Lee interpreted this as a semi-retreat of the Army of the Potomac to Fredericksburg, and so informed his government. Accordingly he ordered Longstreet's corps—now commanded by Anderson—to move in the morning (the 8th) to Spotsylvania. But the woods being still on fire, Anderson could not go into bivouac, and marched directly on to his destination that night. By this accident Lee got possession of Spotsylvania. It is impossible to say now what would have been the result if Lee's orders had been obeyed as given; but it is certain that we would have been in Spotsylvania and between him and his capital. My belief is that there would have been a race between the two armies to see which could reach Richmond first, and the Army of the Potomac would have had the shorter line. Thus, twice since crossing the Rapidan we came near closing the campaign, so far as battles were concerned, from the Rapidan to the James River or Richmond. The first failure was caused by our not following up the success gained over Hill's corps on the morning of the 6th: the second, when fires caused by that battle drove Anderson to make a march during the night of the 7th-8th which he was ordered to commence on the morning of the 8th. But accident often decides the fate of battle.

Warren assumed the enemy in his front was just the Confederate cavalry that Sheridan had driven off earlier, so at 8 a.m. he sent John C. Robinson's division forward to the attack. Robinson, however, received a rude shock when he ran up against Anderson's entrenched troops and was driven back with heavy losses. Warren organized for another attack, but it took time as most of the men were by now near exhaustion after their all-night march. Just before noon he attacked again with his whole corps, but the attack was made piecemeal with one division at a time

and consequently failed to dislodge Anderson. Grant, who was anxious to crush Anderson before Lee could get the rest of his army up, now ordered Sedgwick, who was at Piney Branch Church, to Warren's support for another attempt. But Sedgwick for some reason was slow in getting up to form on Warren's left, and it was five o'clock before they could attack. But again the assault was made piecemeal and was not pushed on a wide front, probably because of the physical condition of the troops. During the fight Ewell appeared on the field and came into line on Anderson's right. Hill's corps, now under Early because of Hill's illness, would form on Ewell's right when it reached the field early the next morning.

That night Grant ordered Sheridan and his cavalry to make a raid around Lee's army to disrupt his communications with Richmond, and then to proceed south to re-provision his force from Butler's army south of the James River. Grant hoped that this would force Lee to send Stuart's cavalry after Sheridan, which in effect would protect the Federal supply trains from Confederate cavalry raids. Lee did send Stuart after Sheridan, and in a later engagement of the two cavalry forces at Yellow Tavern, on the outskirts of Richmond, Stuart was mortally wounded.

THE next day, May 9, was spent mostly in getting the remainder of the army into position and entrenching, although sharpshooting and skirmishing was heavy at times, and one of the casualties was the most liked general of-

Map of the Battle of Spotsylvania, May 10-12, 1864. (*Lossing's* Civil War in America)

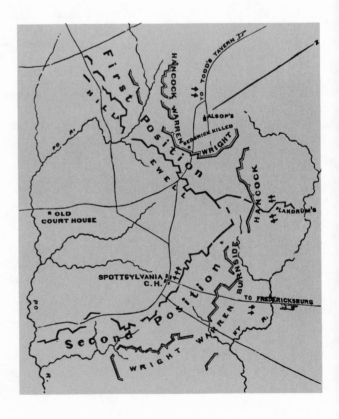

ficer in the Army of the Potomac. In an effort to convince his men in the VI Corps that the sharpshooters "couldn't hit an elephant at this distance," Sedgwick rode forward to an elevated position in his front and fell dead with a bullet in his head. General Horatio Wright then assumed command of the VI Corps.

Later in the day, misled by reports that Lee was withdrawing from the Federal right, Grant ordered Hancock across the Po River to take Lee in flank and rear. Before Hancock could make contact, however, the mistake was realized and he was recalled. In recrossing the river he was attacked by Early whom Lee had sent over from the Confederate right to block Hancock's advance. Hancock extricated himself from this dangerous position and then came into line on Wright's left. Burnside, meanwhile, had come down the Fredericksburg road and now held the extreme Federal left, next to Hancock.

Grant believed that Lee had weakened other parts of his line in order to drive Hancock back, so on the afternoon of May 10 he sent Warren and Wright to attack the left center of the Confederate position. Lee now had Anderson on his left opposite Warren and Wright, Ewell was in front of Hancock, and Early on the right faced Burnside. All were strongly entrenched behind powerful breastworks. There was one weak spot in the line, however. Ewell's entrenchments jutted out in a U-shaped salient beyond the rest of the lines. Being elevated, it was a good spot for artillery, which was why Ewell wanted it in the first place, and he placed twenty-two guns there to hold it. It was nearly a mile deep and about half a mile wide. But the Mule Shoe, as the Confederates called it, made an inviting target. Colonel Emory Upton, of Wright's corps, was selected to lead the attack against the west side of the Mule Shoe with twelve picked regiments, to be supported by Mott's divisin of Hancock's corps. Upton ordered the assault to be made with four lines of three regiments each. When the first line breached the salient, he ordered them to fan out to the left and right to take Ewell's troops in flank, while the other regiments coming up behind could go straight ahead through the opening to stop any reinforcements that might be sent up. Also, they were to make the initial charge across an open field without stopping to fire and reload.

ABOUT 6 p.m. Upton's men charged out of the woods that concealed them, with a cheer, raced across the open ground and charged into the salient, the fading sun glistening on the steel bayonets. After some brief, but desperate, hand-to-hand fighting, the surprise attack succeeded, the plan working just as Upton had predicted it would. The impregnable line of earthworks had been breached with a narrow but deep penetration, and about 1,000 of Ewell's men had been captured along with several pieces of artillery. Now if Mott's division charged through the opening promptly, the Army of Northern Virginia would be in a critical position. But, as Grant later wrote, Mott "failed utterly." Coming to Upton's support and with

Brevet Major General Emory Upton. He led the first Union assault on the "Mule Shoe" salient. (Battles and Leaders of the Civil War)

only about half a mile to go, Mott's troops came under heavy artillery fire, broke, and then retreated in confusion. There was nothing left for Upton to do now but withdraw. He took his prisoners with him but was forced to abandon the guns he had captured. Grant promoted him to general on the spot, later confirmed by the President.

That night Wright told Meade, "General, I don't want Mott's men on my left; they are not a support; I would rather have no troops there." A few days later the division was broken up and Mott's brigades transferred to Birney's division.

Elsewhere the attack had not gone any better. Warren was beaten back and Wright could not make any permanent advances. The next day Grant wrote to Washington: "We have now ended the sixth day of very heavy fighting. The result to this time is much in our favor. But our losses have been heavy, as well as those of the enemy. . . . I am now sending back to Belle Plain all my wagons for a fresh supply of provisions and ammunition, and propose to fight it out on this line if it takes all summer."

GRANT had been much impressed with Upton's success, and before starting another flanking movement around Lee's right decided to attack him in his entrenched position once more, using Upton's tactics on a much larger scale against the same position. That afternoon he wrote an order to Burnside: "Major-General Hancock has been ordered to move his entire corps under cover of night to join you in a vigorous attack against the enemy at 4 a.m. of to-morrow, the 12th instant. You will move against the enemy with your entire force promptly and with all possible vigor at precisely 4 o'clock to-morrow morning. Let your preparations for this attack be conducted with the utmost secrecy, and veiled entirely from the enemy. . . . Generals Warren and Wright will hold their corps as close to the enemy as possible, to take advantage of any diversion caused by your and Hancock's attack, and will push in their whole force if any opportunity presents itself."

In the predawn darkness of May 12 rain set in, wrapping the area in a sullen mist. The drops ticked off the leaves monotonously as Hancock's and Burnside's men formed for the attack, stumbling through the dark and the rain and the mud. Their noisy approach alerted the Confederate pickets that this would be no small attack, and now Ewell's division and brigade commanders were really concerned.

Ewell was well aware that the apex of the salient was his weakest point and consequently had placed the twenty-two artillery pieces there. But Lee, misled by a report that Grant was moving around his right flank again had ordered the guns to the rear to be ready to move quickly if necessary. Alerted by the reports of the pickets, they were now frantically galloping up to the front again in the rainy darkness, and would arrive just in time for twenty of them to be captured without having fired a shot.

IN the early morning rain the massed Federal column hit the apex, Hancock's corps at the center and Burnside's on the east side. Francis Barlow, commanding Hancock's leading division, broke through, closely followed by Birney's division. The blue-clad troops poured through the gap and advanced. Without the necessary artillery support, Ewell's troops were forced back, losing the twenty guns in the process, in addition to General Johnson and about 3,000 of his men.

But then things began to go wrong for the Federals. Instead of fanning out to the left and right, as Upton's regiments had done, to widen the breach and enable Burnside to come through, they went straight ahead and jammed up. The supporting troops coming in behind them crowded up so closely that organization and control was just about impossible, and the 3,000 prisoners only added to the confusion. The delay enabled Lane's brigade of Hill's corps (temporarily under Early during Hill's absence), which was immediately on the right of the captured works, to fall back to an unfinished line in the rear and pour a telling flanking fire on Hancock's left, which stopped the advance. Then Gordon's division of Ewell's corps, which was being held in reserve, was thrown in front of the Federal column, slowly forcing Hancock's men back to the Confederate entrenchments in their rear. About 6 a.m. Grant ordered Warren and Wright to Hancock's support, but another breakthrough was not achieved. In the initial assault Potter's division of Burnside's corps momentarily broke through the east side of the salient but was quickly driven out again by Early's troops who came over to their left to support Ewell.

Again, as in The Wilderness, Lee now appeared on the field to rally his men in this critical moment. If the assault succeeded, the Army of Northern Virginia might be cut in two and destroyed piecemeal. All day long and into the night the battle raged along the whole line with increasing fury. One Confederate officer remembered that "there was one continuous roll of musketry from dawn until midnight." Lee made five separate assaults in a vain attempt to recover his position. Although he failed in this, the Confederates did hold so that he could have new works constructed at the base of the Mule Shoe to straighten out his line.

A FEW hundred yards west of the salient the Confed-

Union troops hold a captured trench in the struggle for the salient. Drawing by Alfred R. Waud. (Library of Congress)

Union artillery lumbering through the mud created by the early morning rain of May 12, 1864. Many horses died from exhaustion in their struggles against mud. Etching from a drawing by Edwin Forbes.. (Thirty Years After: An Artist's Story of the Great War)

erate trenches made a slight bend to the south, known as the "angle," and later as the "Bloody Angle." Here the men of Wright's corps came face to face with Ewell's veterans in a vicious hand-to-hand fight. Clubbed muskets and bayonets were used freely, as the rain poured down in sheets and the trenches ran red with blood. In some places the wounded and dying of both sides were trampled into the mud to drown or suffocate in the frenzied fighting. "The flags of both armies waved at the same moment over the same breast-works," one soldier noted, "while beneath them Federal and Confederate endeavored to drive home the bayonet through the interstices of the logs." Colonel Porter, of Grant's staff, later described the scene as he remembered it. "The battle near the 'angle' was probably the most desperate engagement in the history of modern warfare, and presented features which were absolutely appalling. It was chiefly a savage hand-to-hand fight across the breastworks. Rank after rank was riddled by shot and shell and bayonet-thrusts, and finally sank, a mass of torn and mutilated corpses; then fresh troops rushed madly forward to replace the dead, and so the murderous work went on. Guns were run up close to the parapet, and double charges of canister played their part in the bloody work. The fence-rails and logs in the breastworks were shattered into splinters, and trees over a foot and a half in diameter were cut completely in two by the incessant musketry fire. A section

of the trunk of a stout oak-tree thus severed was afterward sent to Washington, where it is still on exhibition at the National Museum."

Despite the intensity of the battle, neither side could advance, and later that night Lee's men withdrew to their new line at the base of the salient. Then a tragic silence settled over the bloody field. In the dark woods surgeons were busy amputating by the eerie glow of lanterns. The next day Porter again visited the area of the heaviest fighting. "Our own killed were scattered over a large space near the 'angle,' while in front of the captured breastworks the enemy's dead, vastly more numerous than our own, were piled upon each other in some places four layers deep, exhibiting every ghastly phase of mutilation. Below the mass of fast-decaying corpses, the convulsive twitching of limbs and the writhing of bodies showed that there were wounded men still alive and struggling to extricate themselves from their horrid entombment. Every relief possible was afforded, but in too many cases it came too late. The place was well named the 'Bloody Angle!' "

A COMPARATIVE lull settled over the area for the next several days, as each army tried to catch its breath and the rain continued to pour down. "Since the 3rd we had been marching, fighting, and building earthworks so continuously," wrote a soldier in the 13th Massachusetts Volunteers, "that no opportunity had been afforded

The struggle for the works at the "Bloody Angle." (Battles and Leaders of the Civil War)

to change any of our clothing." On the 16th Grant reported to Washington: "We have had five days' almost constant rain without any prospect yet of its clearing up. The roads have now become so impassable that ambulances with wounded can no longer run between here and Fredericksburg. All offensive operations necessarily cease until we can have twenty-four hours of dry weather." He had suffered over 17,000 casualties at Spotsylvania Court House and he now requested replacements be sent to him. But he did not want anyone in Washington to get the idea that he intended to stop fighting or retreat. "You can assure the President and Secretary of War," he wrote, "that the elements alone have suspended hostilities and that it is in no manner due to weakness or exhaustion on our part."

Grant was gradually getting to know the Army of the Potomac and, more important, the caliber of its generals. He was becoming dissatisfied with Burnside and Warren for their dilatory tactics and lack of drive and initiative. There seems little doubt that had they attacked at Spotsylvania with the force and coordination that Hancock and Wright used, that the Army of Northern Virginia might very well have been destroyed. Of Warren he later wrote: "Warren's difficulty was two fold: when he received an order to do anything, it would at once occur to his mind how all the balance of the army should be engaged so as properly to cooperate with him. His ideas were generally good, but he would forget that the person giving him orders had thought of others at the time he

had of him. In like manner, when he did get ready to execute an order, after giving most intelligent instructions to division commanders, he would go in with one division, holding the others in reserve until he could superintend their movements in person also, forgetting that division commanders could execute an order without his presence."

ALTHOUGH he did not seem to realize it, a similar criticism, in a sense, could be levelled against Grant. As General Humphreys wrote later: "There were two officers commanding the same army. Such a mixed command was not calculated to produce the best results that either singly was capable of bringing about. It naturally caused some vagueness and uncertainty as to the exact sphere of each, and sometimes took away from the positiveness, fullness and earnestness of the consideration of an intended operation or tactical movement that, had there been but one commander, would have had the most earnest attention and corresponding action."

And Lee by now was getting to know Grant. He had no illusions anymore about Grant retreating, even after his heavy losses in the Wilderness and at Spotsylvania. He was acutely aware that Grant was probably just waiting for replacements before again moving south. On the 18th he sent a long dispatch to Jefferson Davis describing the situation as he saw it: "[Grant's] position is strongly entrenched, and we cannot attack it with any prospect of success without great loss of men which I wish to avoid if possible. The enemy's artillery is superior in weight of metal and range to our own, and my object has been to engage him when in motion and under circumstances that will not cause us to suffer from this disadvantage. . . . Neither the strength of our army nor the condition of our animals will admit of any extensive movement with a view of drawing the enemy from his position." Then he told Davis, "The importance of this campaign to the administration of Mr. Lincoln and to General Grant leaves no doubt that every effort and every sacrifice will be made to secure its success." In effect, he was warning the Confederate Government in Richmond that Grant would get all the replacements and supplies he needed in order to continue to carry the war to the South, regardless of the casualties Lee might be able to inflict along the way. He was also implying that with an election coming up in November, Lincoln could not afford to let the Army of the Potomac retreat again, regardless of its losses. And, although his casualties at Spotsylvania were unknown, Lee informed Davis that if Grant was to be kept away from Richmond the Army of Northern Virginia had to have reinforcements. "The question," he warned, "is whether we shall fight the battle here or around Richmond. If the troops are obliged to be retained at Richmond I may be forced back."

AS early as the day after the hard fighting at the salient,

Grant had decided that he would again move around Lee's right flank rather than attempt to attack him in his entrenched position. He wrote to Meade: "I do not desire a battle brought on with the enemy in their position of yesterday, but want to press as close to them as possible to determine their position and strength. We must get by the right flank of the enemy for the next fight." That night, the 13th, Warren and Wright pulled back and marched behind the rest of the army to a new position east of Spotsylvania Court House. The heavy rains then held up further movement. Lee, of course, then extended his right to meet this shift. On the theory that Lee had probably weakened his left and center by this move, Grant agreed to another assault against the salient. On May 18 Hancock, supported by Wright, made a last attempt to break Ewell's line, but this time the attack was blasted by thirty massed cannon and beaten back before it even reached the Confederate position. The next day Ewell tried to find a weak spot on the Federal right flank but was quickly repulsed, although the attack did delay the departure of the Federals for another twenty-four hours. During the night of the 20th the Army of the Potomac once again was put in motion, sliding leftward and southward, always edging closer to Richmond, on the long road to the North Anna, Cold Harbor, Petersburg, Richmond, Appomattox, and the end, the end of the long dying.

One of General Ewell's men killed in the fighting of May 19, 1864. Photograph by Timothy H. O'Sullivan. (Library of Congress)

Detour on the Road to Richmond
by Joseph P. Cullen

IN the inky blackness of the relatively quiet night of May 20, 1864, the Union Army of the Potomac started its march away from the battlefield of Spotsylvania Court House, Virginia. The men of General Winfield S. Hancock's II Corps stumbled along the unfamiliar country roads, falling into ditches, tripping over the underbrush, walking into bushes and limbs of trees. Some fell asleep marching; imagination played havoc with tired eyes; a clump of trees became a group of the enemy—a runaway horse, a cavalry charge. Dead faces of lost comrades seemed to stare out between the silent trees. "It is no small tax upon one's endurance to remain marching all night," one veteran recalled. "During the day there is always something to attract the attention and amuse, but at night there is nothing."

Hancock's orders were "to get as far towards Richmond" on the line of the Richmond, Fredericksburg & Potomac Railroad as he could, "fighting the enemy in whatever force" he could find him. The other three corps would follow as soon as possible. Having failed to crush General Robert E. Lee in the Wilderness, and again at Spotsylvania, Grant was trying either to maneuver Lee into a position where he could be attacked in the open or, failing in that, to get between him and Richmond.

ATTEMPTING to lure Lee out in the open where he could be attacked before he had time to entrench, Grant deliberately sent the II Corps ahead of the rest of the army to act as bait. But Lee apparently was incapable of assuming the offensive at this time; his only objective was to keep his army between Grant and Richmond in order to protect the Confederate capital. Consequently, as soon as he learned of Hancock's move he ordered a withdrawal to Hanover Junction, just south of the North Anna River and about twenty-five miles from Richmond. Here the Virginia Central and the R.F.&P. railroads crossed. Explaining the withdrawal, Lee stated: "I should have preferred contesting the enemy's approach inch by inch; but my solicitude for Richmond caused me to abandon that plan."

The North Anna here flows in a southeasterly direction between high, steep bluffs. Just north of Hanover Junction was the R.F.&P. railroad bridge, and west of it Chesterfield (or Fox's) Bridge on the Telegraph Road (nearly congruent

Jericho Mills and the pontoon bridge over which both the V and VI Corps crossed the North Anna River. Photograph by Timothy H. O'Sullivan. (Library of Congress)

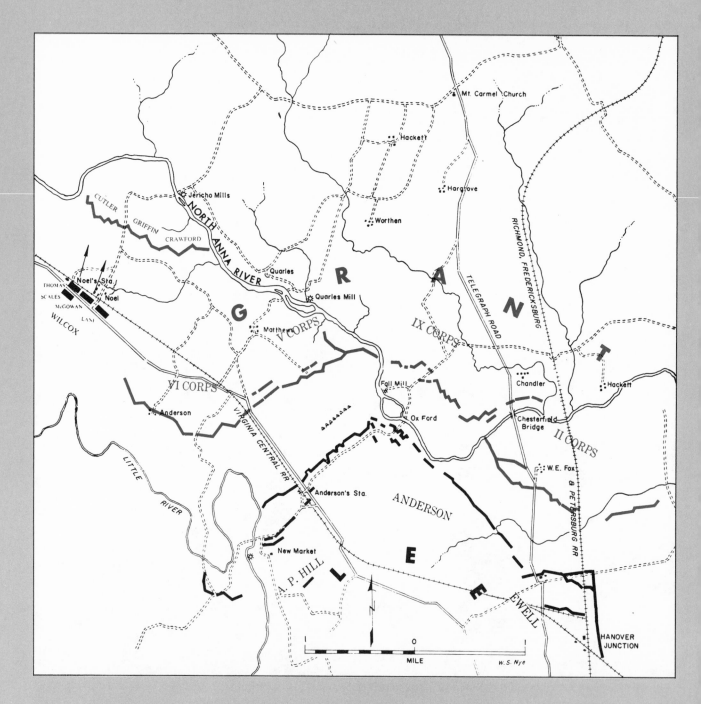

After the Battle of Spotsylvania Court House, Lee marched his forces to a convex position south of the North Anna River, with his right resting near Hanover Junction. The Army of the Potomac followed, arriving along the river on 23-24 May. Wright's VI and Warren's V Corps crossed above Ox Ford and Hancock's II at Chesterfield Bridge. Burnside, dilatory as usual, got only one division of the IX across. Both armies entrenched and there was some fighting. However, Grant decided that the Confederate position was too strong to be taken in a general assault. He continued his movement by the left flank.

This map, being based on an accurate topographic map with some place names, roads, and troop positions as in the Atlas to the Official Records, is probably the first reasonably accurate diagram of the operation. The troop positions shown are, with one exception, the entrenchments occupied at the close of the operation. The exception is on the left, between Noel's Station and the river. The map shows the positions from which Wilcox's division attacked three of Warren's divisions about six o'clock in the evening of May 23. The Federals entrenched at the close of this action, as shown.

with U.S. Route #1). Nearly two miles upstream was Ox Ford, and three miles beyond that was another ford at Jericho mills. It was a gently rolling country of soft ridges and quiet woods interspersed with cleared lands and cultivated fields, unspectacular but pleasing and colorful to the eye.

LEE did not plan to contest seriously the crossing of the river, because the north bank in most places was higher than the south bank, and the Federal artillery would be in command. The one exception to this was at Ox Ford where the high ground on the south dominated the river. Here a Federal crossing could be contested. Accordingly, Lee adopted a novel system of defense. His line was in the form of a wide inverted V with the Apex at Ox Ford facing generally north. Here he placed R. H. Anderson's (formerly Longstreet's) First Corps. A. P. Hill's Third Corps, on Anderson's left, was drawn back on a line running southwest through Anderson's Station on the Virginia Central Railroad to the Little River. And Richard S. Ewell's Second Corps, on Anderson's right, stretched southeast to a swamp just east of Hanover Junction. With the North Anna guarding his front and both flanks well secured—the left by Little River and the right by swampy ground—Lee was in a powerful defensive position. So long as he held Ox Ford he could quickly and easily reinforce one wing from the other and at the same time compel the enemy to attack him with separated wings.

By late afternoon of May 22 all three Confederate corps were in position and strongly entrenched, and Lee's strength had been increased by the arrival of George E. Pickett's division, Robert F. Hoke's brigade, and two brigades under John C. Breckinridge, giving him a total force of about fifty thousand, as opposed to over one hundred thousand for Grant. Pickett was attached temporarily to Hill, while Hoke's brigade was returned to Jubal A. Early's division of corps. Breckinridge's two brigades remained as an independent command under the direct orders of Lee and were put into line between Anderson's right and Ewell's left.

ABOUT noon on the twenty-third the head of General Gouverneur K. Warren's V Corps reached the ford at Jericho Mills and started to cross. Wading in water up to their waists, the Federals quickly brushed aside the small confederate force guarding the ford. Pontoons were then laid and by 5 p.m. the whole corps was across and advancing southward through densely wooded country towards the Virginia Central Railroad, driving off Hill's skirmishers. Although the initial crossing had been made at noon, it was 3 p.m. before Hill was notified. He immediately ordered Cadmus M. Wilcox's division to advance and attack. Moving up a road just south of the Central Railroad and parallel to it, Wilcox then turned and formed line of battle facing north, with Lane's brigade on the right, McGowan's in the center, and Thomas's on the left. Scales's brigade was in rear of Thomas. It was now almost dusk.

Advancing across the railroad tracks and into the woods, Wilcox caught the leading Union division, Cutler's, just coming into position and temporarily drove it back in confusion, but the attack was uncoordinated and poorly supported. Thomas's brigade broke and gave way when Federal reinforcements appeared, leaving McGowan's left flank in the air and creating a gap in the line through which the Federals advanced. Scales, who was supposed to move around Thomas's left and hit the enemy in flank, made the move but did not press the attack and was quickly repulsed. Hill later sent Henry Heth's division to Wilcox's support but it did not arrive in time to have any appreciable effect. Wilcox suffered over six hundred casualties and gained absolutely nothing. With the coming of darkness Hill withdrew behind his entrenchments, and Warren's corps proceeded to dig in unmolested.

A soldier in the 13th Massachusetts Volunteers recorded a humorous incident in the aftermath of the fight:

> We were now occupying a piece of woods from which the enemy had just been driven. As soon as it was dark we were ordered to lie down on the ground, in line of battle, with guns in readiness, at a moment's notice, to continue the fight. We were to remain absolutely quiet and not to strike a match, even for lighting a pipe. Not a sound could be heard along the line so perfect was the stillness. While we were lying there, completely hidden from sight by the impenetrable darkness of the woods, watching with ears strained to catch the slightest sound, and eyes struggling to pierce the gloom, the crackling sound of footsteps was heard, and suddenly a tall specimen of the Southern chivalry appeared. With gun on his shoulder and an air of confidence, such as a soldier has when fancying himself safely within his own lines, he walked up to the very muzzles of our rifles before being challenged. To his inexpressible astonishment he received the order to "*Halt!* Who comes there?" to which he responded, "Second South Carolina, by Gawd!" One of the boys, imitating the tone of his voice, replied, "Well, we're the Thirteenth Massachusetts, by Gawd!" At this unexpected salutation, which surprised him as much as if he had been suddenly challenged by St. Peter, he unclasped his belt and threw it, with his gun, on the ground to the great amusement of the boys, who in spite of orders to the contrary, could not restrain their laughter. "How did you like the fight, Johnnie?" he was asked by one of the boys. "Wall, you 'uns fire shell a derned sight worse than we 'uns do." The necessity for silence prevented our carrying on the conversation further.

MEANWHILE Horatio G. Wright's VI Corps had reached Jericho Mills and was in position to cross to Warren's aid if needed, while Ambrose E. Burnside's IX Corps was now at Ox Ford. Near nightfall, Hancock, coming down the Telegraph Road, found a small force of Confederates entrenched on the north bank of the river guarding the railroad and Chesterfield bridges. Two brigades of David B. Birney's division quickly charged the Confederates and drove them back across the river, leaving one bridge intact.

Early next morning Wright's corps crossed at Jericho Ford and took up position on Warren's right, thus extending the Union right flank south of the Virginia Central Railroad and facing almost directly east, opposite Hill and Anderson's left. Hancock also crossed unopposed and came

40

Losses on the North Anna
Federal reports show 223 killed, 1,460 wounded, 290 missing—a total of 1,973 casualties. No Confederate reports are available other than the 600 casualties Wilcox's division suffered. Phisterer estimates the total Confederate losses at 2,000.

into line opposite Ewell and Anderson's right. But when Burnside in the center attempted to cross at Ox Ford he was easily repulsed.

Not yet realizing the strength of Lee's position, Grant ordered Burnside to send one division to Hancock and another to Warren, with a view to marching on Ox Ford by the south bank of the river and from opposite directions. If successful, this would clear the way for Burnside's remaining division to cross, and it would also unite the separated wings of the army.

ON the twenty-fourth, Robert B. Potter's division crossed over the Telegraph Road bridge and reported to Hancock. No attempt was made to move on Ox Ford, however, as Hancock realized that the strength of the Confederate position in his front did not justify an attack. Thomas L. Crittenden's division crossed at the newly discovered ford at Quarles Mill, about a mile upstream from Ox Ford. Crittenden then started to move down the south bank, James H. Ledlie's brigade in the lead, only to be attacked by Billy Mahone's division and driven back with heavy losses,

Ledlie's brigade narrowly escaping capture. The division then fell back and connected with Samuel W. Crawford's division of Warren's corps behind strong entrenchments. That ended action on the 24th except for skirmishing.

As in The Wilderness and at Spotsylvania, both armies were again at a stalemate. Grant had his whole army south of the river with the exception of one division on the north bank at Ox Ford, which would move in either direction to the support of either wing if the necessity arose. But both forces were entrenched so strongly that frontal assaults would be suicidal, and at the same time there was no place to maneuver. As Grant stated in his report to Washington:

> To make a direct attack from either wing would cause a slaughter of our men that even success would not justify. To turn the enemy by his right, between the two Annas, is impossible on account of the swamp upon which his right rests. To turn him by the left leaves Little River, New Found River, and South Anna River, all of them streams presenting considerable obstacles to the movement of our army, to be crossed.

EVEN if Grant succeeded in making a breakthrough, to take advantage of it he would have to cross the river twice before he could reinforce one wing from the other, while Lee could shift his forces quickly and easily on his interior lines. Defensively Lee's position was just about impregnable, but offensively there was no particular advantage to it. Douglas S. Freeman in his biography of Lee implies that if Lee had not been sick and confined to his tent on May 25

Federal troops in newly dug trenches overlooking the North Anna River. A sketch in Battles and Leaders of the Civil War *identifies them as "Confederate trenches at Chesterfield Bridge on the North Anna, half a mile above the railroad bridge." However, Miller's* Photographic History of the Civil War *notes that they were "thrown up in a night by the Federals near North Anna River . . . ." (Library of Congress)*

If the picture above of crossing the North Anna is based on a dependable field sketch, the location is Ox Ford, because only at that point were the river banks, especially on the north, low and relatively flat as shown. Burnside's IX Corps was supposed to cross here but was delayed by entrenched Confederates south of the river. The sketch would therefore have been made after the Confederates withdrew. (Harper's History of the Great Rebellion) *Battery on the North Anna with the left three pieces of a Federal battery of Napoleons in the foreground and other guns nearer the river (below). The latter appear to be somewhat scattered and echeloned in depth; it is likely that they were used individually since echelonment of guns in a battery position was not commonly practiced until World War II.* (Harper's History of the Great Rebellion)

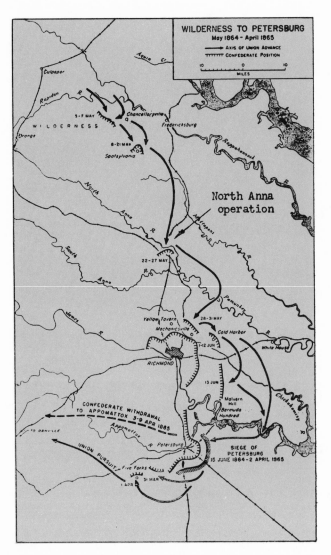

WILDERNESS TO PETERSBURG
May 1864 - April 1865

North Anna
operation

Map of Grant's 1864 campaign and his successive attempts to overcome Lee's army by direct assault, followed in each case by a flank movement. (CWTI Collection)

Potomac, except for two divisions, was south of the river, and earthworks more than compensated for the difference in numbers. If Grant admitted it would have been suicidal for the Union army to make a frontal assault against either of the Confederate flanks, it certainly would have been even more so for Lee to attack Hancock's reinforced corps, after it had thrown up breastworks. If Lee had tried it and failed, as most assuredly would have happened, the Army of Northern Virginia might have been crushed between the two Federal wings.

GRANT recognized his position as being generally useless to his objective of destroying the opposing army, particularly if that army would not come out from behind its entrenchments and assume the offensive, but at no time did he regard it as dangerous. After his failure on the 24th to unite both wings at Ox Ford, there was no further action, but the Army of the Potomac stayed in position on the 25th and 26th, giving Lee plenty of time to attack if he so desired. This was certainly not the action of a field commander who considered his situation as critical. The men of Warren's corps spent these two days destroying long stretches of the Virginia Central Railroad, main connection for the Confederates with the vital food supply of the Shenandoah Valley. They left many tokens of their presence in the shape of Maltese crosses made around trees and stumps by bent railroad iron. At the same time Hancock's men were ripping up miles of the R.F.&P. track.

The fact was that the Army of Northern Virginia had lost its old capacity to seize the initiative and turn a stubborn defense into a daring offense, and no one realized this more than Lee himself. He no longer could afford to gamble; his sole mission was the protection of Richmond.

WHEN it became evident that Lee was not going to make any move, Grant, admitting that "we could do nothing where we were," determined to "draw out of our present position and make one more effort to get between him and Richmond. I had no expectation now, however, of succeeding in this; but I did expect to hold him far enough west to enable me to reach the James River high up."

Consequently, orders were issued to change the Federal base of supplies from Port Royal on the Rappahannock to White House on the Pamunkey River. Then, in the midst of a violent rainstorm on the night of May 26th, both wings started back across the North Anna, as the tired soldiers began yet another session of stumbling through the dark and the rain and the mud, many of them worn out as much from marching as from fighting, in this seemingly endless campaign of "shoot, shovel, and march," as they called it. And when the nauseous odor from the heat-bloated bodies of dead men and horses became almost unbearable at times, a veteran in the 9th New York Heavy Artillery remembered some wag remarking, "Any man that'll take more'n one sniff of that's a hog," as they headed for yet another river crossing at Hanovertown and a rendezvous with destiny at a crossroads called Cold Harbor.

he might have been able to destroy one or the other of the separated Federal wings. This statement had led other historians to assert that Grant blundered badly by putting his army into a positon where it could have been destoyed and probably would have been but for the fact that Lee was indisposed at the critical moment.

For a few precious hours on the 24th, after Hancock's corps crossed the North Anna and before his troops had entrenched, Lee had the opportunity, if his divisions moved promptly, to strike Hancock's corps a terrible blow. Until reinforced by Potter's division, Hancock's command numbered about twenty thousand. At this time, the Federal army was divided into two wings neither of which could reinforce the other without crossing the river twice. Leaving seven thousand men to hold the west face of the entrenchments and the apex at Ox Ford, Lee might have assailed Hancock with more than thirty-six thousand footsoldiers, but time was critical. Hancock's troops by early afternoon on the 24th had entrenched and had been reinforced by Potter's four thousand-man division. Now the Army of the

Drewry's Bluff and Cold Harbor

Grant's campaign strategy had envisaged a simultaneous advance by all Union armies in Virginia to prevent Lee from calling in reinforcements from detachments in the Shenandoah Valley and near Richmond. The largest Union force in this theater, other than the Army of the Potomac, was the 30,000–man Army of the James commanded by Benjamin Butler, a political general with a checkered military career during the War. Grant ordered Butler to advance from his base at Hampton Roads up the James on May 5 and cut the railroad between Richmond and Petersburg. Had he acted boldly, Butler might have smashed into Richmond from the south, for the city was defended by no more than 5,000 troops plus a few thousand emergency militia. Fighting desperately in the Wilderness and at Spotsylvania sixty miles to the north, Lee could spare no troops to reinforce General P.G.T. Beauregard, who had been called to Virginia to command Richmond's defenses.

Butler fumbled his opportunity. He advanced slowly and timidly, probing for the railroad with detached brigades instead of moving with his whole force. This enabled Beauregard to scrape together reinforcements from the Carolinas and create an army of 18,000 men, with which he attacked Butler's advance units of equal size on May 16 near Drewry's Bluff eight miles south of Richmond. In a hard-fought battle the Confederates drove Butler's men back to their trenches across a neck between the James and Appomattox Rivers just north of Petersburg. The southerners entrenched their own line and sealed off Butler's army "as if," in Grant's caustic words, "it had been in a bottle strongly corked." Beauregard could even spare some men from this line, so he sent 7,000 much-needed reinforcements to Lee.

Disgusted by this failure, Grant ordered 10,000 reinforcements from Butler to the Army of the Potomac at the beginning of June. By then Grant confronted Lee along six miles of trenches near the dusty crossroads hamlet of Cold Harbor, ten miles northeast of Richmond. In four weeks of fighting and flanking Grant had driven Lee nearly fifty miles, at the cost of 44,000 Union casualties and at least 25,000 Confederate casualties. It was a campaign unprecedented in its relentless intensity and duration. In previous years these two armies had fought each other in several big battles, followed by the retreat of one or the other behind the nearest river. Both armies would then rest and recuperate for a month or more before going at it again (the sole exception was the two-and-one-half-week interval between Second Manassas and Antietam). In the 1864 campaign, though, the armies had never been out of contact with each other. Some kind of fighting along with a great deal of marching and digging took place virtually every day, and a great many nights as well. Mental and physical exhaustion began to take a toll; officers and men suffered from what in later wars would be called shell shock. One Union officer noted that in three weeks men "had grown thin and haggard. The experience of those twenty days seemed to have added twenty years to their age." Captain Oliver Wendell Holmes, Jr., observed that "many a man has gone crazy since this campaign began from the terrible pressure on mind and body."

All of this was on Grant's mind as the armies confronted each other at Cold Harbor. Grant's strategy in this campaign is often called a war of attrition. That is a mistake. Grant sought to maneuver Lee into open-field battle where the superior

"Building breastworks at Cold Harbor." Here, on June 3, the Yankees under Grant suffered 7,000 casualties; Lee's Confederate troops had fewer than 1,000. (Grey Castle Press)

weight of northern artillery and numbers would tell. It was Lee who turned it into a war of attrition by anticipating Grant's maneuvers and entrenching his army at every turn. At Cold Harbor Grant could undertake another flanking move to the left. But Lee had the inside track and could pull back into the immensely strong fortifications ringing Richmond or slide south to link up with Beauregard in the equally strong fortifications protecting Petersburg. So Grant decided to attack at Cold Harbor, hoping for a breakthrough that would puncture Lee's defenses and open the road to Richmond.

At dawn on June 3, half of the Army of the Potomac went over the top in an assault on the Confederate trenches that anticipated similar attacks along the western front in World War I. And the assault at Cold Harbor turned out the same way as most such attempts did in World War I—a bloody, demoralizing repulse. In less than half an hour the Union attackers suffered 7,000 casualties. This horrible experience took the fighting edge off the Army of the Potomac. Its striking power was never quite the same again. Grant confessed his mistake. "I regret this assault more than any one I have ever ordered," he said that evening.

But part of Grant's genius lay in his iron will. Unlike previous Union commanders in the Virginia theater, he did not allow tactical setbacks to dissuade him from his strategic goal. Instead of pulling back, he prepared for another long swing southward, this time all the way across the James River in an attempt to capture the network of railroads that joined at Petersburg. These railroads were vital to the survival of Richmond and of Lee's army. Grant knew that Lee would have to fight to defend them. On June 12 he began the move that would take both armies to Petersburg.

—James M. McPherson

THE SIEGE
OF PETERSBURG

by Joseph P. Cullen

IN MARCH 1864 President Lincoln appointed Lieutenant General Ulysses S. Grant commander in chief of all the armies of the United States. Fresh from his recent dramatic victories at Vicksburg and Chattanooga, Grant now wore three stars—more than any officer had ever worn, except George Washington and old Winfield Scott. He now commanded twenty-one army corps and eighteen military departments, for a total of more than half a million men. In a little more than a month he would turn 42. His appointment would change the whole course and direction of the war.

Of medium height (5′ 8″), Grant was not impressive physically. Round-shouldered with a slovenly posture, his favorite dress was a private soldier's uniform with officer's insignia stitched on the shoulders. A native Midwesterner from Ohio, he was generally looked down on by the more polished Eastern officers in the Army of the Potomac. But the enlisted men quickly noticed one of his strongest characteristics—dogged determination. As one of them noted when Grant galloped past, "He looks as if he meant it." And over in Robert E. Lee's Army of Northern Virginia, General James Longstreet warned, "That man will fight us every day and every hour till the end of the war."

Although he had spent the war so far in the West, Grant was well aware of what had been happening in the Eastern theater. As he stated: "In the east the opposing forces stood in substantially the same relations toward each other as three years before, or when the war began; they were both between the Federal and Confederate Capitals. Battles had been fought of as great severity as had ever been known in war. . . from the James River to Gettysburg, with indecisive results." He planned to change that by putting pressure on all Confederate armies at the same time, something that had never been done before.

LEE'S strategy had always been to "risk some points in order to have a sufficient force concentrated, with the hope of dealing a successful blow when opportunity favors." He believed "as the enemy cannot attack all points at one time. . .the troops could be concentrated. . . where an assault should be made." With its interior, or shorter, lines of communication the South could so concentrate its forces, shifting troops from east to west, or the reverse, as the need arose.

This is exactly what Grant realized and wished to prevent. The way to stop the Confederates from so concentrating, as he saw it, was to put and keep pressure on all points at all times, so that the South would be unable to continue its thus-far-successful strategy. Consequently, he organized a unified plan of operations. General Benjamin F. Butler, with the Army of the James, was to march up the south side of the James River and attack Petersburg or Richmond or both; General Franz Sigel would push down the Shenandoah Valley driving General John C. Breckinridge before him, thereby protecting Washington; General Nathaniel Banks in New Orleans to march on Mobile; General William T. Sherman to cut across Georgia, driving General Joseph E. Johnston before him, take Atlanta, and if still necessary swing north to Richmond; while General George Meade's Army of the Potomac, with Grant actually in command, pushed to stop Lee's Army of Northern Virginia and capture Richmond. As Grant stated "To get possession of Lee's Army was the first great object. With the capture of his army Richmond would necessarily follow."

LEE was well aware of Grant's determination and ability, and he also realized that this was an election year in the North. He wrote to President Jefferson Davis: "The importance of this campaign to the administration of Mr. Lincoln and to General Grant leaves no doubt that every effort and every sacrifice will be made to secure its success." Consequently, he believed he had to destroy Grant's army before it reached the James River. "If he gets there it will become a siege, and then it will be a mere question of time." To accomplish this, Lee's strategy would be to try to inflict such heavy losses on Grant that either he would abandon the campaign or the North would become tired of so costly a struggle and not re-elect Lincoln, in which event the South hoped for a negotiated peace.

The campaign began in May when the Army of the Potomac crossed the Rapidan River and the Army of Northern Virginia blocked its path in The Wilderness. After a particularly vicious and costly battle Grant, instead of retreating to re-group and re-plan as other Federal commanders had done, executed a left flank movement, still heading south and trying to get between Lee and Richmond. A few days later the two armies clashed again at Spotsylvania Court House in a series of grim battles, but still indecisive so far as major objectives were concerned. Although Grant suffered staggering losses, he was slowly but methodically destroying Lee's ability to wage offensive war.

Again Grant executed a left flank movement to get around Lee, and then, by a series of flanking marches which the Confederate soldiers called the "sidling movement," and the Federal soldiers the "jug-handle movement," Grant worked his way down to the outskirts of Richmond. At the Battle of Cold Harbor in early June he attacked Lee's veterans in their well-entrenched positions but suffered defeat with heavy losses. This battle finally convinced Federal officers that well-selected, well-manned entrenchments, adequately supported by artillery, were practically impregnable to frontal assaults. Consequently, the results of this battle changed the course of the war in the East from a war of maneuver to a war of siege.

GRANT now had to decide what action he would take next. It was obvious that Lee with his numerically inferior force had no intention of coming out from behind his

Gathering bodies for burial, April 1865. This photograph was taken at Cold Harbor, a bloody battle in Grant's Overland Campaign prior to Petersburg. (U.S. Army Military History Institute)

Pontoon bridge on the Appomattox River below Petersburg, at Point of Rocks, Butler's headquarters. Drawing by Alfred R. Waud. (LC)

entrenchments to fight; it was equally obvious that to attempt to storm those entrenchments again would be nothing less than mass murder. And another left flanking movement was out of the question because Grant had run out of room in which to maneuver. That left only two courses of action open; withdraw to Washington and start all over again, or head south. Grant never even considered withdrawal. On June 5 he wrote to Army Chief of Staff Henry W. Halleck in Washington: "My idea from the start has been to beat Lee's army, if possible, north of Richmond; then after destroying his lines of communication north of the James River, to transfer the army to the south side and besiege Lee in Richmond, or follow him south if he should retreat."

To isolate Richmond Grant needed to cut the railroads which supplied it. Twenty-three miles south of the Confederate Capital stood the city of Petersburg, with a population of about 18,000. Nestling on the south bank of

Grant's crossing of the James River, June 14-16, 1864, one of the most brilliant actions in military annals.

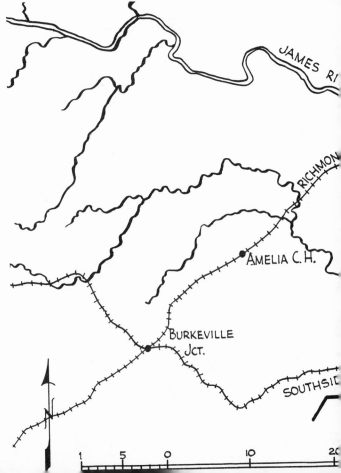

the Appomattox River, Petersburg by 1864 had become the main source of supply for both Richmond and the Army of Northern Virginia. Five railroads converged there, and through it passed a constant stream of war materials and necessities of life from farther south to sustain the war effort. Tracks radiated in all directions. The Richmond & Petersburg Railroad left the city to the north; the Southside Railroad ran west to Lynchburg; the Weldon Railroad connected with North Carolina and points south, and also connected with the Richmond & Danville Railroad (which did not go through Petersburg) at Burkeville, about forty miles west; the Norfolk Railroad; and the City Point Railroad which ran to the hamlet of City Point at the junction of the James and Appomattox Rivers, about eight miles away.

AS early as 1862 the need for fortifications to protect Petersburg was recognized. Work began that summer under the direction of Captain Charles H. Dimmock, and a year later a chain of massive breastworks and artillery emplacements ten miles long stood completed. A huge semi-circle began east of the city on the Appomattox River and ended on the river west of the city, thus protecting all but the northern approaches. The fifty-five artillery batteries were numbered consecutively from east to west. Generally referred to as the "Dimmock Line," its very length and size required a formidable number of troops to man it properly.

Grant's original plan, of course, called for Butler's Army of the James to march up the south side of the James

and attack Petersburg. But largely through the ineptness of his Regular Army subordinates Butler, a politically appointed general, was bottled up in a curve of the river at Bermuda Hundred by a much smaller Confederate force and never did reach Petersburg and, although frequent raids on the railroads were made, the damage was usually quickly patched up. It was obvious that if these railroads were to be permanently shut off the Federal forces would have to take physical possession of them. Consequently, Grant decided to by-pass Richmond, move the army quickly across the James River and attack Petersburg before Lee got in position to defend it. With the capture of that railroad center Lee would be besieged in Richmond with most of his supply lines cut and the end of the war would then be a mere question of time, as Lee himself recognized.

On June 6 Grant withdrew General Gouverneur K. Warren's corps from the lines at Cold Harbor and, supported by General James H. Wilson's cavalry division, used it to secure the passages across the Chickahominy River and down to the James. The rest of the army would move behind this screen. On June 7 he sent "Little Phil" Sheridan with the remaining two divisions of cavalry west to raid Charlottesville and disrupt Confederate communications. To counter this, Lee was forced to send Wade Hampton's cavalry after Sheridan, leaving himself without adequate cavalry for reconnaissance. Then during the night of June 12 Grant secretly moved all the troops out of the trenches, without Lee's being aware of the move until the following morning.

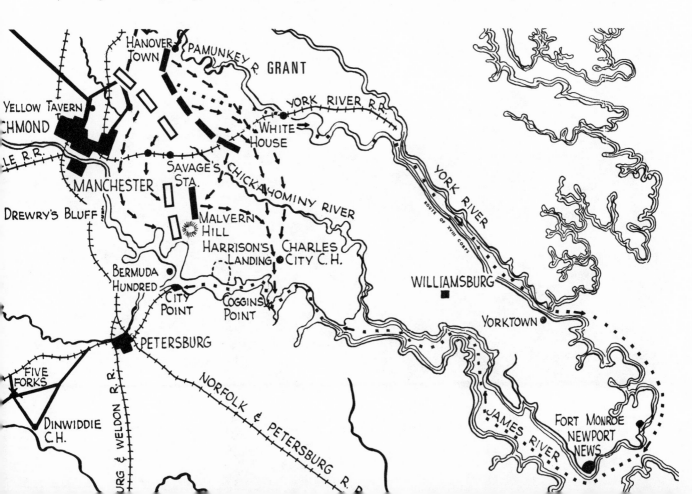

GENERAL William F. Smith's XVIII Corps, which Grant had borrowed from Butler's Army of the James for the fight at Cold Harbor, moved first. Immediately after dark it withdrew from the line quietly and proceeded on a short march behind General Ambrose Burnside's IX Corps to White House Landing on the Pamunkey River, where the troops boarded transports for the return voyage to Bermuda Hundred on the James. General Winfield S. Hancock's II Corps also pulled back at dark and went in the opposite direction towards the Chickahominy behind the screen of the V Corps.

While this move was taking place, Grant went to Bermuda Hundred to confer with Butler regarding the forthcoming attack on Petersburg. It was agreed that Smith's corps, which would be the first to arrive, would, if considered feasible, attack Petersburg, supported later by the II Corps when it arrived. Grant's verbal orders to Butler and Smith may have been definite and dynamic, but his written instructions certainly were not. "I do not want Petersburg visited," he wrote, "unless it is held, nor an attempt to take it unless you feel a reasonable degree of confidence of success." To timid generals like Butler

and Smith, this type of instruction gave them a wide degree of latitude in their interpretation of orders.

Early on the morning of June 15 Smith's troops crossed the Appomattox on a pontoon bridge at Broadway Landing, about a mile above City Point. His corps was below its usual strength as one division was left at Bermuda Hundred and he had suffered heavy losses at Cold Harbor. To bring him up to near normal strength, a small division of colored troops commanded by General Edward W. Hinks had been assigned to the XVIII Corps. All in all, Smith probably had about 15,000 men.

PUSHING westward on the City Point Road, Smith ran into a handful of Confederate cavalry under General James Dearing behind breastworks. This held up the ever-cautious Smith for several hours, so it was almost noon when the head of his column reached the outer defenses of Petersburg on the east side. And these defenses looked formidable indeed, particularly to anyone who had just experienced the awful slaughter inflicted by the Confederates from their entrenchments at Cold Harbor. A long, uneven ridge ran south for several miles, and crest-

Quarters of Company 1, 7th Rhode Island Infantry at Fort Sedgwick, a Union defense erected as operations at Petersburg turned into a siege. (U.S. Army Military History Institute)

ing the ridge at intervals were strong redoubts connected by raised breastworks. In front of these breastworks yawned ditches six to eight feet deep and fifteen feet wide, and a few yards out in front of the ditches were felled trees with the branches interlaced. For a half mile or so the ground beyond the slashings was open so it could be swept by fire from the fortifications. Smith decided that a very careful survey was necessary before any attack could take place. "As no engineer officer was ordered to report to me," he stated, "I was obliged to make the reconnaissance in person, and some time was unnecessarily wasted on that account." As a matter of fact, he wasted several hours.

As a result of his survey, Smith concluded that the Confederate works were as strong as they looked, with but one glaring weakness—they were seriously undermanned. The theatrical and controversial General P. G. T. Beauregard commanded everything south of the James with about 9,000 troops, but most of them were at Bermuda Hundred to hold the cork in Butler's bottle. In front of Petersburg he had only about 2,200 men. "These troops," he wrote later, "occupied the Petersburg line on the left from Battery No. 1 to what was called Butterworth's Bridge, toward the right, and had to be so stationed as to allow but one man for every 4 1/2 yards. From that bridge to the Appomattox—a distance of fully 4 1/2 miles—the line was defenseless." He had requested reenforcements that morning and was informed that General Robert Hoke's division was on the way back to him from Drewry's Bluff but would not reach him until later that night. Until then he was on his own. He also warned the Confederate War Department in Richmond that "We must now elect between lines of Bermuda Neck and Petersburg. We cannot hold both."

BY the time Smith had finished his personal reconnaissance it was almost 4 p.m. He believed the Confederate works to be lightly held, so decided to attack by using a succession of skirmish lines rather than a massed assault which could be torn apart by the artillery. If the trenches were lightly held, then the skirmish lines would be sufficient; if they were not, then no method of attack could succeed anyway in Smith's estimation. So he ordered an assault for 4 o'clock. But no one had informed the chief of artillery that an attack was imminent, and he had sent the artillery horses back to be watered. As artillery was considered necessary for the success of the whole operation, the attack had to wait until the horses returned to get the artillery into position. By the time this was accomplished it was 7 p.m. and darkness approached.

Shortly after 7 o'clock Smith attacked and overwhelmed the small force in his front. Entering a ravine between Batteries 7 and 8 the Union soldiers approached Battery 5, one of the strongest Confederate fortifications, from the rear, the direction from which an attack was least expected. Within a few hours Beauregard lost not only Battery 5 but all the line for more than a mile south. The Confederates withdrew to a new line a short distance to the

Incident at Petersburg: the capture of a Confederate cannon by Hinks's Federal Negro troops in the first day's fighting.

rear of the captured works and threw up a hasty entrenchment along Harrison's Creek.

Hinks's colored troops, who had captured six guns and many prisoners, were jubilant, as was Hinks himself. He suggested to Smith that if they continued the attack they could probably walk right into Petersburg. To be sure, it was dark, but the moon was out and its dim light showed the ridges and fields and roads leading into the city. Beauregard also believed this. As he wrote later, "Petersburg at that hour was clearly at the mercy of the Federal commander, who had all but captured it, and only failed of final success because he could not realize the fact of the unparalleled disparity between the two contending forces." Smith, however, had no intention of advancing, being interested only in defending what he had already captured, despite the fact that by now two of Hancock's divisions had arrived on the field.

HANCOCK'S II Corps experienced a most exasperating and frustrating day. By early that morning all his troops had crossed over the James from Wilcox's Landing. The evening before he had received the following dispatch from Meade: "General Butler has been ordered to send to you . . . 60,000 rations; so soon as they are received and issued you will move your command by the most direct route to Petersburg, taking up a position where the City Point railroad crosses Harrison's Creek, where we now have a work." There was no indication that Hancock was to be at any designated area at any specified time; there was no mention of his supporting Smith; there was no word of any impending attack on Petersburg. And, although Hancock could not know it then, Harrison's Creek was behind the Confederate lines.

At 4 a.m. and again at 6:30 Hancock notified headquarters that no rations had arrived. When they still hadn't come by 9 o'clock, he gave the order to move

Wartime view of the important rail center of Petersburg, Va. Whoever held Petersburg controlled Richmond. (Nat'l Archives)

without them. General David Birney's division finally got in motion about 10:30, and then the real trouble started. As Hancock reported: "It is proper to say in this connection that it afterward appeared my orders were based on incorrect information, and the position I was ordered to take did not exist as it was described on my instructions; Harrison's Creek proved to be inside the enemy's lines and not within miles of where it was laid down on the map with which I was furnished to guide me. The map was found to be utterly worthless, the only roads laid down on it being widely out of the way." None of the white natives would or could give him any information concerning the creek, but finally he obtained some Negro guides and the column started toward Petersburg. The day turned excessively hot. "The road was covered with clouds of dust, and but little water was found on the route, causing severe suffering among the men."

THEN between, 5 and 6 p.m., Hancock received messages from both Grant and Smith telling him to hurry to Smith's aid in the attack on Petersburg. Smith, of course, had not attacked yet and would not do so for another hour, but these messages were the first intimation Hancock had received that Petersburg was to be attacked that day. "Up to that hour," he reported, "I had not been notified

Edwin Forbes called this sketch "Burnside's corps charging the Confederate position on the right of their line of defense." (Reproduced from "The Soldier in Our Civil War" v. II)

from any source that I was expected to assist General Smith in assaulting that city." Regardless of the delay over the rations, he insisted that had he known what was expected of his corps he could have joined Smith by 4 p.m. at the latest, in which case the whole course of the war probably would have been changed. With Petersburg in Union hands Lee's situation in Richmond would have been untenable. As it was, the II Corps did not reach Smith until the attack was over after dark.

And when Hancock's men finally did get there, Smith did nothing with them except to relieve Hinks's men in the captured trenches. When the battle-wise veterans of the II Corps saw what Hinks's colored troops had captured, they concluded that if those inexperienced troops could do that then it meant that Lee's veterans of the Army of

Northern Virginia had not yet reached Petersburg. Consequently, they wanted to attack at once before Lee's men got there, and were furious when all they did was bivouac. As one soldier wrote later: "The rage of the enlisted men was devilish. The most bloodcurdling blasphemy I ever listened to I heard that night, uttered by men who knew they were to be sacrificed on the morrow."

BUT it wasn't just Smith who was hesitant. Grant himself did not seem to understand the situation, nor did Meade, despite the fact that Smith telegraphed Butler that "unless I misapprehend the topography, I hold the key to Petersburg." But the key should have been turned that night because by the next morning the Confederates had changed the lock. Later that night Hancock received

a message from Grant stating that "the enemy were then throwing reenforcements into Petersburg, and instructed me that should Petersburg not fall on the night of the 15th it would be advisable for General Smith and myself to take up a defensive position and maintain it until all of our forces came up." Burnside's IX Corps was expected momentarily, to be followed by Warren's V Corps. But the fighting for the 15th was over.

As darkness settled down that night, Hoke's division began arriving to bolster Beauregard's meager forces in the trenches. Earlier he had informed the Richmond authorities that he could not hold both Petersburg and the Bermuda Hundred lines with the forces presently available to him, and he was hopeful that they would tell him which he should hold. But when no word was forth-

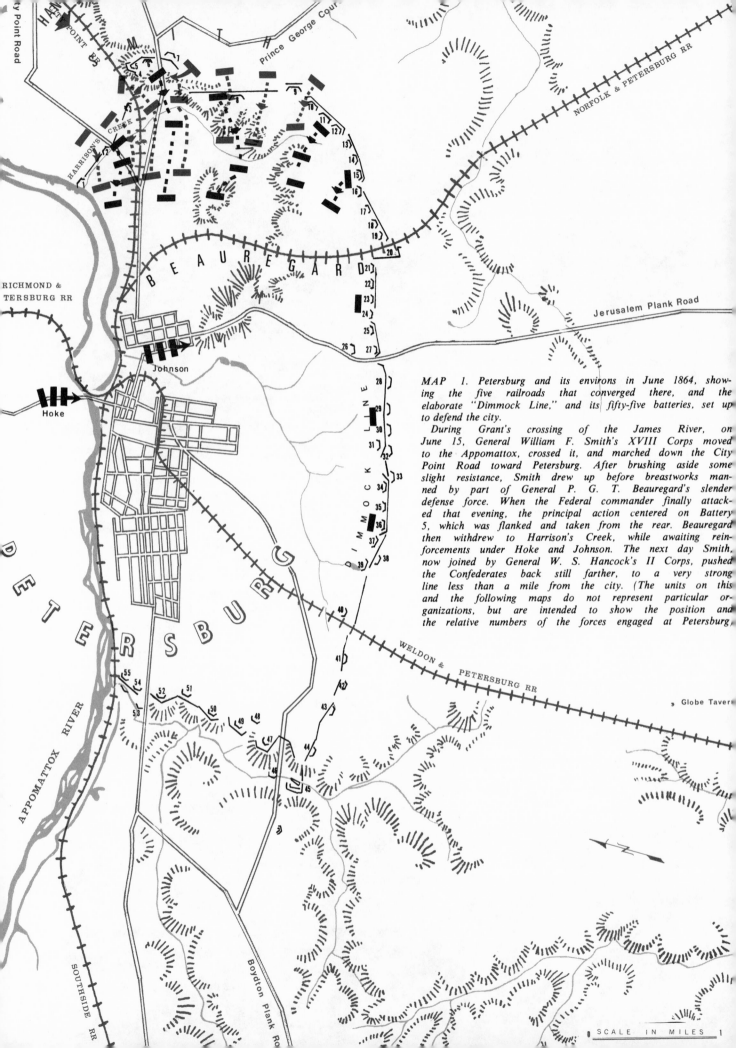

MAP 1. Petersburg and its environs in June 1864, showing the five railroads that converged there, and the elaborate "Dimmock Line," and its fifty-five batteries, set up to defend the city.

During Grant's crossing of the James River, on June 15, General William F. Smith's XVIII Corps moved to the Appomattox, crossed it, and marched down the City Point Road toward Petersburg. After brushing aside some slight resistance, Smith drew up before breastworks manned by part of General P. G. T. Beauregard's slender defense force. When the Federal commander finally attacked that evening, the principal action centered on Battery 5, which was flanked and taken from the rear. Beauregard then withdrew to Harrison's Creek, while awaiting reinforcements under Hoke and Johnson. The next day Smith, now joined by General W. S. Hancock's II Corps, pushed the Confederates back still farther, to a very strong line less than a mile from the city. (The units on this and the following maps do not represent particular organizations, but are intended to show the position and the relative numbers of the forces engaged at Petersburg,

SCALE IN MILES

coming from higher authorities that night, Beauregard made the decision himself. He ordered Bushrod Johnson's division down from Bermuda to Petersburg, thus uncorking Butler's bottle, and so informed Richmond. "I have abandoned my lines on Bermuda Neck to concentrate all my forces here." This brought his strength up to about 10,000 effectives, as opposed to over 40,000 Federals, and over 60,000 when the IX Corps arrived. The odds were still mighty high against the Confederate commander, but they were better than they had been the day before.

ANOTHER of Beauregard's troubles was that Lee was not yet convinced that Grant had moved his whole army south of the James. As he regarded the safety of Richmond as his first responsibility, he was reluctant to strip the north side of the James of troops in case Grant should mount an attack along that line. Although Beauregard reported fighting the XVIII Corps, Lee regarded that corps as part of Butler's Army of the James and not the Army of the Potomac, and many of Beauregard's reports to Richmond never did reach Lee, as Beauregard at that time exercised a command independent of Lee. The fact is that since the morning of June 13 Lee did not know the whereabouts of the Army of the Potomac or its commander's intentions. He did take some precautions, however, as General Braxton Bragg's dispatch of June 14 to Beauregard attests: "General Lee reports Grant has abandoned his depot on the York and moved to James River, he supposes about McClellan's old base at Harrison's Landing. Lee is on a line from Malvern Hill to White Oak Swamp. He has sent Hoke's division to Drewry's Bluff, with a view to reenforce you in case Petersburg is threatened." In Lee's view that was all he could do until he knew something more definite.

Early the next morning, June 16, Hancock conducted a reconnaissance in force while Burnside's IX Corps came into position on his left. Grant and Meade were both on the south side of the river that morning, and after an inspection of the front Grant told Meade that "Smith has taken a line of works stronger than anything we have seen this campaign. If it is a possible thing I want an assault made at six o'clock this evening." Grant apparently was not the least disturbed that Petersburg did not fall to Smith and Hancock, although he stated years later in his *Memoirs* that he believed it should have been captured on the 15th. And as all his troops were massed on the east side of the city, he seemed totally unaware that there were practically no Confederate troops in the lines west of the Jerusalem Plank Road. As Beauregard admitted later, if Grant or Meade had sent a large force up that road to swing west and then north, "I would have been compelled to evacuate Petersburg without much resistance." But for the time being at least, Grant seems to have been basking in the glow of having deceived Lee completely and successfully outflanked him. Not usually given to boasting, Grant could not help telling Wash-

Union pickets at breastworks of Fort Mahone following its capture in April 1865. (Library of Congress)

ington: "Our forces drew out from within fifty yards of the enemy's intrenchments at Cold Harbor, made a flank movement of an average of about fifty miles' march, crossing the Chickahominy and James rivers, the latter 2,000 feet wide and 84 feet deep at point of crossing, and surprised the enemy's rear at Petersburg. This was done without the loss of a wagon or piece of artillery and with the loss of only about 150 stragglers, picked up by the enemy." All of which was true. By late that night or early the next morning the Army of the Potomac with its more than 100,000 men, 5,000 wagons and ambulances, 56,000 horses and mules, and 2,800 head of cattle, would be safely across the James River. And that night Lee would telegraph in desperation: "I do not know the position of Grant's army."

IT IS a paradox of the war that Grant seldom if ever receives credit for this successful change of base in the face of an aggressive enemy. And yet such an astute military historian as Colonel Mathew Steele has written: "When one considers how unexpected the movement was to General Lee, and how long he was left in doubt and uncertainty; how skillfully all the difficulties of logistics were surmounted, and how quickly the movement was made, one must reckon it, in conception and execution, among the very finest achievements of strategy to be found in our military history."

Unfortunately, however, the staff work and tactics following this great strategic movement were something

2d Corp Army of the "Potomac"
Before Petersburgh Va.
July 17th 1864

Dear Brother David,

From the Potomac to here Virginia is one vast scene of desolation. Villages and farms are deserted and in ruins—the plough remains standing in the unculti-vated fields—the village Blacksmiths and Carpenters Shop are no more—the flour mill is burned and level-led with the ground—entering a romantic glen one day on the march there was the remains of a flour mill still burning with all the machinery still in motion. It was driven by water, and as the sluices had not been closed there the machinery kept working away amidst the silent woods. If ever a country experienced the horrors of war it is Va. We came through some fine sections of country, but the most of our way was through gigantic forests and over terrible roads. We suffered a good deal for want of water crossing the Peninsula, besides had serious encounters with the Rebels. Owing to the heavy woods Artillery and Cav-alry could not be brought into use, but with what cool-ness the cavalry dismounted and pushed into the woods on foot with their carbine in their hand driving the Rebs before them.

About a mile from where we lay at present is the extreme front. Our lines and the Rebels lines are with-in 50 yds of one another. We are encamped in woods and from here to the front the Rebels when they held this place had cut down the woods to give their artil-lery play to sweep us down, their works are very strong, and you would almost think it an impossibility to have captured them. But our Boys took them on the charge.

I was over at the front this morning, but did not stay long, there was such a heavy musketry fire going on. If you dare to show your head above the rifle pits you are a gone goose. Some parts of our walking pit is ex-posed to the Rebel Sharpshooters where it makes ab-rupt turns, and to pass that you have to make a run for it.

Hoping this will find you all well, I remain your aff. brother
Jas. Mitchell
3d N.J. Lt. Artillery
Arty. Brigade, 2d Corps.
Army of the Potomac
U.S.

This and following letters from James Mitchell were furnished through the kindness of a descendant of the writer, Mr. David Mitchell of Lewiston, New York.

less than brilliant, with both Grant and Meade equally responsible. Hancock and Burnside attacked again that evening as ordered and fought bitterly for over three hours, with little effect. Some more ground was gained, particularly by Birney's division of Hancock's corps, but darkness put an end to it and the Confederates simply threw up a new line during the night. Hancock and Meade both noticed that the men seemed to be wearied and did not attack with their usual persistence.

Meade reported to Grant: "Our men are tired and the attacks have not been made with the vigor and force which characterized our fighting in The Wilderness; if they had been I think we should have been more successful. I will continue to press."

That night Warren's V Corps came up and held the extreme left of the Federal line, and Grant wired Meade to get it over on the Jerusalem Plank Road. One division of General Horatio Wright's VI Corps also came up. Meade issued his orders that night: "A vigorous assault on the enemy's works will be made tomorrow morning at 4 o'clock by the whole force of the Fifth, Ninth, and Second Corps." Smith's corps and the one division of the VI Corps would be held in reserve ready to support any significant breakthrough.

WARREN moved out early the morning of the 17th toward the Jerusalem Road, ran into heavy skirmishing, stopped to reconnoiter, and never did get going again. On his right there was heavy fighting all day by Hancock and Burnside, with two significant hills captured, the Shand house hill and the Hare house hill; on the latter the Federals would later erect Fort Stedman. But the attack was generally uncoordinated, the tactics and lead-ership faulty, and again nothing decisive was accom-plished, except that Beauregard had held again even though he lost another section of the line.

Time was fast running out now for the Federals. Lee, convinced at last that Grant actually was on the south side of the river, put his army in motion for Petersburg. They began arriving that night and early next morning, with Lee himself on the field by 11:30 a.m. With the arrival of the Army of Northern Virginia the Confederates would have something over 50,000 troops to man the trenches, as opposed to about 90,000 Federals. And during the night Beauregard selected a new line only about a mile in front of Petersburg and withdrew his forces to it under cover of darkness. All night they worked feverishly to fortify and strengthen it. An aide to Beauregard later recalled that "without a moment's rest the digging of the trenches was begun, with such utensils as had been hastily collected at Petersburg, many of the men using bayonets, their knives, and even their tin cans, to assist in the rapid execution of the work."

ANOTHER general assault was ordered by Meade for the morning of the 18th, but it turned out to be more of a fiasco than the previous one. All the divisions were late getting started; first one attacked and then the other; and some never did get going at all until late in the after-noon. Finding the Confederates in their new line seems to have had a confusing effect on the Federal line officers, most of whom believed it should be felt out cautiously before any assault was made. The veterans quickly realized that the Army of Northern Virginia now stood behind those entrenchments, and they had no intention of assault-ing them. They knew it would be nothing but Cold Har-

Federal sharpshooters at work in front of Petersburg. (FL)

bor all over again, and they had had enough of that kind of fighting. One regiment volunteering to make a charge, the 1st Maine Heavy Artillery, suffered the highest losses of any regiment in a single engagement in the entire war. About 4 p.m. this unit, about 850 strong, charged from concealment along the Prince George Court House road. Met by a heavy crossfire, it withdrew in less than thirty minutes with 632 casualties.

In the rear Meade was fast losing his temper in a futile effort to bring about a coordinated attack. Shortly after 2 p.m. he telegraphed Warren and Burnside: "What additional orders to attack you require I cannot imagine. My orders have been explicit and are now repeated, that you each immediately assault the enemy with all your force, and if there is any further delay the responsibility and the consequences will rest with you." But it was far too late by then; the Federals' last chance for success by assault had gone. To another general Meade stated that "It is of the utmost importance to settle today whether the enemy can be dislodged." Now he had his answer—they could not. That night he reported to Grant that "our losses, particularly today, have been severe. . . .It is a source of great regret that I am not able to report more success." In the past four days' fighting the Federals suffered approximately 10,000 casualties in killed, wounded, and missing. And Grant telegraphed back: "Now we will rest the men and use the spade for their protection until a new vein can be struck."

A ND SO the decision was made—the war in the East would now be primarily a siege operation. So the campaign that began early in May in The Wilderness ended some six weeks later in the trenches around Petersburg. And in those six weeks Grant had suffered between 60,000 and 70,000 casualties, and Lee's army still stood undefeated, and to some, particularly President Lincoln's political enemies, it all seemed like wasted effort. What they could not understand was that the war

would never be the same again. Now it was only a question of time, provided the North did not become impatient and fail to re-elect Lincoln who would support Grant to the end. The failure to capture Petersburg quickly was tragic, to be sure, as it would have shortened the war immeasurably and, thereby, saved many lives, but the fact was that Lee now lay pinned down on the Petersburg-Richmond defense line and could not get out. Never again would he assume the offensive, threatening to win the war by bold, aggressive moves with the famed and feared Army of Northern Virginia. As one Confederate general wrote later, "However bold we might be, however desperately we might fight, we were sure in the end to be worn out. It was only a question of a few months, more or less."

Things remained fairly quiet for several days while the men dug fortifications and trenches and the weather grew hotter. Then Meade ordered the II and VI Corps to extend to the left and march on the Weldon Railroad which Grant was anxious to cut off from Petersburg. Lee himself went over to the right of the line on June 22 to observe the action. General William Mahone reported to him that he believed he saw an opportunity for a flank attack, and Lee agreed. What Mahone observed was a gap carelessly left between the two Federal corps, and here he struck swiftly, rolling up two divisions and capturing over 1,500 prisoners. The Federals then withdrew and the railroad was saved for awhile longer, but Grant's left now extended west of the Jerusalem Plank Road, so that important artery was lost to the Confederates and Lee had to extend his defense line. Now investing Petersburg Grant had the IX Corps on his right, then the V, the II, and the VI held the left of the line on the south. Butler's Army of the James held its position at Bermuda Hundred and was also responsible for the ground the Federals held north of the James River.

THUS the siege of Petersburg, which would last almost ten months, began. Almost every hill and rise of

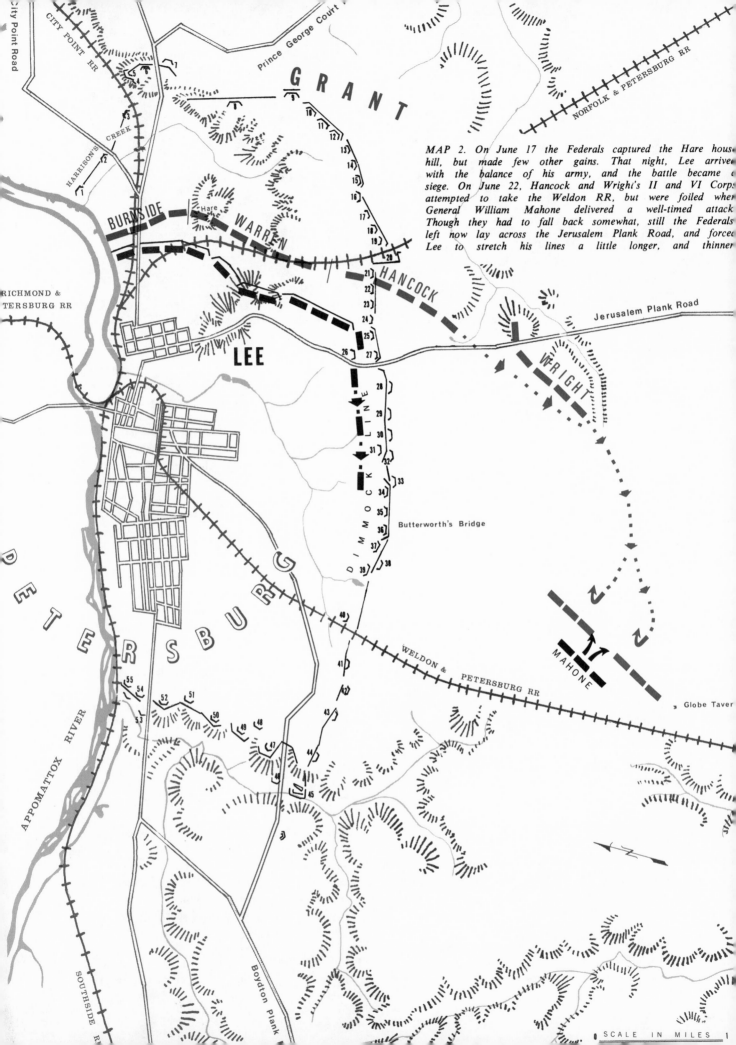

City Point Road

CITY POINT RR

HARRISON'S CREEK

Prince George Court

G R A N T

NORFOLK & PETERSBURG RR

Hare

BURNSIDE

WARREN

HANCOCK

RICHMOND & PETERSBURG RR

Jerusalem Plank Road

LEE

WRIGHT

DIMMOCK LINE

Butterworth's Bridge

MAP 2. On June 17 the Federals captured the Hare house hill, but made few other gains. That night, Lee arrived with the balance of his army, and the battle became a siege. On June 22, Hancock and Wright's II and VI Corps attempted to take the Weldon RR, but were foiled when General William Mahone delivered a well-timed attack. Though they had to fall back somewhat, still the Federals left now lay across the Jerusalem Plank Road, and forced Lee to stretch his lines a little longer, and thinner.

P E T E R S B U R G

APPOMATTOX RIVER

WELDON & PETERSBURG RR

MAHONE

Globe Tavern

Boydton Plank

SOUTHSIDE RR

SCALE IN MILES

Lieutenant Colonel Henry Pleasants engineered the mine.

ground was capped with a fort and artillery batteries, along both the Union and Confederate lines, and in some places the lines lay less than 400 feet apart. There was little if any chance that any part of either line could be taken by direct assault so long as the defenders remained alert. One Federal soldier wrote later: "In building our works we utilized the dead bodies of the rebels by burying them in the earth which we threw up from the trenches, serving the double purpose of burial and increasing the size of the breastworks." In this vast maze of trenches, forts, redoubts and tunnels the soldiers of both sides lived, suffered, and died. Constant skirmishing and sharpshooting took its deadly toll. Constant shelling back and forth was just another of the nerve-wracking hardships the men had to endure, along with scorching heat and choking dust, then mud and constant wetness, followed by freezing cold and utter loneliness. But in the mud and general filth of the trenches, disease was the greatest killer of all, and one of the most depressing things that had to be endured was complete boredom.

IT was this boredom, more or less, that led to the next significant action. As the days wore on and the awful monotony of siege tactics became apparent to the soldiers, some members of the 48th Pennsylvania Volunteers in General Robert B. Potter's division of the IX Corps, many of whom had been coal miners from

the upper Schuylkill coal region, came up with an idea. In front of their position stood a Confederate work known as Elliott's Salient, a particularly strong point in the line near a ridge called Cemetery Hill. Behind earthen embankments lay a battery of four guns, with two veteran South Carolina infantry regiments stationed on either side. Behind these were other strong defensive works. At this point the two lines lay less than 400 feet apart. One day Lieutenant Colonel Henry Pleasants, the commanding officer of the regiment and a mining engineer by profession, heard one of the enlisted men mutter, "We could blow that damned fort out of existence if we could run a mine shaft under it."

From this and other remarks grew the idea of a Union mine under the Confederate fortification. When Pleasants told his regimental officers, "That God-damned fort is the only thing between us and Petersburg, and I have an idea we can blow it up," they were receptive. The division commander then passed the idea along to Burnside who was agreeable and passed it up to Meade. Meade was lukewarm to the whole idea and his engineer officers thought it all "clap-trap and nonsense" because, they said, the shaft or tunnel leading to the mine could not possibly be ventilated without being observed by the Confederates. But Grant said to go ahead with it.

Work started on June 25, but Pleasants soon discovered that, although higher ups promised all the help he would need, none was forthcoming. "My regiment was only about four hundred strong. At first I employed but a few men at a time, but the number was increased as the work progressed, until at last I had to use the whole regiment—non-commissioned officers and all. The great difficulty I had was to dispose of the material got out of the mine. I found it impossible to get any assistance from anybody; I had to do all the work myself. I had to remove all the earth in old cracker-boxes; I got pieces of hickory and nailed on the boxes in which we received our crackers, and then iron-

"The Forty-eighth Pennsylvania, Colonel Pleasants, mining the Confederate works in front of Petersburg, July 15-20, 1864."

Carrying powder to the mine. From drawing by A. R. Waud. (HW)

clad them with hoops of iron taken from old pork and beef barrels—Whenever I made application I could not get anything . . . . I could get no boards or lumber supplied to me for my operations. I had to get a pass and send two companies of my own regiment, with wagons, outside of our lines to rebel saw-mills, and get lumber in that way, after having previously got what lumber I could by tearing down an old bridge. I had no mining picks furnished me, but had to take common army picks and have them straightened for my mine picks. . . .''

DESPITE the lack of cooperation, the work went ahead day after day. Every night the men cut bushes to cover the fresh dirt at the mouth of the tunnel; otherwise the Confederates would have known what was going on. However, the biggest problem with the 510-foot shaft was ventilation. Generally it had been considered impossible to dig a tunnel for any considerable distance without spacing shafts at regular intervals to replace the polluted air with a fresh supply. In this instance, of course, that was out of the question because of the proximity of the enemy. But Pleasants and his men came up with an ingenious solution, based on the application of the simple physical principle that warm air tends to rise. Behind the Federal picket line and to the right of the tunnel, although connected with it, the miners dug a ventilating chimney. Between the chimney and the tunnel entrance they put up an airtight canvas door. Through the door and along the floor of the tunnel they laid a square wooden pipe. A fire was then built at the bottom of the ventilating chimney, and as the fire warmed the air it went up the chimney, and the draft thus created drew the foul air from the end of the tunnel where the men were working. As the foul air rushed out, of course, fresh air was drawn in through the wooden pipe to replace it.

By July 17 the diggers were directly beneath the battery in Elliott's Salient, twenty feet from the floor of the tunnel to the enemy works above. The average height

of the tunnel was five feet, with a base four and a half feet in width, tapering to two feet at the top. By now the Confederates had become suspicious, as the faint sounds of digging could be heard issuing from the earth. Consequently, they sank countermines of their own in an effort to locate the Union shaft. When they failed to locate anything suspicious, their fears diminished, helped along, no doubt, by the belief that it was impossible to ventilate a tunnel of any length over 400 feet without air shafts above it.

THE next step in Pleasant's plan was to burrow out into lateral tunnels at the end of the long shaft. Accordingly, on July 18 work began on two branches extending to the right and left, paralleling the Confederate fortifications above. When completed on July 23, these additional tunnels added another seventy-five feet to the total length of the excavation, for a grand total of a little over 585 feet. Then 320 kegs of black powder, weighing on the average twenty-five pounds each, were placed in the two lateral tunnels in eight magazines. The total charge was thus about four tons or 8,000 pounds. The men sandbagged the powder to direct the force of the explosion upward, and spliced two fuses together to form a 98-foot line.

BY JULY 27 all stood ready with the explosion set for 3:30 a.m. July 30. Burnside submitted his plan of attack, which was to have the division of colored troops now under General Edward Ferrero go in first and fan out to the left and right along the line, then the other

Entrance to Confederate countermine in Fort Mahone. (From LC)

divisions would go forward and take the crest of Cemetery Hill. Grant and Meade, however, objected to this plan on two counts. Meade was afraid they would be blamed for putting the colored troops in first, and Grant agreed, primarily for political reasons. As Grant later stated: "General Meade said that if we put the colored troops in front (we had only one division) and it should prove a failure, it would then be said, and very properly, that we were shoving these people ahead to get killed because we did not care anything about them. But that could not be said if we put white troops in front." Unfortunately this decision was not relayed to Burnside until the night of July 29, which, of course, necessitated last minute changes in his battle orders.

The other objection was to the first division through the gap fanning out to the right and left. Meade, with Grant's approval, changed the orders so that the leading division would charge straight ahead for the crest of Cemetery Hill, the next two divisions advance to the left and right of the crest to protect the flanks, and then the colored division followed by the V Corps, and if necessary the XVIII, would come through for the general advance all along the line. A total of 110 guns and 54 mortars would be alerted to begin a bombardment as soon as the explosion occurred.

Burnside had the commanding generals of the three white divisions draw straws to see who would lead the charge. General James Ledlie of the First Division won the draw. He had been with the division just six weeks.

In the meantime, Grant sent the II Corps over to the north side of the James at Deep Bottom as a diversionary tactic, and Lee reacted to it by withdrawing troops from Petersburg, so that on July 30 the Confederates had only about 18,000 troops in the lines around the city. Then Meade ordered Hancock to make a night march and be in rear of the XVIII Corps by daylight to support the attack if needed. And Meade reminded all corps commanders that "promptitude, rapidity of execution, and cordial cooperation, are essential to success."

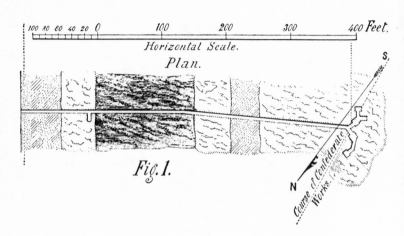

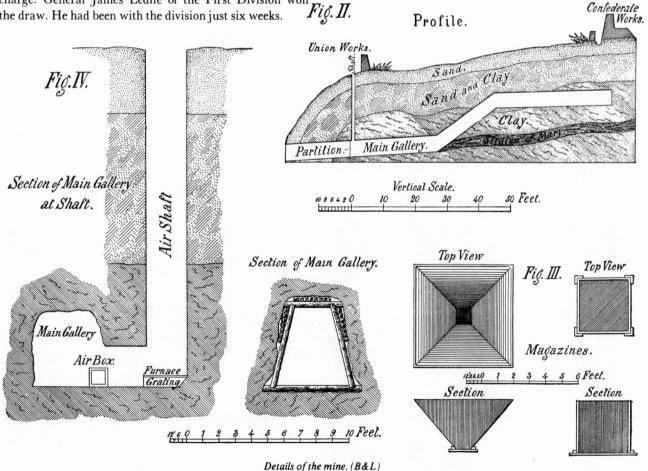

Details of the mine. (B&L)

BELOW: "Before Petersburg, July 30, 1864. Explosion of the mine, and charge on the Confederate works." (Both drawings reproduced from "The Soldier in Our Civil War." Vol. II)

ABOVE: "The Fifth Army Corps awaiting the order to advance, after the explosion of the mine, Petersburg, July 30, 1864."

Petersburg Railroad   Confederate Fort.   Confederate Mortar Battery.   City of Petersburg.   Ninth Co

BY 3 A.M. on July 30 the IX Corps lay assembled in the ravine behind the mine entrance, the First Division at the head of the column. Three-thirty came and went and nothing happened. Then the first grey fingers of dawn began to appear. "Four o'clock arrived, officers and men began to get nervous, having been on their feet four hours; still the mine had not been exploded." Pleasants had lit the fuse at 3:15. By 4:15 he knew something was wrong. Sergeant Henry Rees and Lieutenant Jacob Douty volunteered to crawl in and find out what had happened, and discovered that the fuse had died out at the first splicing. Quickly they relighted it and scrambled to safety. At 4:45 the earth erupted with a terrifying roar. "It was a magnificent spectacle," an officer present remembered, "and as the mass of earth went into the air, carrying with it men, guns, carriages, and limbers, and spread out like an immense cloud as it reached its altitude, so close were the Union lines that the mass appeared as if it would descend immediately upon the troops waiting to make the charge. This caused them to break and scatter to the rear, and about ten minutes were consumed in re-forming for the attack."

But that was just the beginning of their troubles. Incredible as it now seems, no one made provision for ladders for Burnside's troops to get out of their own entrenchments. As Major Houghton of the 14th New York Heavy Artillery reported: "Our own works, which

Brigadier General James H. Ledlie (seated left) and staff at Petersburg. Ledlie was in command of the First Division, IX Corps, at the Battle of The Crater. (Library of Congress)

osion of the Mine.

Brigadier General Edward Ferrero. He commanded the Fourth (Colored) Division at the Battle of The Crater. (From NA)

The Battle of The Crater. This original drawing by Alfred R. Waud depicts the Fourth (Colored) Division going into action. Regimental colors are being planted on the rim of The Crater in the background. The artist was apparently intending to indicate the detail of the sole of the soldier's shoe for the "Harper's" engraver by drawing the oversized foot. (LC)

were very high at this point, had not been prepared for scaling . . . ladders were improvised by the men placing their bayonets between the logs in the works and holding the other end . . . thus forming steps over which men climbed." Then, after this second delay, the men were not prepared for what they would see at the "crater," the hole caused by the explosion, and it struck them dumb with astonishment. The hole, about 30 feet deep, 60 to 80 feet wide, and 170 feet long, was "filled with dust, great blocks of clay, guns, broken carriages, projecting timbers, and men buried in various ways—some up to their necks,

View of the Confederate works after the explosion of the mine and the battle of July 30, 1864. Sketch by Mullen. (SCW)

others to their waists, and some with only their feet and legs protruding from the earth." The explosion wounded, buried or killed about 278 Confederates and completely destroyed two guns of the battery. Soon one brigade after another of gaping soldiers milled in and around the crater, but no one was moving forward; brigades and regiments soon became inextricably mixed in the confusion. When finally some did try to get out of the crater, they discovered to their chagrin that they again had no ladders and "owing to the precipitous walls the men could find no footing except by facing inward, digging their heels into the earth, and throwing their backs against the side of the crater." Neither Burnside, Ledlie, nor Ferrero were with their troops to lead them on and help bring order out of chaos.

THESE delays proved fatal. In a short time the Confederates recovered from their shock and soon shells poured in on the IX Corps from both the right and left

Brigadier General William Mahone led the successful Confederate defense in the bloody Battle of The Crater. (Photo from LC)

flanks. The only outfit that actually went forward and got close to the crest of Cemetery Hill was Potter's Second Division, but Lee quickly rushed Mahone's division from farther south into the breach and forced the Federals back. Many, however, got caught in the crater and soon Confederate mortar shells started to drop on them with deadly effect. Meade, observing the scene with Grant, ordered a withdrawal about 9 o'clock, but it was past noon before Burnside transmitted it as he kept insisting that a victory could still be won. Many soldiers by then had chosen to run the gantlet of fire back to their own lines, but others remained clinging to the protective sides of the crater.

Shortly after 1 p.m. a final charge by Mahone's men succeeded in gaining the outside slopes of the crater. Then some of the Confederates put their hats on ramrods and lifted them over the rim. They were promptly torn to shreds by a volley, but before the Federals could reload Mahone's men jumped into the crater where a desperate hand-to-hand struggle with bayonets, rifle butts, and fists ensued. The scene in the crater was now appalling. As Major Houghton described it, "The sun was pouring its fiercest heat down upon us and our suffering wounded. No air was stirring within the crater. It was a sickening sight; men were dead and dying all around us; blood was streaming down the sides of the crater to the bottom, where it gathered in pools for a time before being absorbed by the hard red clay."

ALTOGETHER Grant suffered some 4,400 casualties in killed, wounded, and missing, as opposed to about 1,500 for Lee. And neither Grant nor Meade was very happy about the way the whole operation had been conducted. Meade's official report to Grant was unusually accurate and detailed:

On the 30th, owing to a defect in the fuse, the explosion of the mine was delayed from 3:30 to 4:45 a.m., an unfortunate delay, because it was designed to assault the crest of the ridge occupied by the enemy just before daylight, when the movement would, in a measure, be obscured. As soon as the mine was sprung the First Division, Ninth Corps, Brigadier-General Ledlie commanding, moved forward and occupied the crater without opposition. No advance, however, was made from the crater to the ridge, some 400 yards beyond, Brigadier-General Ledlie giving as a reason for not pushing forward that the enemy could occupy the crater in his rear, he seeming to forget that the rest of his corps and all the Eighteenth Corps were waiting to occupy the crater and follow him. Brigadier-Generals Potter and Wilcox, commanding the Second and Third Divisions, Ninth Corps, advanced simultaneously with Ledlie and endeavored to occupy parts of the enemy's line on Ledlie's right and left, so as to cover those flanks, respectively, but on reaching the enemy's line Ledlie's men were found occupying the vacated parts, both to the right and left of the crater, in consequence of which the men of the several divisions got mixed up, and a scene of disorder and confusion commenced, which seems to have continued to the end of the operation. In the meantime the enemy, rallying from the confusion incident to the explosion, began forming his infantry in a ravine to the right and planting artillery, both on the right and left of the crater. Seeing this, Potter was enabled to get his men out of the crater and enemy's line, and had formed them for an attack on the right, when he received an order to attack the crest of the ridge. Notwithstanding he had to change front in the presence of the enemy, he succeeded not only in doing so, but, as he reports, advancing to within a few yards of the crest, which he would have taken if he had been supported. This was after 7 a.m., more than two hours after Ledlie had occupied the crater, and yet he had made no advance. He, however, states he was forming to advance when the Fourth Division (colored troops), General Ferrero commanding, came rushing into the crater and threw his men into confusion. The Fourth Division passed beyond the crater and made an assault, when they encountered a heavy fire of artillery and infantry, which threw them into inextricable confusion, and they retired in disorder through the troops in the crater and back into our lines. In the mean time, in ignorance of what was occurring, I sent orders to Major-General Ord, commanding Eighteenth Corps, who was expected to follow the Ninth, to advance at once on the right of the Ninth independently of the latter. To this General Ord replied the only debouches were choked up with the Ninth Corps, which had not all advanced at this time. He,

Union Fort Morton, opposite The Crater. (LC)

however, pushed a brigade of Turner's division over the Ninth Corps' parapets, and directed it to charge the enemy's line on the right, where it was still occupied. While it was about executing this order the disorganized Fourth Division (colored) of the Ninth Corps came rushing back and carrying everything with them, including Turner's brigade. By this time, between 8 and 9 a.m., the enemy, seeing the hesitation and confusion on our part, having planted batteries on both flanks in ravines where our artillery could not reach them, opened a heavy fire not only on the ground in front of the crater but between it and our lines, their mortars at the same time throwing shells into the dense mass of our men in the crater and adjacent works. In addition to this artillery fire, the enemy massed his infantry and assaulted the position. Although the assault was repulsed and some heroic fighting was done, particularly on the part of Potter's division and some regiments of the Eighteenth Corps, yet the exhaustion incident to the crowding of the men and the intense heat of the weather, added to the destructive artillery fire of the enemy, produced its effect, and report was brought to me that our men were retiring into our old lines. Being satisfied that the moment for success had passed, and that any further attempts would only result in useless sacrifice of life, with the concurrence of the lieutenant-general commanding, who was present, I directed the suspension of further offensive movements, and the withdrawal of the troops in the crater when it could be done with security, retaining the position till night, if necessary. It appears that when this order reached the crater (12:20) the greater portion of those that had been in were out; the balance remained for an hour and a half, repulsing an attack of the enemy, but on the enemy's threatening a second attack, retreated in disorder, losing many prisoners. This terminated this most unfortunate and not very creditable operation. I forbear to comment in the manner I might otherwise deem myself justified

in doing, because the whole subject, at my request, has been submitted for investigation by the President of the United States to a court of inquiry, with directions to report upon whom, if any one, censure is to be laid.

GRANT agreed with Meade's request for a Court of Inquiry. "So fair an opportunity will probably never occur again for carrying fortifications," he wrote to Meade the next day. "Preparations were good, orders ample, and everything so far as I could see, subsequent to the explosion of the mine, shows that almost without loss the crest beyond the mine could have been carried. This would have given us Petersburg with all its artillery and a large part of the garrison beyond doubt."

The Court of Inquiry concluded that if Meade's orders had been carried out the attack would have been successful. Burnside was censured for not obeying the orders of the commanding general, specifically regarding a prompt advance after the explosion, and for not "preparing his parapets and abatis for the passage of the columns of assault." As for Ledlie, the Court concluded that instead of leading his troops he "was most of the time in a bomb-proof ten rods in rear of the main line of the Ninth Corps works," and that Ferrero was also in a bomb-proof "habitually, where he could not see the operation of his troops." Burnside and Ledlie later resigned, and Ferrero was transferred elsewhere.

IT WAS certainly evident by now, if not before, that storming the Confederate fortifications by any means was out of the question. But the usual siege tactics, that is, a series of regular approaches by which heavy artillery could get close enough to flatten the enemy's fortifications, would not be effective either against earthen works. And at that rate, both armies could sit there facing each other forever. The only option open, it seemed, was for Grant to continually keep Lee off balance and under pressure with surprise attacks north of the James on the Richmond front, while at the same time extending his left to the west and north, forcing Lee to stretch his thinly held line, until Petersburg was completely encircled and all railroads and roads blocked. If nothing else, this would starve Lee into surrender or force him to abandon Richmond and flee south.

The first move in this new strategy was another attack on the Weldon Railroad. On August 18 Warren's V Corps marched three miles westward and seized the railroad in the vicinity of Globe Tavern, then marched northward towards Petersburg. The next day Lee sent A. P. Hill to attack Warren and recover the railroad. Hill inflicted serious losses and captured 2,700 prisoners, forcing Warren back to the area of Globe Tavern, but here the V Corps held despite repeated desperate attacks by the Confederates. Now Lee's lines were stretched almost to the breaking point, and he had lost another vital line of supply. As an indication of things

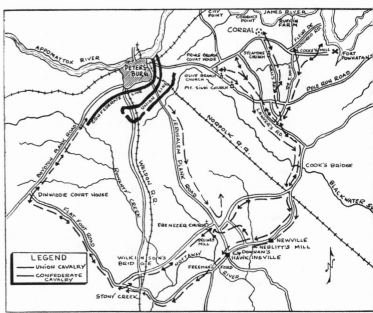

Map of Hampton's "Beefsteak" raid.

to come, he wired Richmond: "Our supply of corn is exhausted today, and I am informed that the small reserve in Richmond is consumed." Starvation was now a strong possibility. Only the Southside Railroad connected Petersburg with the rest of the South, and the Richmond & Danville Railroad was the only direct connection with Richmond, while Grant with his huge supply base at City Point could haul supplies on the City Point Railroad and now the Weldon Railroad in all kinds of weather.

General Warren's headquarters at the Globe Tavern. From a contemporary sketch which appears in "Battles and Leaders, etc."

IN A desperate move to alleviate the hunger of the Army of Northern Virginia its cavalry commander, Wade Hampton, in mid-September led a daring raid of 4,000 mounted troopers around the entire rear of the Army of the Potomac and succeeded in returning to Petersburg September 17 with over 2,000 head of cattle and more than 300 surprised prisoners, while losing only about 60 of his own men. Although this raised the morale of the Confederates temporarily, it had no lasting effect on the campaign. Grant just continued to tighten the noose and keep the pressure on.

His next move took place just twelve days later. In the pre-dawn darkness of September 29 he quietly slipped Birney, now commanding the X Corps, and Ord's XVIII Corps back across the James in a surprise move against the outer defenses of Richmond. The primary purpose was to prevent Lee from reenforcing General Jubal Early in the Shenandoah Valley. If, however, any weakness was discovered it could be exploited fully, and it might force Lee to weaken some part of the Petersburg line. Ord successfully stormed heavily armed but badly undermanned Fort Harrison on the Varina Road, but Birney was repulsed a mile and a half farther north in a similar attack on Fort Gilmer on the New Market Road. Lee, however, regarded the loss of Fort Harrison as serious enough to demand his personal attention. The next day, with reenforcements rushed from Petersburg, including Generals Archibald Gracie's and Hoke's divisions and four of General George Pickett's regiments, he directed several vigorous assaults against the fort. However, the Federal forces had closed in the rear of the work and also strengthened it and, armed with new repeating rifles, successfully beat back the attacks and inflicted heavy losses on the Confederates.

MEADE took advantage of this diversion to send a reconnaissance in force to the west again, but Hampton's cavalry and Johnson's division of infantry stopped them at the area known as Peebles' Farm. However, Meade had extended his left flank another three miles west of the Weldon Railroad, again forcing Lee to stretch his line of defense. Lee was now holding a 35-mile line from north of Richmond to the west of Petersburg with fewer than 50,000 troops, and with no relief in sight. "The enemy's position enables him to move his troops to the right or left without our knowledge," he informed Richmond, "until he has reached the point at which he aims, and we are then compelled to hurry our men to meet him, incurring the risk of being too late to check his progress and the additional risk of the advantage he may derive from their absence." For the first time during the whole war, Lee now began to sound pessimistic. "Without some increase of strength, I cannot see how we can escape the natural military consequences of the enemy's numerical superiority," he declared. "If things thus continue, the most serious consequences must result."

Grant gave the weary, half-starved Confederates no rest. On October 27 he sent Hancock's II Corps and two divisions of Warren's V, with a cavalry screen, west to the Boydton Plank Road. But when the two Federal commanders carelessly let a gap develop between the two forces, Hampton's cavalry and Generals Henry Heth's and Mahone's divisions quickly struck hard at Hancock at Burgess' Mill, where the road crossed a creek called Hatcher's Run. The Federals were forced to withdraw to their old positions and the Boydton Plank Road remained in Confederate control.

THIS was the last major action of the year, as the two armies settled into the awful monotony of living in the trenches through the cold winter. And as the long winter months of the siege dragged on, the Confederate soldiers began to know real despair for the first time. In the Shenandoah Valley Sheridan had crushed Early's forces at Cedar Creek October 19 and now that indispensable source of supply was lost to the Confederates. Far to the south Sherman had captured Atlanta in September, insuring Lincoln's re-election, and Savannah surrendered December 21. Sherman prepared to march north to join Grant in the spring.

So even the coming of spring could bring no hope to Lee's men, starving and freezing in the filthy trenches. Death, disease, and desertion were slowly destroying the once proud Army of Northern Virginia. In one five-week period that winter 2,934, nearly 8 percent of the effective strength, slipped off in the darkness to go home and not return. Recruiting and drafting could not keep up with the losses. "The men coming in do not supply the vacancies caused by sickness, desertions, and other casualties," Lee admitted sadly. And the caliber of the new men was not what the Army of Northern Virginia was used to, thus tending to destroy the morale of the remaining veterans. But Lee's biggest problem that winter was subsistence. He candidly told the authorities in Richmond, "Unless the men and animals can be subsisted, the army cannot be kept together, and our present lines must be abandoned." He even made a special trip to Richmond to appeal in person to the Confederate Congress, but on his return told his son Custis, "I have been up to see the Congress and they do not seem to be able to do anything except to eat peanuts and chew tobacco, while my army is starving." As one Maryland soldier wrote in January 1865: "There are a good many of us who believe this shooting match has been carried on long enough. A government that has run out of rations can't expect to do much more fighting, and to keep on is reckless and wanton expenditure of human life. Our rations are all the way from a pint to a quart of cornmeal a day, and occasionally a piece of bacon large enough to grease your plate."

EARLY AND SHERIDAN IN THE SHENANDOAH VALLEY

The Battle that Saved Washington by Robert E. Morsberger

The Battle of Winchester by Joseph P. Cullen

Fishers Hill by Jeffry Wert

Cedar Creek by Joseph P. Cullen

The Battle that Saved Washington
by Robert E. Morsberger

In the early summer of 1864, Ulysses S. Grant's hammering campaigns were threatening Richmond. At Petersburg, a greatly outnumbered Lee was making a dogged defense, exacting a fearful toll of Union casualties, while Grant tried to spread the undermanned Confederate forces thin enough to open an approach to the Rebel Capital. In Washington, D.C. a complacent War Department bureaucracy bumbled on, secure in the knowledge that their city was a safe distance from the front. Suddenly the tables were turned as a daring Confederate raid slipped behind Federal lines, invaded the North, and advanced to the fortifications of Washington itself. The capture of the city hung in the balance of a battle fought at a small river in Maryland—the Monocacy.

Ironically, the invasion was triggered by a Federal attack up the Shenandoah Valley of Virginia, intended to divert some of Lee's defenders from Petersburg. Major General David Hunter had captured Staunton and Lexington at the upper end of the Valley, had burned the Virginia Military Institute, and was advancing on the railroad center at Lynchburg. He had to be stopped, and the hard-pressed Lee decided to gamble by sparing some troops from Richmond to reinforce Major General John C. Breckinridge in his attempt to intercept and defeat Hunter's raiders. On June 12 Lee summoned Lieutenant General Jubal Anderson Early and ordered him to withdraw his Second Corps from Richmond, defend Lynchburg, smash Hunter's expedition, and then move north into enemy territory to threaten Washington and occupy it if possible. One corps could not hope to hold the city; but if Early could seize it briefly, he would provide a great boost to Confederate morale and an equal blow to Union prestige.

Early, a bearded, 47-year-old bachelor, had won a reputation for aggressiveness, durability, and dependability. The rank and file were intensely loyal to "Old Jube" or "Old Jubilee," as they called him; but he

Long-range skirmishing between Early's Confederates and the Union defenders of Washington. Sketch by George H. Durfee.

Frank Leslie's Illustrated Newspaper, August 13, 1864

With Hunter's forces racing into the mountains of southwestern Virginia too rapidly for the pursuit to catch up, Early called a halt and redirected his men northeast down the Shenandoah Valley to take pressure off Richmond from that direction. Confederate forces had already retaken Staunton and Lexington. At Lexington the army marched through the cemetery and paid homage at the grave of Stonewall Jackson. At Staunton, Early paused to reorganize his corps and to procure food and supplies, including shoes for the half of his army that had been marching barefoot. Though the shoes failed to arrive, on the morning of June 28 Early ordered his ragged, unshod legions north. Having cleared the upper Shenandoah Valley and preserved its record harvest for the ill-nourished Confederacy, by July 2 they reached Winchester. Critics later claimed that Early had lingered in the Valley, that he could have advanced his troops much more rapidly; but they failed to consider his depleted provisions. If he had moved ahead precipitately, he would have had to stop at some point to thresh wheat and grind it for flour and bread. Fortunately for him, Major General Franz Sigel, commanding the Federal forces in Early's front, abandoned Martinsburg on July 3 and fled across the Potomac, leaving warehouses full of stores the Yankees could not load in time on the escape trains. Early ad-

Lieutenant General Jubal Anderson Early, audacious commander in the Confederate raid on Washington.

often antagonized his subordinate officers by his sarcasm, irritability, and reluctance to take suggestions. Ambitious, Early was also arrogant and eloquently profane in his high tenor voice. By Southern standards of gentility he was not a gentleman, but Lee knew him to be a fighter.

On June 13, at 2:00 a.m., Early set out with 8,000 men and twenty-four cannon. Looking for Breckinridge, he rapidly marched eighty miles to Charlottesville. There he received a wire from Breckinridge, urging him to save Lynchburg from Hunter, whose forces were only twenty miles away. Meanwhile, within striking distance of Lynchburg, Hunter hesitated, lost his thrust, and became timorous in response to conflicting rumors of enemy activity. Early, sixty miles from Lynchburg, loaded his men onto cars of the Orange & Alexandria Railroad on the morning of June 17, and despite the crawling pace of the train he arrived ahead of Hunter. The next day Early made a sortie that Hunter misinterpreted as a major offensive; apprehensive about the arrival of more reinforcements by train, the Union general assumed he was outnumbered and ordered a retreat. While Early planned to attack at daybreak on the 19th, Hunter stole away by night.

Major General David Hunter, whose advance up the Shenandoah Valley ended in inglorious retreat and freed Early for his Washington raid.

vanced to Bolivar Heights above Harpers Ferry, which Brigadier General Max Weber held for the Union. Weber, uncertain of the enemy's numbers and confused by Early's maneuvers, evacuated the town on July 4 and crossed the Potomac to Maryland Heights, heavily fortified with cannon with which he could shell the Confederates if they tried to hold Harpers Ferry.

Accordingly, Early decided to bypass the town and on July 5 ordered Breckinridge's command to cross the Potomac into Maryland. Many of the Rebels forded the river with no shoes, their already tortured feet further agonized by the rocky river bed and the shells in its granite bottom. The next day, in a daring and desperate venture, Early moved his entire army over into an invasion of the Union. Near Sharpsburg he revisited Antietam battlefield, where two years earlier the bloodiest fighting of the war had taken place. Tassels of corn were now growing high in fields that had been full of corpses and wounded writhing in agony. While General John Gordon's men destroyed as much as they could of the Chesapeake & Ohio Canal, Brigadier General John McCausland was ordered to hold Hagerstown for $200,000 ransom. Misreading the order, McCausland asked for and received only $20,000. Elsewhere, Early's men created confusion and rumors of massive Confederate strength ravaging the North as far as Pennsylvania.

It was only gradually that the Union command became aware of Early's actions, and only one man took decisive action. He was Major General Lew Wallace, commanding the Middle Department in Baltimore. A frustrated romantic who was later to write *Ben-Hur* and other historical novels, Wallace had begun the war with brilliant promise as commander of the 11th Indiana Volunteers, a Zouave regiment that soon won prominence by defeating a superior Confederate force at Romney, Virginia. Before the end of 1861, Wallace was promoted to brigadier general. He helped the Union win its first major victory at Fort Donelson by stopping a Confederate assault and was rewarded by promotion to major general at 34, the youngest in the army. But a few weeks later, at the battle of Shiloh, Wallace was made a scapegoat for the Federal near-disaster in the first day's fighting. Following Grant's hasty and unclear order, Wallace marched his reserves in the wrong direction and did not appear on the battlefield until sundown. Though his division took the initiative the next day, being first in the field and driving the enemy to rout, he incurred the ire of Major General Henry W. Halleck, the Federal chief of staff. Halleck removed Wallace from field command and tried to keep him inactive for the rest of the war. But events conspired to give Wallace opportunities for decisive action in times of crisis. When the Confederate forces of General Kirby Smith threatened Cincinnati,

Major General Lewis ("Lew") Wallace. His valiant battle along the Monocacy delayed Early long enough for Union reinforcements to arrive for the defense of the Capital.

only Wallace was available to take command and defend the city successfully. Now that a graver crisis was at hand—a threat to the national Capital itself—Wallace seized the initiative while Halleck at first dawdled and then was frantically ineffectual.

Wallace first received warning on July 2 from John W. Garrett, president of the Baltimore & Ohio Railroad, whose agents reported Early's actions in the Shenandoah Valley. Garrett, concerned that Washington was defended by insufficient troops, suggested that Wallace survey the region between Monocacy Junction and Harpers Ferry. Though Wallace thought this a sensible precaution, he answered that such action was beyond his jurisdiction; his department stopped at the Monocacy River by the city of Frederick, about forty miles west of Baltimore. Beyond this was General Hunter's domain. But Wallace had no idea where Hunter was after his battle at Lynchburg, where Wallace had heard (inaccurately) that he was victorious. Aside from Sigel's troops, the route was wide open from the Shenandoah Valley to Washington or to Baltimore. From Harpers Ferry, the obvious route was to Frederick. There the highway forked into the Baltimore and Washington pikes. Just east of the city each pike had to cross the Monocacy by the railroad junction. Three bridges spanned the river; a stone bridge to

Prewar sketch of Washington from the unfinished dome of the Capitol.

Baltimore, an iron railroad bridge, and a wooden bridge (with a macadamized road bed) to Washington.

Wallace determined not to let a Rebel army pass Monocacy Junction without a fight. At first he thought that his defenses there—a blockhouse with two companies of infantry and two guns, one of them a 24-pound howitzer, would suffice. But impressed by Garrett's urgency, Wallace began to consider whether Washington was threatened, and if so, by whom. The city had massive fortifications—it was ringed by fifty-three forts and twenty-two batteries on a thirty-seven-mile perimeter—but at least 34,000 men were needed to garrison them. Actually there were fewer than 10,000 troops on hand, many of them convalescent invalids or unseasoned militia. Halleck could spare no men to put into the field; the best he could hope was to withstand a siege. None of the bridges over the Potomac had sufficient guards. Many blockhouses were unmanned; some batteries were manned by a commander and crews who knew nothing about the operation of their cannon, not even how to load them. Halleck was supposed to advise Grant if Washington needed relief, but it might take two days for troops to arrive after being summoned. Basking in a false security, the Capital was extremely vulnerable.

On July 3, Wallace learned of rumors that Hunter was in the Kanawha Valley, leaving the Shenandoah undefended all the way to Winchester. In fact, Early had already reached Winchester the day before. On July 4 Wallace received a telegram from Sigel at Martinsburg: "I have reports of an advance of the enemy in force down the Shenandoah Valley. His advance is at Winchester." Wallace had already mustered what troops the department could spare; now he ordered his brigadiers to have their commands ready to move. He sent Brigadier General E. B. Tyler's brigade from the Relay House on the rail line to Washington on to Monocacy Junction. Telegrams began to come in from all directions with reports of enemy activity; Tyler reported that Sigel had evacuated Martinsburg and was falling back toward Harpers Ferry. At 2 p.m. Tyler wired again, "Telegraphic communication cut west of Frederick. Operator at Point of Rocks says the enemy have crossed [the Potomac] one-half mile west of that point." The Confederate strength was uncertain, but General Weber at Harpers Ferry reported ten to twenty thousand men.

Washington did not receive reports of Early's activity until during the July 4 celebrations, when fugitives from around Harpers Ferry arrived with what sounded like extravagant rumors. Unable to get accurate figures, Halleck dismissed the news as exaggerated accounts of a minor raid. The night before, Grant had wired from the front, "Early's corps is now here." When Halleck so informed Secretary of War Stanton, the latter exploded, "I do not want to know where they should be but where they are!"

With no more reliable information than Halleck had, Wallace did not just wait and hope things would work out; he seized the initiative. He determined to go to the front himself, but knowing of Halleck's animosity toward him and fearful of alarming Baltimore, he kept his departure secret. Accompanied only by his aide-de-camp, he left Camden Street station at midnight in a special locomotive provided by Mr. Garrett. His plan was to find the enemy, determine his numbers and his objective, and delay him as long as possible.

At daybreak, Wallace surveyed the unfamiliar terrain that was shortly to become Monocacy battlefield. To the right of the blockhouse was the stone bridge, to its front the iron railroad bridge, and several hundred yards downstream the macadamized Washington pike crossed the river on a wooden covered bridge. The railroad on the western bank branched to Frederick and to Harpers Ferry, and beyond the branch a level valley stretched through ten miles of wheat fields to the blue ridge of the Catoctin Mountains. Somewhere beyond them was Early's army. The river bluff on the east was fifty-five or sixty feet high. Also to the east, near the blockhouse, was a grist mill by a ranch in a hollow, and behind, "rough, dark-wooded hills." Wallace concluded that with the bluff commanding a river too deep for fording, a small force could hold off a larger one attacking from the west.

Meanwhile, rumors kept drifting in; Sigel was holed up with Weber on Maryland Heights. Enemy strength

Above: Major General Henry Wager Halleck refused to believe in the seriousness of Early's raid. Below: Map of the area of Early's advance to Washington. The Monocacy River is just left of center.

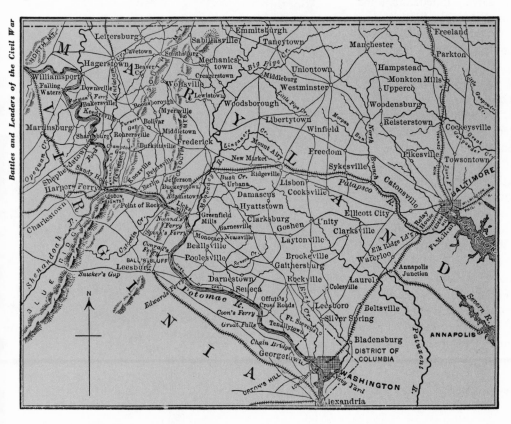

was reported to be from five to thirty thousand men, with Early, Gordon, Breckinridge, Ransom, and Bradley Johnson in command. One fugitive insisted that Lee was commanding in person. No one knew exactly where the enemy was. Wallace arranged for half a dozen civilians to reconnoiter west of the Catoctin Mountains and bring news of the size of the Rebel army and its whereabouts. All reported that they had been stopped by mounted squads, whom Wallace took to be advance pickets of an army heading his way. Deducing that their goal must be Washington, which they could reach in

Confederate commanders under Early. Left to right: Major General John B. Gordon, Major General Robert Ransom, Jr., and Major General Stephen D. Ramseur.

two forced marches once they held the pike at Frederick, he had all spare troops from his district moved up to join him at Monocacy. By noon on July 6, Wallace received a telegram from Sigel, whose skirmishers were fighting with a large Confederate force that seemed to be moving on Frederick. Wallace forwarded the dispatch to Halleck, who refused to believe it. More favorably, Wallace learned that Lieutenant Colonel David Clendenin had five squadrons of the 8th Illinois Cavalry near the mouth of the Monocacy, searching for Mosby's raiders. He urged Clendenin to join him, which the latter did, though Wallace was not authorized to issue him orders. Now that Wallace had some cavalry, he instructed Clendenin to take two pieces of field artillery and ride over the mountains until he either encountered the Confederates or determined that they were not there.

"You see, colonel," Wallace explained, "as yet nobody seems to know how strong the enemy is, or what he has in aim. Suppose it Washington, and it should turn out that he is in force to take it. How can we here in his front hope ever to be excused if he pockets the great prize through our failure to unmask him? We all look to General Grant to save the city. Is it probable he will detach a corps, or even a division, from his work in hand upon nothing better than a rumor or a conjecture?"

Frederick, Md. during Confederate occupation in early September 1862.

Early, meanwhile, was having problems of his own. On July 6, while he was considering driving Weber and Sigel off Maryland Heights, Robert Lee, the commander in chief's youngest son, arrived with a dispatch ordering Early to create a diversion near Baltimore in order to assist a vague plot to free 18,000 Confederate prisoners at Point Lookout. This many men would add a corps to the undermanned Rebels; joined to Early, they could give him a force strong enough to ravage the North with overwhelming numerical superiority. But as yet, half of Early's men were barefooted. The shoes finally arrived on the evening of July 7. That morning, while Gordon attacked the Federals at Maryland Heights, the rest of Early's army evaded a major engagement and slipped through the passes of South Mountain and Catoctin Mountain.

On the morning of July 7, Wallace made a point of getting to know the officers now under his newly organized command. Enjoying the serene view of farms and fields to the west, he suddenly heard distant cannon fire in the mountains. An hour later, a courier galloped in with a dispatch from Clendenin at Catoctin Pass, reporting that he had been driven back by a superior force. Half an hour later, another rider brought a note that Clendenin would be in Frederick within two hours.

Harper's Weekly, September 27, 1862

Wallace debated seriously whether he should hold his ground. At the moment, he had only 2,300 men, many of them untried in combat, against an evidently much larger force. "Had I a right," he wondered, "morally speaking, to subject those under me to the perils of a battle so doubtful, if not so hopeless?" Being directly in the enemy's road, he would have to evacuate or fight. On the other hand, if Washington rather than Baltimore were the Rebel objective, he imagined "a kind of horrible schedule" resulting from the capture of the Capital. The navy yard and its ships would be burned. At the Treasury Department millions of bonds would be seized. The city would be looted and storehouses full of medical, military, and commissary supplies would be plundered for enemy use. Finally, there was the loss of prestige and confidence and the "apparition of President Lincoln, cloaked and hooded, stealing like a malefactor from the back door of the White House just as some gray-garbed Confederate brigadier burst in the front door." But by forcing a battle, Wallace could make the enemy reveal his strength and his route and could perhaps hold him long enough, if Washington was the goal, for Grant to provide reinforcements to defend the Capital. Wallace therefore determined to make a stand at Monocacy Junction, though it would probably result in a fight against fearful odds.

Having made his decision, Wallace sent Colonel Charles Gilpin's regiment to Frederick to cover the city and support Clendenin's retreat. On the return trip, the train was to bring away the city's public stores and those invalids who could be moved from the hospital. At that point, a wire arrived from Garrett of the B & O in Baltimore, stating that an unspecified large force of veterans had arrived up the Chesapeake and would be forwarded immediately. "I saw my role distinctly," thought Wallace; "it was to hold the enemy back until the reinforcements reached me, and then do the fighting behind the river where I was, holding the three bridges."

Clendenin, meanwhile, held up the enemy as best he could while retreating. Whenever the position was favorable, he would dismount his cavalry, wheel his guns into battery, and resume combat until flankers moved in on him, whereupon he would remount, move back, and make another delaying fight. His opponent was Colonel Bradley T. Johnson, who drove the 8th Illinois through Catoctin Pass and back to Frederick. There, ragged fighting continued all afternoon. When the Federals asked for reinforcements, Wallace said he could spare no more men without endangering the junction. Instead, he urged the city's defenders, "The fellows fighting you are only dismounted cavalry, and you can whip them. Try a charge on them."

But by evening, Gilpin was apparently retiring from the city, and Wallace directed him to fall back and hold "at all hazards" the Baltimore pike's crossing of the Monocacy. Bradley Johnson, whose home had been in Frederick, was planning a flanking operation that he was sure would enable him to enter the city behind Union lines, when Major General Robert Ransom arrived and ordered him, to his chagrin, to fall back toward Catoctin Mountain. Wallace thought that he had won the day. To Halleck he wired that "after a severe fight," the enemy "were handsomely repulsed," and to Colonel Lawrence in Baltimore he sent the exuberant message, "Think I have had the best little battle of the war." But later in the evening he informed Lawrence, "The fighting has just begun. It will be heavier and more uncertain tomorrow."

Early considered the fighting around Frederick to be a minor action, but he realized the Federals were becoming alerted. Baltimore was full of fearful rumors. Meanwhile, Wallace waited anxiously for the expected reinforcement of veterans. In Washington, Stanton and Halleck had no plan and took no resolute action for the defense of the city. Their hope was that Hunter might arrive in time to attack Early from the rear. When Grant suggested on July 5 sending a corps of reinforcements, Halleck wired back that this was not necessary. But Grant belatedly realized that Early's corps was gone from the Petersburg defenses, so he sent the 3d Division of the VI Corps under Brigadier General James B. Ricketts. The men reached Baltimore by water on the afternoon of July 7 and were put on a train for Harpers Ferry. In the pre-dawn hours of July 8, the first cars were stopped by Wallace's guards at the iron bridge over the Monocacy. When the officer in charge, Colonel Henry, demanded by what authority he was stopped, Wallace suggested that the troops stay with him to defend Frederick until the division commander, General Ricketts, arrived to give authorized commands. Wallace then joined Henry's regiment on the train to Frederick. There he had them maneuver to give the enemy the impression of a large body of reinforcements; they marched and countermarched until they themselves were confused.

Fortunately for Wallace, Early delayed the battle for another day. On July 8, he moved the Army of the Valley only to the western base of Catoctin Mountain. Summoning Colonel Bradley Johnson back from Frederick, Early instructed him to take 800 cavalry, bypass Frederick to the north, and ride across country to Baltimore, cutting telegraph lines, burning bridges, and tearing up railroad track en route. By July 12 Johnson was to be at Point Lookout to help with whatever attempt was being made to free the prisoners. If the operation succeeded, he should take the freed forces to Washington and join Early, who would arm them with weapons from the city's arsenal.

During most of July 8, the rattle of small arms fire between skirmishers sounded west of Frederick. All during the two days' fighting, a crowd of townspeople, including women and children, sat on a fence within bullet range, watching the show. By 4 p.m., Wallace could see "three long, continuous yellow cloud-lines, apparently on as many roads, crawling serpent-like slowly down towards the valley." These were clearly strong columns of thousands of infantry with artillery trains. Wallace realized for certain that he had been fighting only the advance-guard. To General Tyler he said, "The enemy outnumbers us, that is plain, but because we don't know how much, we must fight." Though he hated to abandon Frederick, he thought it essential that he cover the road to Washington and decided to withdraw his forces to Monocacy Junction.

That night he was unable to sleep, worrying about his right to expose his men to probable defeat and wondering whether he was exceeding his authority in this desperate venture. If he lost the battle, "as seemed inevitable," it would give Halleck his long-awaited chance to ruin Wallace. While he was tossing sleeplessly, Ricketts arrived with the rest of the 3d Division of the VI Corps. Ricketts was amazed at the audacity with which Wallace had planned to resist Early with only 2,300 men; now Wallace had over 5,000 troops to put into action though the odds were still dismay-

Kean Archives

Brevet Major General James Brewerton Ricketts. His division arrived in time to bolster Wallace's forces along the Monocacy.

Brigadier General John McCausland, cavalry commander under Early.

deployment. Cautiously, he began to organize the attack, while artillery blasted at each other across the river. During the morning, Early held the city of Frederick for $200,000 ransom lest he burn it, as his forces under McCausland were to set the torch to Chambersburg, Pennsylvania three weeks later. The mayor asked for some time to raise the money; but when it was clear that Wallace could not save them, the city banks produced the funds. Unable to get compensation later from the Federal Government, the city assumed the debt, which was not paid off until 1951.

Early then rode out to survey the field of the imminent battle. He could see how the Baltimore pike forked to the left and the Washington pike to the right, with the B & O railroad between them. Wallace's forces, posted along a two-mile front, covered all these routes and the three bridges. In the center was Wallace's one formidable piece of artillery, the 24-pound howitzer. Early realized that a direct frontal assault would result in enormous numbers of casualties, but he thought that with Wallace's lines extended so far, he was most vulnerable to an attack on the flank. The obvious flank was Wallace's left and Early's right, south on the road to Washington. But Early could not use the wooden bridge. Clearly, Wallace would burn it if it were too closely threatened, and Early did not know where the river could be forded.

Meanwhile, casualties were mounting. A Confederate sharpshooter sent a ball between Ricketts and Wallace at their command post, and they rode back to higher ground. Near the mill, Wallace established a field hospital. While he was inspecting the arrangements, a victim was carried in screaming in agony; a shell fragment had ripped across his chest, tearing and exposing the lungs. Wallace wondered whether in such cases where death is inevitable, the surgeons should not put the suffering out of their misery.

Near 11 o'clock McCausland's cavalry found a ford about a mile below the wooden bridge. Observing Confederate skirmishers advancing south of the cornfield to Ricketts' left, Wallace sent his orderly to suggest that Ricketts change his front to face them and to move his men forward in concealment behind the cornfield's near fence, even though they would be exposed to enfilading fire from enemy gunners. In the field the corn was green and waist-high. Wallace could see the dismounted Rebel cavalry clear the fence on the other side of the field. Some fence rails were torn down to open gaps for the mounted officers. Then the Confederates advanced at a run, giving the Rebel yell, which sounded to Wallace like the yelping of wolves. As they trampled through the corn, Ricketts' men held their fire. The Confederates did not bother to shoot as they advanced; apparently they thought the resistance

ing. He explained to Ricketts that if Early were not held up, he could reach Washington by the evening of July 10. In fact Early should have been there already; had he not dallied with Hagerstown and Frederick, he could have moved directly on the Capital. Halleck meanwhile sent Wallace neither men nor encouragement; instead, Brigadier General Albion Howe had urged him to join the useless forces at Maryland Heights, leaving Early a clear road to Washington. Apprised of the situation, Ricketts agreed to join Wallace's command and fight in the morning. Since the VI Corps were the most seasoned fighters, Wallace assigned them to hold the left and told Ricketts, "I put you across the Washington pike because it is the post of honor. There the enemy will do his best fighting." After Ricketts left, Wallace slept soundly.

On July 9 skirmishers began firing at sunrise. By 8 o'clock Major General Stephen Ramseur's division drove the Federal skirmishers back through Frederick and pursued them southeast toward the Monocacy. Through the clear and cloudless air, Wallace and Ricketts could see two regiments advancing on the Washington pike towards the wooden bridge and another column veering to the Union left. Breckinridge and Gordon were leading their divisions south of the city and against Wallace's extreme left flank, while Rodes's division moved against his right. Ramseur opposed the center.

When Early arrived in Frederick he held up the advance until he could determine enemy strength and

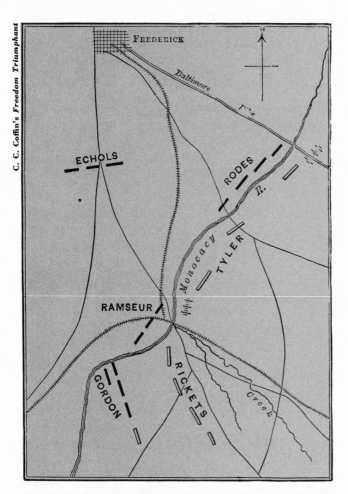

The Battle of Monocacy. Positions during the latter part of battle.

would flee in the face of the howling charge. Ricketts' men reminded Wallace "of hunters in a broad runway, the deer in sight and speeding down upon them." When the distance closed to about 125 yards, the Federals rose, laid their rifles on the top fence rail, and fired a ragged volley, followed by firing at will. The dead and wounded, fallen beneath the corn, were invisible to Wallace, who could see only riderless horses galloping wildly, and retreating foot soldiers climbing over the far fence, tearing down sections of it in their frantic flight.

It was now noon, and Wallace had delayed Early for five hours. Outnumbered at least three to one, he knew he could not hold out when the main enemy force was on his side of the river. But he was now certain that Washington was Early's objective. If he could hold on until 5 or 6 o'clock and then burn the wooden bridge, he could keep Early from moving before the next morning. After the first repulse, there was a lull in the fighting, while skirmishing continued beneath the artillery duel.

But at 2 p.m., it was clear that another attack on Ricketts' left was building up. McCausland had crossed

impetuously and attacked against too heavy odds, so Early ordered Breckinridge to send Gordon's veterans against Ricketts. The Confederates crossed the river under cover of the steep bank on the east but had difficulty climbing up the muddy slope, at the top of which they were picked off by enemy musketry while Gordon deployed them into battle order. Gordon recalled that he had tried to ford the river unobserved, but Wallace "discovered the maneuver of my division before it could drag itself through the water and up the Monocacy's muddy and slippery banks. He at once changed front and drew up his lines in strong position to meet the assault." Wallace ordered his artillerymen to train the howitzer on the advancing battle line but learned to his chagrin that a green gunner had put it out of commission by ramming down a shell before the cartridge. Meanwhile, Ricketts' brigades endured a murderous enfilade from Confederate cannon across the river. With enemy infantry advancing in force, Wallace burned the wooden bridge, even though doing so would leave his skirmishers stranded on the opposite bank.

This time the Confederates had to charge through a wheat field. Gordon's men were cut down by bullets while climbing fences, and they could not maintain order or return fire around the stacks of grain. In Gordon's reminiscences: "Deadly missiles from Wallace's ranks were cutting down the line and company officers with their words of cheer to the men but half spoken. It was one of those fights where success depends largely upon the prowess of the individual soldier." From a distance of several hundred yards, the opponents poured a furious fire into each other, until the Confederate right flank began to give way. Wallace ordered a charge which Ricketts' men carried out boldly, driving the Rebel rout across the recently reaped wheatfield, corpses lying among the sheaves.

This encounter lasted about forty minutes. At 3 p.m., Wallace dictated a telegram to Grant:

I have been fighting General Early here since seven o'clock. With General Ricketts' aid have repulsed two attacks. A third and heavier is making ready. It is evident now he is aiming at Washington. He has been fighting us with eighteen or twenty thousand men, and has others, apparently a corps, in reserve, with field artillery in proportion. If you have not already strengthened the defensive force at Washington, I respectfully suggest the necessity for doing it amply and immediately.

He wrote a similar wire to Halleck to goad him into action. But finding that the telegraph operator had fled, he was obliged to send the messages by mounted courier to the nearest telegraph office. Wallace then consulted with Ricketts on whether to withdraw or hold out a few hours longer. They agreed to stay, even though Ricketts was running low on ammunition. But knowing retreat to be inevitable, Wallace gave instructions to his commanders for the conduct of the withdrawal. Tyler was to hold the stone bridge until Ricketts' force gained the Baltimore pike. Colonel Landstreet was to use his regiment as a rearguard to cover the retreat and keep it orderly instead of a rout.

Near 4 p.m., after the two repulses, Gordon launched a massive attack that drove the first two Federal lines back upon the third, which held, pouring a deadly fire into his left. Wallace's skirmishers, trapped west of the river, suddenly crawled back off the field to the railroad bridge. There they leapt to their feet and began running across the bridge, exposed to enemy fire. The bridge was at least sixty yards long, forty feet above the swirling river. At it was unfloored, the men had to run or rather quick step in a column on the cross ties. Enemy artillery held its fire, but Confederate riflemen dropped a number of victims through the ties or over the side into the river bed below. Most of the

men crossed safely; on the other side, they turned and fired a final round, then cheered and marched off in good order.

On the left, there was desperate fighting back and forth at close quarters across a stream in a narrow ravine, until the water ran crimson. Again, Gordon pulled back and reorganized. Then he sent Brigadier General William Terry's fresh brigade forward against the stubborn Federal infantry. Terry's attack turned into an impetuous, irresistible charge that broke Ricketts' front.

Shortly after 4 p.m. Wallace ordered a withdrawal. Ricketts retreated across the stone bridge, which Tyler held until after 5 o'clock, when his men under attack fought their way out through the woods. The Confederates were too badly battered to offer a vigorous pursuit, and Wallace and Ricketts managed to bring their men off in a semblance of order, with the rearguard occasionally pausing to fight back. At Urbana, Clendenin and his men raced through the village and held up on the hill beyond. Looking back, they saw the Rebels break rank and start pillaging, whereupon Clendenin's cavalry galloped back with drawn sabers and captured the regimental flag of the 17th Virginia.

House near Fort Stevens, showing effects of shot during Early's attack on July 12, 1864.

Wallace insisted that his men were not whipped but withdrew still fighting on an unbroken front. But almost half of his fighting men were casualties, and Gordon wrote that "The Confederate victory was won at fearful cost. . . ." Wallace reported a total of 1,880 casualties: 98 killed, 594 wounded, and 1,188 missing; and Early estimated that his forces suffered about 700 casualties. To Halleck, Wallace wired:

> I fought the enemy at Frederick Junction from 9 a.m. till 5 p.m., when they overwhelmed me with numbers. I am retreating with a foot-sore, battered, and half-demoralized column. Forces of the enemy at least twenty thousand. They do not seem to be pursuing. You will have to use every exertion to save Baltimore and Washington. . . . I think the troops of the 6th Corps fought magnificently. . . . I shall try to get to Baltimore.

En route, he was ordered to halt at Ellicott's Mills (now Ellicott City) to try to stop any Confederate drive toward Baltimore.

Soon Baltimore was in a panic because of Bradley Johnson, who was ravaging the territory north of the city. Along the way, his cavalry cut telegraph lines, tore up railroad track, and burned bridges over the Gunpowder River on the roads from Baltimore to Harrisburg, Philadelphia, and Wilmington. One of Johnson's detachments, under Lieutenant Colonel Harry Gilmor of Baltimore, burned two passenger trains that they ran out on a wooden bridge across the Gunpowder. Among the passengers was Major General William B. Franklin, who was taken prisoner. But Franklin's exhausted guards fell asleep, and the general made his escape in the dark. Johnson's men threatened Baltimore's northern outskirts as close as Cockeysville and Towson and burned the country home of Governor Bradford just across the city line.

But Early's goal was Washington. As Wallace hoped, he mauled Early's army too badly for it to move until Sunday morning. Fighting for time, he had gained a day for the Capital's defense. By Sunday night, Early was only on the outskirts of Rockville, with twenty miles yet to go. Not until Monday afternoon did the Confederate advance reach the fortifications defending the city's outskirts. Early galloped ahead of his army to find his advance cavalry stopped before Fort Stevens on the Seventh Street road. As he considered attacking the works, hoping to be in Washington that evening, he saw reinforcements march smartly into the fort. Early was too late by a day—the day lost at Monocacy. On Sunday, only 209 soldiers manned Fort Stevens, but by Monday afternoon the rest of the VI Corps arrived, followed by three more brigades the next morning,

President Lincoln (in stovepipe hat) during the attack of July 11, 1864 on Fort Stevens.

adding 10,000 able troops for the city's defense. Bradley Johnson sent word of rumors that Grant's entire army was on the move. The projected prison break from Point Lookout failed to materialize, and the anxious Early ordered Johnson to return to the main force.

During Monday afternoon and all of Tuesday, an artillery duel and skirmishing continued between Fort Stevens and Early's advance troops, while the Confederate cavalry cut telegraph wires and tore up railroad tracks. Curious crowds of sightseers took streetcars out North Seventh Street to see the excitement. Among the spectators was President Lincoln, who was under fire both days at Fort Stevens. On Tuesday afternoon, when a brigade of the VI Corps made a sortie to drive off enemy sharpshooters, Lincoln climbed up on the parapet, where a surgeon within three feet of him was shot dead. General Wright ordered Lincoln to step down; and as the President still delayed, Wright's aide, Captain Oliver Wendell Holmes, Jr., shouted, "Get down, you fool!" The President obeyed promptly. During the sortie, Colonel Bidwell's brigade lost about 300 of its 1,000 men.

Despite extensive casualties on both sides, the fight at Fort Stevens was not a major battle. Early decided not to risk his army in an all-out engagement. That evening he withdrew, and the next morning the road before Fort Stevens lay empty. As the VI Corps started in pursuit they found the path of Early's army battle-scarred, with dead and wounded, charred houses,

Frank Leslie's Illustrated Newspaper, August 13, 1864

trampled farms, fences demolished, and homes ransacked. The mansions of Governor Bradford of Maryland and of Postmaster General Montgomery Blair at Silver Spring were burned in retaliation for Hunter's burning of the home of Governor John Letcher and the Virginia Military Institute.

Pursued by General Wright, Early recrossed the Potomac and withdrew to the Shenandoah Valley. For the next several months, he stayed in the Valley and raided out of it, sending McCausland marauding as far as Pennsylvania. In response, Grant put Philip Sheridan in command of the Federal forces in the Shenandoah. On September 18 Sheridan defeated Early at Winchester, pursued him south to Staunton, and drove him into the mountains. Early returned with reinforcements, surprised the VI Corps at Cedar Creek on October 19 and almost routed it before Sheridan arrived with reinforcements from Winchester and practically annihilated the Confederate army, thus ending the fighting in the Shenandoah Valley.

Early's raid had given Washington a serious scare, but he had otherwise failed to accomplish his objectives. He had not helped free the Confederate prisoners at Point Lookout, he had not occupied Washington and carried off its stores, and he had not deflected a significant number of Grant's troops from Petersburg, but he had shaken Union confidence and given a brief

boost to Confederate morale. As he told one of his officers, "Major, we haven't taken Washington, but we've scared Abe Lincoln like hell!"

As for Wallace, he was at first blamed for not beating Early at Monocacy. He called the battle "the most trying, and, in point of service rendered, the most important of my life. It was a battle . . . given upon my own judgment and responsibility, without an order from any of my superiors or their knowledge." Halleck and Stanton belittled him and Lincoln sent a cold dispatch to Grant telling of Wallace's defeat. For three days, Grant relieved Wallace of his command. But as panic died down, the perspective shifted and Wallace received credit for saving the Capital. Postmaster General Blair called Wallace a bolder and better officer than any in Washington. Newspapers praised his gallant stand, and Horace Greeley insisted that Wallace held out four hours longer than honor required. In September Wallace had a cordial meeting with Grant. By September 23 he could write to his brother that "a defeat did more for me than the victories I've been engaged in. In truth, the battle of Monocacy saved Washington, and the authorities acknowledge the service and are grateful for it."

About thirty-five years later Wallace met General Gordon, then a U.S. Senator, at the White House, and they reminisced about Monocacy. Gordon said he had wished for a long time to make the acquaintance of "the only person who had whipped him during the war." Wallace demurred that the Confederates were left holding the field. "But," said Gordon, "you snatched Washington out of our hands—there was the defeat. . . . The duty of driving you off the road fell to me; and I did it, but not until you had repulsed several attacks, and crippled us so seriously we could not begin pushing our army forward until next morning about ten o'clock."

Grant wrote in his memoirs of Wallace's accomplishment by leading his men in "what might well be considered almost a forlorn hope. If Early had been one day earlier he might have entered the Capital before the arrival of the reinforcements I had sent. Whether the delay caused by the battle amounted to a day or not, General Wallace contributed on this occasion, by the defeat of the troops under him, a greater benefit to the Cause than often falls to the lot of a commander of an equal force to render by means of a victory." On one of the monuments at Monocacy battlefield is Wallace's inscription, "These men died to save the National Capital, and they did save it."

The Battle of Winchester
by Joseph P. Cullen

THE summer of 1864 was one of the most critical periods of the war for the Union cause. There was growing war-weariness in the North—a hopeless feeling that the conflict would never end. Since spring, the South had based its hopes for termination of the war and resultant independence on this pessimistic attitude, provided of course that it could hold its own against the Union armies.

This hope was further bolstered when the Democratic convention in Chicago in late August adopted a peace plank in its platform and nominated George B. McClellan as its presidential candidate. The platform was ingeniously contrived to appeal to all those opposed to President Lincoln and the war, and yet was flexible enough to be governed by the military events between then and the election. And the South believed—probably because it wanted to—that the Democrats would win. As young General Dodson Ramseur of North Carolina wrote his wife, "McClellan will be elected and his election will bring peace. . . ."

Even Lincoln was not immune to this belief. Late that summer he had expressed the thought that he was likely to lose the election. For although Grant had Lee pinned down along the Richmond-Petersburg axis and Sherman was threatening Atlanta, no dramatic victories had been achieved. More important politically, however, was the fact that the Federal campaign in the Shenandoah Valley had been a dismal failure. Sigel, defeated by Breckinridge at New Market on May 15, had been replaced by Hunter, only to have Early drive him into western Virginia and thus gain undisputed control of the Valley once again for the Confederacy.

TAKING advantage of this opportunity, "Old Jube," as Early's men called him, crossed the Potomac in July and struck the outskirts of Washington itself, creating near panic in the Federal Capital and seriously damaging Republican prospects for victory in November. Militarily, of course, Early's small force did not pose any real threat and he was quickly forced to withdraw, but because of the political situation Grant had to send large reinforcements from Petersburg to the Valley. On August 7 he appointed Major General Philip H. Sheridan to command all the forces there, later to be known as the Army of the Shenandoah. Politically, a successful Valley campaign was now vital.

When news of Sheridan's appointment reached Early, he decided to keep the new Federal com-

The Battle of Winchester. This drawing by Alfred R. Waud depicts Ricketts' advance against Rodes' division on the morning of Sept. 19, 1864. (B & L)

Sheridan and subordinates. From left to right, Maj. Gen. Philip H. Sheridan, Col. James W. Forsyth, his chief of staff, Maj. Gen. Wesley Merritt, commanding the cavalry corps, Brig. Gen. Thomas C. Devin, commanding 1st Cavalry Division, and Brig. Gen. George A. Custer, commanding 3d Cavalry Division. (LC)

mander off balance by a strategy of ceaseless maneuver which resulted in a succession of marches and demonstrations that accomplished little except to cause Sheridan and Grant to over-estimate the size of Early's force. As Major General John B. Gordon, commanding one of Early's divisions, wrote sarcastically: "Early's little army was marching and countermarching toward every point of the compass in the Shenandoah Valley, with scarcely a day of rest, skirmishing, fighting, rushing hither and thither to meet and drive back cavalry raids, while General Sheridan gathered his army of more than double our numbers for his general advance up the valley."

WHEN Sheridan refused to accept any of the invitations to battle, as Early called these maneuvers, the Confederate commander became overconfident. He convinced himself that Sheridan lacked initiative and boldness. "The events of the last month," he declared, "satisfied me that the commander opposed to me was without enterprise, and possessed an excessive caution which amounted to timidity." A dangerous mental attitude indeed for a general on the verge of battle. And on the surface at least an amazing conclusion,

General Jubal Early. (LC)

particularly as it came after the Battle of Yellow Tavern and Sheridan's ride around the Army of Northern Virginia, threatening Richmond itself. Indeed, Sheridan's reputation in the West had been one of recklessness, rather than timidity.

Actually, however, in refusing these challenges Sheridan was acting under orders. Because of the successful maneuvering of the Confederates in the Valley, Grant believed that Early had about 40,000 men and that this was "too much for Sheridan to attack." Consequently, he increased the pressure on Petersburg, suffering casualties to be sure, but forcing Lee to order Kershaw's division back to Petersburg from the Valley, thus leaving Early with approximately 10,000 infantry and about 4,000 cavalry, as opposed to Sheridan's 40,000, of whom about 6,400 were cavalry. And while the Confederates wore themselves out in marching and countermarching, their Federal counterparts welcomed the opportunity to rest while their commander familiarized himself with his new command and the surrounding terrain, carefully built up his supplies, and very meticulously organized his lines of supply. "We guard wagon-trains," wrote a veteran in the 9th New York Heavy Artillery, "pick blackberries and raspberries, with which the fields abound, read the papers, draw rations, have inspections, dress-parade, and even get back to an old-fashioned drill."

But their rest would soon be over. Learning of Kershaw's withdrawal on September 15, Grant proceeded to Charlestown for a conference with Sheridan, and as a veteran Vermont sergeant growled on seeing Grant, "When that old cuss is around there's sure to be a big fight on hand."

SINCE August 17 Early, described by one observer as "solemn as a country coroner going to his first inquest," had used Winchester, about four miles west

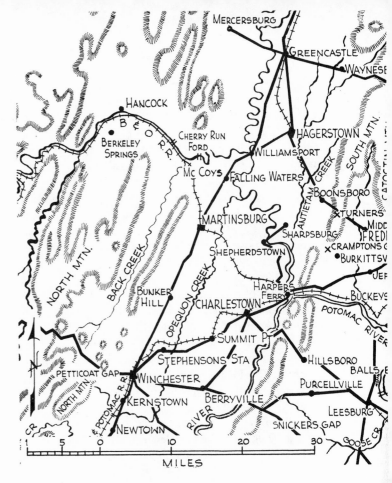

Map 1. Theater of Operations.

of Opequon Creek, as his base of operations, thereby threatening the Baltimore & Ohio Railroad and the Chesapeake & Ohio Canal, and posing a constant danger to Maryland and Pennsylvania.

Now, on September 18, as if in open contempt of his adversary's ability, he had his small force dangerously split. After a reconnaissance in force against some Federal cavalry at Martinsburg, Gordon's division encamped that night at Bunker Hill, about thirteen miles north of Winchester, with orders to pro-

Sheridan's wagon trains in the Valley in the early morning. Drawing by A. R. Waud. (HW)

ceed to Stephenson's Depot on the Winchester & Potomac Railroad by sunrise the following morning. Rodes's and Breckinridge's divisions were at the Depot, about five miles north of Winchester, while Ramseur's division straddled the Berryville Pike on an elevated plateau between Abraham's (Abram's) Creek and Red Bud Run, about a mile east of Winchester. Lomax's cavalry screened his right flank along Senseney Road and Fitz Lee's the left on the Martinsburg Pike. The Confederates, in effect, were in a perfect position to be defeated piecemeal and utterly destroyed.

AWARE of the general disposition of Early's forces, that is exactly what Sheridan planned to do, with Grant's assent. The Opequon here presented a formidable barrier to any attacking force. It flowed generally northward through high, steep bluffs, and except at the fords it ran deep. The two major crossings were at the Charlestown Road and the Berryville Pike. Sheridan planned a concentric attack using all his forces. Merritt's cavalry division would force a crossing at the Charlestown Road and push on to hook-up with Averell's division, coming south on the Martinsburg Pike, where the Charlestown Road joined the Pike in the vicinity of Stephenson's Depot. Both were under the command of Brigadier General A. T. A. Torbert. According to his orders, Merritt's immediate objective was "to prevent Breckinridge, who was known to be in our front, from sending his corps to join the rest of Early's forces near Winchester. . . ." Then both divisions would sweep down the Martinsburg Pike to hit Early's left flank.

Wilson's cavalry division, meanwhile, was to clear the crossing at Berryville Pike for the infantry. Wright's VI Corps would cross first, taking a position south of the Berryville Pike, followed by Emory's XIX Corps, also under Wright's command, to form north of the Pike and thus hopefully to outflank Ramseur on his left. Crook's VIII Corps would be held temporarily in reserve east of the Opequon, but if everything went according to schedule he would cross the creek and take the Senseney Road to the Valley Pike south of Winchester, thereby cutting off Early's only retreat route.

That Sheridan expected the attack to begin at an early hour in the morning is evidenced by his statement that "The utmost promptitude should be exercised in the formation of this line of battle." He hoped to attack about 6 a.m.

IN THE chilly, pre-dawn darkness of 2 a.m. on the 19th the Union army began to move. Just before daylight Wilson's troopers splashed across the creek, drove off the few cavalry pickets, and headed into a long, narrow gorge blocked at the west end with small earthworks. Coming under fire from these fortifications, McIntosh's brigade, armed with the Spencer repeating carbine, made a daring charge and in a combined mounted and dismounted attack quickly captured the works and held them against numerous counterattacks.

As a rich, crimson sun rose slowly in the clear blue sky, signaling a beautifully mild late summer day, the leading elements of Wright's VI Corps filed through the gorge and deployed south of the Berryville Pike, passing on the way cavalrymen stretched out in death, which seemed, as one soldier remarked, to have effectually answered Joe Hooker's earlier sarcastic question, "Whoever saw a dead cavalryman?"

Right on schedule the veterans of the VI Corps formed line of battle, but then things started to go wrong. When Emory tried to bring his XIX Corps

---

For Portfolio of Maps on Winchester, See Next 3 Pages

Map 2. Battle of Winchester, September 19, 1864—the opening phase, at about 8:45 a.m. This and the succeeding maps of the battle were adapted by W. S. Nye from those in the "Official Records," and were used originally in E. J. Stackpole's "Sheridan in the Shenandoah." "Ridgway's Ford" in the upper right-hand corner of the map is known locally as Clevenger's Ford, and Abraham's Creek is more correctly "Abram's Creek." Troop operations for this phase were briefly as follows:

Federals. Wilson's cavalry division crossed the Opequon on the Berryville Road and moved rapidly west to attack Ramseur's advanced brigades, which were in earthworks astride the road, as shown. Wilson took this position, and held it against several counterattacks until about 9:00 a.m., when leading units of the VI Corps arrived and began to relieve the cavalry. At the northeast corner of the battlefield Lowell's cavalry brigade of Merritt's division, followed later by Devin's brigade, forced a crossing at Ridgway's Ford. Custer's brigade crossed a mile farther north and linked up with Lowell. Averell's cavalry division, not shown on this map, is moving south astride the Martinsburg Pike.

Confederates. The bulk of Early's infantry up to this time has been concentrated at Stephenson's Depot, with Ramseur guarding the approaches to Winchester from the east, as shown. Johnson's cavalry brigade of Lomax's division, after screening the front of Ramseur, and picketing the crossings of the Opequon in that front, has fallen back and taken positions on either flank of Ramseur. The map also shows the locations of Lomax's other three brigades—McCausland, Imboden, and Jackson. Fitzhugh Lee's cavalry division is falling back in front of Averell.

When Early became aware of the advance of the Federal columns at Ridgway's Ford and the Berryville Crossing, he started Breckinridge's two brigades under Wharton to reinforce McCausland, and Gordon's and Rodes' divisions to extend Ramseur's position. These movements are shown as just getting under way at about 8:45 a.m.

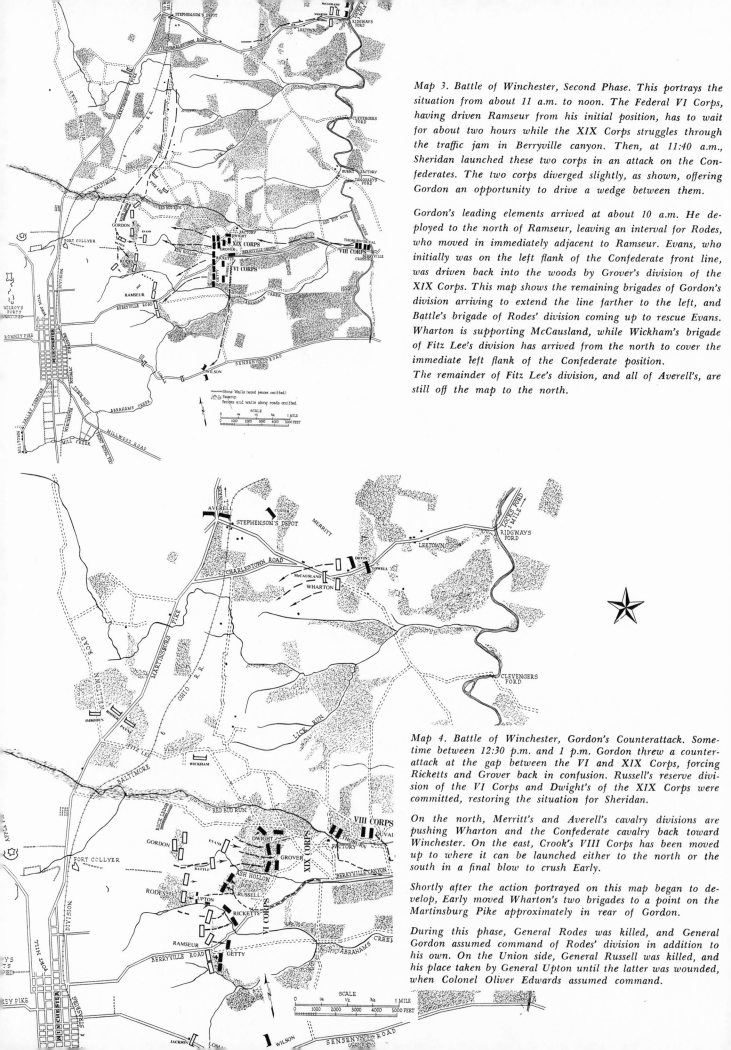

Map 3. Battle of Winchester, Second Phase. This portrays the situation from about 11 a.m. to noon. The Federal VI Corps, having driven Ramseur from his initial position, has to wait for about two hours while the XIX Corps struggles through the traffic jam in Berryville canyon. Then, at 11:40 a.m., Sheridan launched these two corps in an attack on the Confederates. The two corps diverged slightly, as shown, offering Gordon an opportunity to drive a wedge between them.

Gordon's leading elements arrived at about 10 a.m. He deployed to the north of Ramseur, leaving an interval for Rodes, who moved in immediately adjacent to Ramseur. Evans, who initially was on the left flank of the Confederate front line, was driven back into the woods by Grover's division of the XIX Corps. This map shows the remaining brigades of Gordon's division arriving to extend the line farther to the left, and Battle's brigade of Rodes' division coming up to rescue Evans. Wharton is supporting McCausland, while Wickham's brigade of Fitz Lee's division has arrived from the north to cover the immediate left flank of the Confederate position.

The remainder of Fitz Lee's division, and all of Averell's, are still off the map to the north.

Map 4. Battle of Winchester, Gordon's Counterattack. Sometime between 12:30 p.m. and 1 p.m. Gordon threw a counterattack at the gap between the VI and XIX Corps, forcing Ricketts and Grover back in confusion. Russell's reserve division of the VI Corps and Dwight's of the XIX Corps were committed, restoring the situation for Sheridan.

On the north, Merritt's and Averell's cavalry divisions are pushing Wharton and the Confederate cavalry back toward Winchester. On the east, Crook's VIII Corps has been moved up to where it can be launched either to the north or the south in a final blow to crush Early.

Shortly after the action portrayed on this map began to develop, Early moved Wharton's two brigades to a point on the Martinsburg Pike approximately in rear of Gordon.

During this phase, General Rodes was killed, and General Gordon assumed command of Rodes' division in addition to his own. On the Union side, General Russell was killed, and his place taken by General Upton until the latter was wounded, when Colonel Oliver Edwards assumed command.

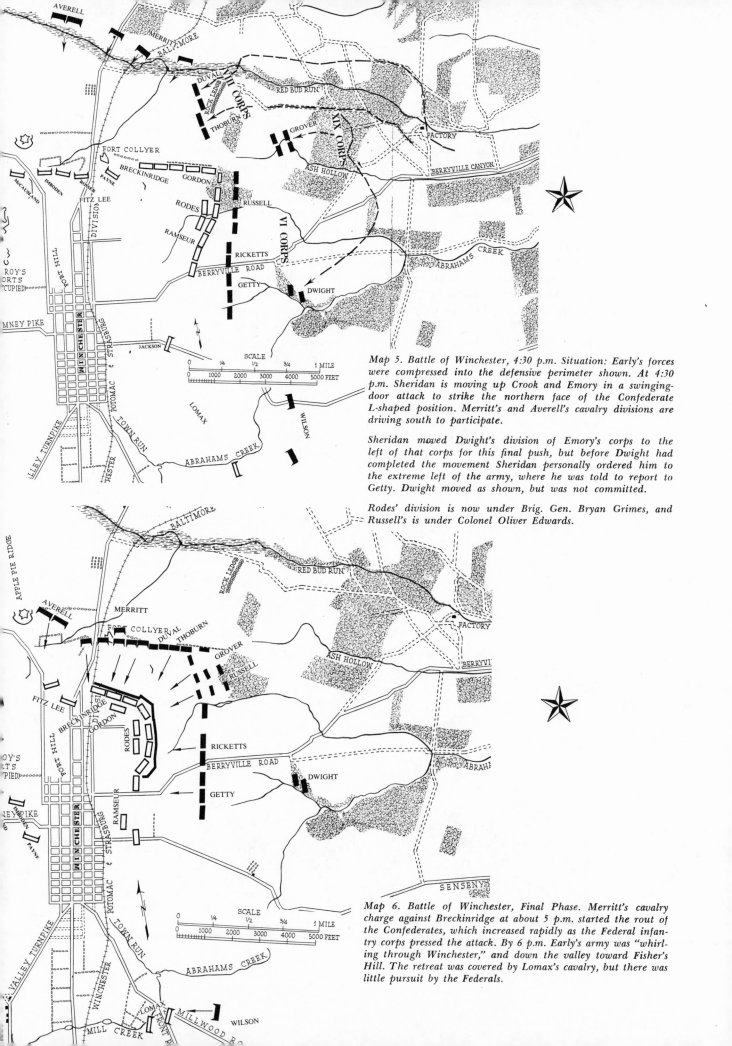

Map 5. Battle of Winchester, 4:30 p.m. Situation: Early's forces were compressed into the defensive perimeter shown. At 4:30 p.m. Sheridan is moving up Crook and Emory in a swinging-door attack to strike the northern face of the Confederate L-shaped position. Merritt's and Averell's cavalry divisions are driving south to participate.

Sheridan moved Dwight's division of Emory's corps to the left of that corps for this final push, but before Dwight had completed the movement Sheridan personally ordered him to the extreme left of the army, where he was told to report to Getty. Dwight moved as shown, but was not committed.

Rodes' division is now under Brig. Gen. Bryan Grimes, and Russell's is under Colonel Oliver Edwards.

Map 6. Battle of Winchester, Final Phase. Merritt's cavalry charge against Breckinridge at about 5 p.m. started the rout of the Confederates, which increased rapidly as the Federal infantry corps pressed the attack. By 6 p.m. Early's army was "whirling through Winchester," and down the valley toward Fisher's Hill. The retreat was covered by Lomax's cavalry, but there was little pursuit by the Federals.

up he found the gorge, with its steep, tree-covered slopes rising sharply on either side of the pike, completely blocked by the supply and ammunition wagons of the VI Corps, despite Sheridan's specific order that the wagons should be held east of the creek until the XIX Corps was in position. Even the slopes were clogged, one soldier remembered, with "the hundreds of men who belong to an army but never fight—the cooks, the officers' servants, the hospital gangs, the quartermaster's people, the 'present sick' and the habitual skulkers."

The key to Sheridan's whole plan was to have these two corps hit Ramseur early and quickly and overwhelm him before he could be reinforced. Now the key was lost and the battle would have to be fought as it developed. It would be several hours before Emory could be in position for the attack.

SHORTLY after dawn Early learned that the Federals had crossed the Opequon at the Berryville Pike and were massing for an attack on Ramseur. He immediately ordered Gordon, at Stephenson's Depot, to come to Ramseur's support, and then Old Jube rode out on the pike to see for himself what the

situation was. Realizing at once that a major attack was in the offing, he ordered his remaining infantry, that of Rodes and Breckinridge, to hurry to the scene of action, although admitting at the same time that he was not surprised that Sheridan at last was willing to fight. At Martinsburg the day before he had "learned that Grant was with Sheridan that day, and I expected an early move." Despite this belief, because of his overconfident attitude and contempt for Sheridan, he ignored the opportunity to unite his forces or even to hold the western opening of the gorge, a move which would have completely thwarted the Federal plan.

Under pressure from Wright, Ramseur now withdrew slowly but skillfully until about 10 a.m. when Gordon and Rodes arrived on the field. Observing the leading elements of Emory's XIX Corps debouching from the gorge and starting to curl around Ramseur's left, Early placed Gordon, the first up, on the extreme left to check this flanking movement, and put Rodes, when he came up, in between Gordon and Ramseur and ordered an attack. Shortly after 11 a.m. they moved out and caught Emory's corps just coming into line and thus off-balance. Then, because of the delay and the peculiarities of the terrain, a dangerous gap developed between Emory and Wright just north of the pike. Although most of the land was generally open with cornfields and meadows, a few houses, and patches of woods, there were also numerous small ravines and marshy areas, combined with stone and

General Cuvier Grover's 2d Division of the XIX Corps at the Battle of Opequon (Winchester) September 19, 1864. Original drawing by A. R. Waud. (LC)

wooden fences which made it difficult to maintain alignment. Rodes and Gordon both saw the opportunity offered and attacked with vigor as Ramseur succeeded temporarily in halting the advance of the VI Corps on the right.

RODES was killed at the start of this attack, but Battle's brigade of that division hit the gap between Grover's division on Emory's left and Ricketts' division on Wright's right and drove them back in confusion, thus widening the gap and pushing in the Federal center. Colonel J. W. Kiefer, commanding the brigade on Ricketts' right flank, had also noticed the gap and on his own initiative ordered three of his regiments to the right in an attempt to fill it. About the same time Evans' brigade of Gordon's division on the Confederate extreme left was first driven back by Emory's right, but a stubborn stand by Braxton's artillery halted the Federals and then started driving them back. The situation for Sheridan was serious, to say the least. In his report Kiefer described what happened:

> As the lines advanced the interval became greater. The enemy discovering this fact hurled a large body of men towards the interval and threatened to take my right in flank. I at once caused the 138th and 67th Pennsylvania and the 110th Ohio to break their connection with the right of the remainder of my brigade, and to move towards the advancing column of the enemy. These three regiments most

gallantly met the overwhelming masses of the enemy and held them in check. . . . The three regiments had arrived within less than 200 yards of two batteries when the 19th Corps, after a most gallant resistance, gave way. The enemy at once came upon my right flank in great force. Successful resistance was no longer possible; the three regiments had already suffered heavily, and were obliged to fall back in some disorder.

At this critical stage David A. Russell's division of the VI Corps came up to plug the gap in the Federal line and hit the shoulder of the Confederate penetration, driving Battle back and thus blunting Early's counterattack. In this crucial action Russell, a close personal friend of Sheridan's, was killed.

THE furious fighting raged for several hours, the lines see-sawing back and forth as neither side asked nor gave quarter. "No earthworks have been thrown up on either side," wrote one veteran, "so it is a fair stand-up fight with no favors, but it is a terrible ordeal through which we are compelled to pass, one to appall the stoutest heart."

The Irish-tempered and profane Sheridan, furious that Emory had not come up in time, dashed about the field on his shiny black charger, orderly and battle flag at his heels, trying to straighten out the line. About noon, believing his right threatened by Gordon's advance, he abandoned his original plan to send Crook's VIII Corps down the Senseney Road behind Wilson's cavalry to envelop Early's right flank. Instead, Crook was ordered to cross the Opequon and come into line on Emory's right flank, with one division extending north of Red Bud Run.

In the meantime, Merritt's cavalry division had also marched at 2 a.m. and before sunrise had forced the fords at the Charlestown Road, scattering Fitz Lee's cavalry pickets. Breckinridge's infantry, encamped at Stephenson's Depot, was ordered out to drive the Federal cavalry back. Strongly entrenched behind the railroad cut, the Confederates poured a heavy fire into the Federals, but in a series of mounted and dismounted charges, Merritt's troopers slowly drove Breckinridge back, but more importantly, they held him on their front for hours. Despite Early's frantic order to join him at once, it was past noon before Breckinridge extricated his force and about 2 p.m. when he actually arrived on the field. With the Federal line finally straightened out and advancing all along the front, Early fell back to a new defensive position, putting two of Breckinridge's brigades on his right to support the hard-pressed Ramseur, and the other on his extreme left next to Gordon. This brigade actually faced to the north at right angles to the rest of the line, so that the Confederate position now took the form of an inverted L.

Early withdraws into the perimeter of Winchester. (KA)

ALTHOUGH he had received his order to move about noon, it was 4 o'clock before Crook came into position on the Federal right. Passing to the rear of the XIX Corps he encountered rough, uneven ground with heavy thickets, tanglefoot underbrush, and the "impossible morass" of Red Bud Run. One division (Thoburn) hit Gordon's left, while the other (Duval) crossed the Red Bud and came down on Breckinridge's brigade from the north.

About the same time Merritt and Averell mounted a frightening, morale-shattering, old-fashioned cavalry charge along the Martinsburg Pike, Merritt on the east and Averell on the west, that came in on Breckinridge's left flank and rear, driving Fitz Lee's broken cavalry through the infantry lines. Although Averell had practically no opposition in his front, his charge was broken and halted temporarily by some horse artillery on Fort Hill, just west and slightly north of the town, and by some deep ditches and steep embankments.

In a whirlwind of galloping horses and slashing sabers, Devin's brigade of Merritt's division charged into the fray, returning with three battle flags and over 300 prisoners. Next Lovell's brigade charged, also capturing flags, prisoners, and two guns. Then the two united for a final charge. Writing his report of the affair Merritt let himself get carried away with the drama of it all. "It was a noble work well done—a theme for the poet; a scene for the painter."

One Federal officer who had the misfortune to be captured in the last charge described the scene within the Confederate ranks:

The confusion, disorder, and actual rout produced by the successive charges of Merritt's division would appear incredible did not the writer actually witness them. To the right a battery of guns disabled and caissons shattered was trying to make to the rear, the men and horses impeded by broken regiments of cavalry and infantry; to the left, the dead and wounded, in confused masses, around their field hospitals—many of the wounded, in great excitement, seeking shelter in Winchester; directly in front, an ambulance, the driver nervously clutching the reins, while six men in great alarm were carrying to it the body of General Rodes.

WITH his left flank now caving in, Early frantically sent Breckinridge's two brigades from the right over to his left, but under the pressure of Crook's attack and the cavalry charge, the lines broke, and as the blood-red sunset faded off into deep purple shadows, the Confederates streamed south through the streets of the town, a broken and decisively defeated army. "It was a sad, humiliating sight," a wounded Confederate recorded in his diary. The battle of Winchester was over. Early reported his casualties at 3,611, while Sheridan suffered about 5,000.

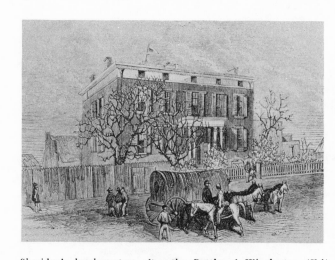

Sheridan's headquarters after the Battle of Winchester. (KA)

But, heartless as it may sound, the casualties were the least significant result of this battle. In a flamboyant telegram to Grant, which quickly made the front page of every newspaper in the North, Sheridan proclaimed pompously: "I attacked the forces of General Early on the Berryville Pike at the crossing of Opequon Creek, and after a most stubborn and sanguinary engagement, which lasted from early in the morning until 5 o'clock in the evening, completely defeated him, and driving him through Winchester captured about 2,500 prisoners, five pieces of artillery, nine army flags and most of their wounded." In another dispatch he stated, "We have just sent them whirling through Winchester, and we are after them tomorrow." Soon the phrase "whirling through Winchester" was on every tongue in the North. This was exactly the dramatic kind of victory report the North so desperately needed. In Washington a hundred-gun salute was fired in celebration, and President Lincoln telegraphed Sheridan: "Have just heard of your great victory. God bless you all, officers and men. Strongly inclined to come up and see you."

THE political significance of the victory was also immediately apparent. Whitelaw Reid of the Cincinnati *Gazette* in a dispatch from Washington voiced the general opinion of those who had sought to replace Lincoln with another candidate. "The general apathy and discontent and the apparent certainty of Mr. Lincoln's defeat" had all changed, he wrote. Horace Greeley, the volatile critic of the Lincoln administration, now declared that his New York *Tribune* would "henceforth fly the banner of Abraham Lincoln for President." While future President James A. Garfield declared that "Phil Sheridan has made a speech in the Shenandoah Valley more powerful and valuable to the Union cause than all the stumps in the Republic can make—our prospects are everywhere heightening." Even the men in the ranks recognized that the victory, as one veteran wrote, "was worth whole tons of campaign literature to the side that was supporting Abraham Lincoln." This, combined with the fall of Atlanta, assured Lincoln's nomination on the Republican ticket and practically guaranteed his re-election.

Since spring the one hope the Confederacy had for success was that the Northern people would tire of the slaughter and force their leaders to quit. After Winchester and Atlanta that hope was futile. And

Sheridan receiving reports after the Battle of Winchester, Sept. 19, 1864. Original drawing by A. R. Waud. (LC)

after Sheridan finished off Early at Fishers Hill on September 22 and Cedar Creek in October, the way was clear to carry out the policy that Grant had mentioned to him earlier in the summer. "If the war is to last another year," Grant had stated, "we want the Shenandoah Valley to remain a barren waste." The great bread basket of the Confederacy, so vital to Lee's Army of Northern Virginia, was at last to be devastated.

IN HIS report of the disaster to Lee, the caustic Early tried to place the blame on factors beyond his control. "The enemy's immense superiority in cavalry and the inefficiency of the greater part of mine has been the cause of all of my disasters." But after studying the various reports Lee knew better. Bluntly he told Early: "As far as I can judge, at this distance, you have operated more with divisions than with your concentrated strength."

Writing his memoirs after the war Early in effect admitted the accuracy of Lee's observation, probably without realizing it, as the main purpose of his state-ment was to deride Sheridan's ability. "A skillful and energetic commander of the enemy's forces," he wrote, "would have crushed Ramseur before any assistance could have reached him, and thus insured the destruction of my whole force." This was also, of course, a tacit admission that the disposition of his troops before the battle was faulty, caused primarily by his overconfidence and his contempt for Sheridan. A well-known fact of military history, however, is that by the faulty disposition of troops a battle can be lost before it even starts. This was the situation at Winchester. There seems little doubt that had Sheridan been able to execute his original plan—and the mix-up in the gorge was the only thing that prevented it—Early's force would have been annihilated.

Pitted against a determined adversary and outnumbered almost three to one, it is difficult to see what Early could have done to change the ultimate result of the whole Valley Campaign. But there is no question that his strategy and tactics could have been improved. His failure to unite his forces in a strong defensive position prior to the attack, and above all his neglecting to hold the western end of the gorge in strength, voided the possibility that the battle might have ended in a standoff, rather than in a dramatic, politically valuable victory for the North.

Fishers Hill
by Jeffry Wert

The Confederate Army of the Valley, Lieutenant General Jubal A. Early commanding, shuffled southward from Winchester, Virginia. Singly, in small clusters, or in remnants around some tattered flag, the Rebels retreated, an army defeated and partially routed at the Third Battle of Winchester, Virginia. A stubborn rearguard and darkness prevented even greater loss for the men who followed the macadamized ribbon up the Shenandoah Valley. "Lucky was the Confederate private who on that mournful retreat knew his own captain," an officer recalled, "and most lucky was the commander who knew where to find the main body of his own troops."

Few words were spoken as the retreat continued throughout the night, only the creaking and rumbling of wagons, caissons and ambulances awoke sleeping residents. In one ambulance were the remains of Major General Robert E. Rodes, a deeply grieved and irreplaceable loss. In the column, also, a carriage carrying the ubiquitous Mrs. John B. Gordon and her son Frank rolled along—Old Jubal cussing the Federal soldiers' failure to capture her. For the soldiers, most of them members of "Stonewall" Jackson's incomparable Second Corps, the retreat marked the first time they had been completely driven from a field of battle. None of them could perceive that it marked the beginning of the end for the Confederacy in Virginia.

By daylight of September 20, 1864, the Confederates filed into their old trenches at Fishers Hill, one mile south of Strasburg, Virginia. Exhausted, hungry, most immediately slumped to the ground and slept. Hundreds, unable to keep pace during the night, straggled in throughout the morning. The defeat of the previous day culminated a month of maneuvers and skirmishes with the Federals, but it had not destroyed their spirit. One veteran, typifying others, said before he rested: "Cheer up, boys; don't be worried. We'll lick them Yankees the first fair chance, and get more grub and guns and things than our poor old quartermaster mules can pull." They now waited for that "first fair chance."

Twenty-one miles to the north at Winchester, the victorious Federal Army of the Shenandoah, Major General Philip H. "Little Phil" Sheridan commanding, started the pursuit at 5:00 a.m. Jubilant, confident, Sheridan's splendid cavalry led the march, two divisions on the Valley Pike, one division to the west on the Back Road. The VI Corps marched beside the pike on the western side, the XIX Corps strode the fields to the east.

Sheridan's headquarters near Cedar Creek.

The wagons followed the road while the Army of West Virginia, or the VIII Corps, trailed the train. The army of roughly 35,000 men was an imposing, formidable sight along the highway.

The warm day and the spirits of the men speeded the march. North of Middletown, Virginia, Brigadier General Wesley Merritt's cavalrymen encountered Confederate pickets and easily brushed them aside. Merritt's troopers proceeded into the town, while Brigadier General James H. Wilson's mounted division, trailing closely, turned eastward onto Front Royal Pike and rode toward that village, where an unknown Confederate force was reputedly located. At 5:00 p.m. Sheridan's infantry relieved Merritt, who rode to the right and encamped near Brigadier General William W. Averell's cavalry division which had followed the Back Road and crossed Cedar Creek.

The veteran infantrymen marched through Middletown, forded Cedar Creek and deployed along some high ground north of Strasburg, a "dingy, dilapidated

village,'' according to one. Major General Horatio G. Wright's VI Corps held the right and Major General William F. Emory's XIX Corps lengthened the line eastward as far as the road from Strasburg to Front Royal. Sheridan halted his wagons north of Cedar Creek and deployed Major General George Crook's VIII Corps in woods nearby. The Federals soon had campfires burning, meals cooking, and equipment stacked.

Their victory at Winchester, or the Opequon, as they would name it after the creek, had forged them into an army. Each corps had suffered previously at the hands of Early's veterans, but now with Little Phil in command they believed in themselves. "An unusual confidence was felt in him," one veteran wrote of Sheridan. "We may have had a blinder faith in McClellan but no such intelligent trust as we now had in Sheridan." That trust was needed as they looked southward toward Fishers Hill, for as one engineer officer said that day, "if they [the Rebels] have prolonged their left sufficiently, they are inattackable [sic]."

The Battle of Fisher's Hill (*CWTI* Collection)

Fishers Hill, a high, steep bluff, had seemingly been heaved up by mistake from the valley floor during the creation. Its eastern heights nestled against the brooding Massanutten mountain range. Three peaks, or the "Three Sisters," of the Massanutten overlooked the Valley at this point. Signal Knob, the western peak, afforded Early an excellent view of the Federal position north of Strasburg. To the west Little North Mountain rose, less than four miles from Signal Knob. At no point in the Shenandoah was the valley so narrow. "The frowning heights of Fishers Hill had long been the bugbear of the valley," according to a Union officer. It was a position, if adequately manned, that was nearly impregnable.

For Jubal Early, "it was the only place where a stand could be made" if he hoped to arrest Sheridan's advance. A month earlier the Union commander had refused to attack Early's forces protected by the sharp bluffs, but then the aggressive Sheridan was under restraining orders not to suffer a defeat—a critical fact unknown to Early. The Confederate commander now reasoned that if he withdrew farther up the Valley he could not stop short of the gaps of the Blue Ridge. "I determined therefore," he subsequently wrote, "to make a show of a stand here, with the hopes that the enemy would be deterred from attacking me in this position."

Old Jubal's reasoning unfortunately did not reflect the altered circumstances. His army, reduced to fewer than 9,000 effectives, had been soundly defeated; the men lacked food, clothing and shoes, and his casualties among the officers seriously impaired the army's effi-

Commanders under Sheridan. Left to right: Major Generals William H. Emory, George W. Getty, and George Crook.

Sheridan's army following Early up the Shenandoah Valley, late September 1864. Pencil drawing by Alfred R. Waud.

ciency. Early assigned Major General Stephen Dodson Ramseur, a very capable officer, to Rodes's division, while giving Brigadier General John Pegram the North Carolinian's command. On the 21st, Major General John C. Breckinridge received orders to report immediately to southwestern Virginia, and he left before nightfall, another loss Early could not afford. At brigade and regimental levels the situation was even more critical as many field officers had already fallen. Early's position now was, as a perceptive Union officer stated, "too big for his enfeebled army."

The Confederate commander compounded the error in judgment by his unwise dispositions, which were completed on the 20th. His right, where Fishers Hill was the steepest and a bend in the North Fork of the Shenandoah River confined the area of attack, was virtually unassailable. Here, however, Early stationed Brigadier General Gabriel C. Wharton's seasoned veterans. Extending Wharton's left was Major General John B. Gordon's excellent division, then Pegram's and finally Ramseur's. His left, where the high bluff sloped down into a small valley before merging with Little North Mountain, Early placed Brigadier General Lumsford

Lomax's undermanned, demoralized cavalry command. If Sheridan hoped to carry the Confederate works, Lomax's position was the vulnerable key, yet here Early placed his weakest command, troops he had no confidence in at all. It was a grievous, inexplicable error on Early's part, and justly controversial.

While the two armies slept, Sheridan conferred with his subordinates at his headquarters located just south of Cedar Creek beside the turnpike. This meeting between Sheridan, Wright, Emory and Crook has generated some controversy as to who proposed the flanking attack. From the available evidence it appears that the four officers unanimously dismissed the idea of a frontal attack. Crook, Sheridan's West Point roommate and close friend, apparently then suggested using his command in a flanking maneuver similar to the one executed at Winchester. Wright and Emory demurred, but Sheridan approved it. Little Phil then sent for Crook's two division commanders, Colonels Joseph Thoburn and Rutherford B. Hayes, to discuss the feasibility of the plan. With the details finally resolved, Sheridan adjourned the meeting.

If Crook proposed the plan, Sheridan unequivocally accepted responsibility for it. "Naturally eager and impulsive," the fiery Irishman wanted to destroy Early's army. As a secondary phase, Sheridan ordered his cavalry commander, Brigadier General A.T.A. Torbert, to take Merritt's division and join Wilson at Front Royal. From there he could sweep down the Luray Valley, cross the Massanutten at New Market Gap and form a barrier across the Valley upon which Sheridan could crush the Rebels. Little Phil always thought in terms of the annihilation of the enemy. He wrote in his report summarizing his entire campaign that his purpose was "to destroy, to the best of my ability, that which was truly the Confederacy—its armies." If the plan worked, Sheridan would have Early's entire army bagged by the 23d.

The Federal movement commenced on September 21, again at five o'clock in the morning when Merritt's cavalry splashed across Cedar Creek, riding northward. Merritt halted to receive his final orders at headquarters before detaching Colonel Thomas Devin's brigade as protection for the army's rear. Continuing, the horsemen forded the North Fork at Buckton's Ford and rode toward Front Royal.

The blue infantrymen, meanwhile, leisurely stirred from their bivouacs. Throughout the morning the veterans rested, except for one of Emory's regiments which engaged Rebel horsemen picketing near the North Fork.

This unit, the 9th Connecticut, forded the river and skirmished with Rebel Brigadier General John McCausland's troopers.

At noon, Wright's and Emory's men formed columns and marched toward the Confederate works, swinging around to the northwest of Strasburg. On Fishers Hill the graybacks, busily constructing stronger works, caught glimpses of the movement across the wooded terrain. To the west, Averell's troopers sniped at Rebel skirmishers and pressed forward on foot. The VI Corps led the rightward sidle, with Brigadier General James B. Ricketts' division in front. Confederate cannon occasionally boomed in defiance, and grayback sharpshooters, at the foot of the hill and north of Tumbling Run, a "brawling brook" which flowed along the entire front of Fishers Hill, fired at the advancing foe. The march consumed most of the afternoon, but the Federals finally halted and deployed.

Blue skirmishers cautiously advanced, while the veterans hastily piled rails across their front. Musket firing increased and Federal cannon joined in. Along one section of the line, the Federals could see puffs of smoke rising from the branches of a large tree. A Union gun crew hurriedly loaded and sent a shell screeching into the tree. Nearly a dozen Rebels dropped to the ground and ran toward the rear. Each side suffered few casualties, but the annoying graybacks successfully held their position.

Sheridan, with Wright, rode along the line inspecting the ground. Sheridan noticed a hill, occupied by Rebels, that was only 700 yards from Early's main line and that would give the Union commander an "unobstructed

view" of the Confederate works. Little Phil ordered Wright to seize the ground, known as Flint Hill. It was now after 5:00 p.m.

Wright returned to his line and ordered Ricketts to send one regiment forward in conjunction with a regiment from Brigadier General George W. Getty's division, which was on Ricketts' left. Ricketts sent the 126th Ohio in on the right, Getty the 139th Pennsylvania on the left. Both regiments charged gamely across the open ground only to be repulsed by fire from Pegram's entrenched skirmishers. Ricketts immediately sent the 6th Maryland forward as support, while Getty hurried Colonel James M. Warner's brigade to the front.

Warner's veteran Pennsylvanians and New Yorkers halted 150 yards before Flint Hill. Reforming ranks and fixing bayonets, the brigade swept across the open field, up the hillside and dislodged the outnumbered Rebels. The soldiers immediately dug rifle pits and awaited nightfall.

Sheridan's line, by sundown, was an unbroken front from the Valley Pike on the left to Ricketts' position opposite Pegram on the right. Brigadier General Cuvier Grover's division of Emory's corps covered the highway. Next to him on the right Brigadier General William Dwight's soldiers connected with Brigadier General Frank Wheaton's VI Corps division. Wheaton, in command of the division for the first time, rested his left on the roadbed of the ruined Manassas Gap Railroad. Getty was closed on Wheaton's right. During the night, however, Sheridan moved Wright's command more than a full division to the right, a maneuver which consumed most of the night because of the rugged terrain. These two corps were positioned to engage the Rebels while Crook outflanked them the next day.

Lossing's Civil War in America

Stone bridge at Fishers Hill, where a large number of Federals were captured by Early.

Harper's Weekly

Sheridan's wagons in the Shenandoah Valley. Engraving from a drawing by Alfred R. Waud.

Crook's soldiers had spent the entire day in the woods north of Cedar Creek, hidden from the Rebel signal station on Signal Knob. After nightfall, Crook marched his divisions across Cedar Creek and into another clump of woods behind Hupp's Hill, a prominence north of Strasburg. From here the command could move the next morning by a concealed route to Little North Mountain and Early's flank and rear.

complied and his veterans marched to the designated point only to be subjected to a fire from graybacks entrenched on two small hills directly in front. Ricketts deployed his two brigades in two lines and charged.

Map of the Battle of Fishers Hill, September 22, 1864.

Rebel sharpshooters renewed their harassment with the dawn of September 22. Federal skirmishers replied and throughout the morning both armies engaged in this fitful firing. "Old Brick Top," as the soldiers called Emory, succeeded, after some confusion, in having his two divisions close on Wright's extended line. Sheridan, constantly riding along the line, could be heard saying, "I'll get a twist on 'em, d—n 'em!" An occasional cannon boom punctured the crackling rifle fire.

About noon Wright ordered Ricketts to continue the latter's sidle to the right to a point opposite Early's left. Ricketts immediately

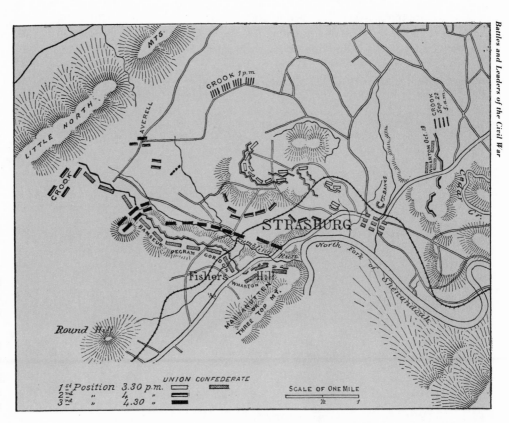

Battles and Leaders of the Civil War

Confederate gunners on Fishers Hill opened fire, but the Federal assault, vigorously executed, routed the gray infantry. "So rapid was their flight," Ricketts reported, "that they abandoned shelter-tents, blankets, and a considerable amount of infantry ammunition." The division entrenched behind the crests and awaited Crook's anticipated attack.

Getty and Wheaton, meanwhile, pushed their brigades forward, suffering also from Rebel artillery fire. Their pickets nearly reached Tumbling Run, where Rebels, some hiding in nearby houses and a distillery, peppered the blue skirmishers. At this point along the line the Federals would have to cross both the creek and a mill race, which provided power for a mill owned by David Fisher for whose family the hill was named. The terrain was broken by ditches, fences, fallen trees and stone walls, while the slope of Fishers Hill was strewn with rocks. The two divisions, with batteries in close support, stood poised to attack at the given signal.

These Union maneuvers, watched closely from the crest, worried the Confederate commander. Early was convinced the advances foreboded a Federal attack the

Battle of Fishers Hill. Charge of Crook's corps on the right. Drawing by James E. Taylor.

next day. He ordered a withdrawal of his army after dark and directed the caissons and ammunition chests be brought forward to the guns to expedite the retreat. Old Jubal apparently worried little about the absence of Crook's command the past two days. Early correctly surmised Sheridan's intentions; unfortunately he miscalculated when the assault would occur and from where it would come. He had never before been so completely surprised.

The missing Union force, Crook's two divisions, had been en route throughout the day as Wright and Emory attended to Early's army. The march progressed slowly, for the two divisions had to remain concealed from the Rebel signal station. "I led the way in person," Crook wrote, "following my way up a succession of ravines, keeping my eyes on the signal station on top of the mountain, so as to keep out of their sight, making the color bearers trail their flags so they could not be seen."

The command crossed the Back Road at St. Stephen's Church, where Averell's troopers provided an impenetrable screen. Reaching the foot of Little North Mountain, Crook halted and brought Thoburn's rear division forward alongside Hayes' soldiers. The corps, in two parallel columns, resumed the march up the rugged slope of the mountain. Crossing an open patch of ground, the Federals encountered Lomax's pickets, who fled after firing a volley. Down in the valley, a Confederate battery sent shells screaming into the trees, the crashing limbs annoying Crook's men but hurting few. Crook again halted the corps at a point beyond Early's left, faced the two columns to the left and waited momentarily to order the attack.

The capable officer instructed his men not to yell until he ordered it, but with the Rebels' shells bursting above their heads, the veterans emitted a tremendous shout. "And unless you heard my fellows yell once," boasted Crook, "you can form no conception of it. It

Brigadier General Williams Carter Wickham.

Colonel Rutherford Birchard Hayes.

beggars all description.'' Down the slope, which was covered by huge boulders and cedar thickets, the two divisions charged. Coordination evaporated almost instantly and the soldiers, sensing the total surprise they had accomplished, raced individually toward the bottom, the stouter, swifter men leading the way. Hayes pictured the scene when his men burst into the open: ''They [the Rebels] were thunderstruck, swore we had crossed the mountain. The men rushed on, no line, no order, all

yelling like madmen. Rebs took to their heels, each striving to get himself out of the way.''

The aroused Federals easily swept over Lomax's line of breastworks, which were perpendicular to Early's main line and parallel to Crook's advance. Lomax's 1,000 troopers were no match for Crook's nearly 6,000 and quickly disappeared into the woods to the south. Lomax, when he discovered the Federal force on the mountain, alerted Ramseur, who commanded the nearest division. This intrepid officer ordered Brigadier General Cullen Battle's brigade to Lomax's support. The remainder of Early's army extended to the left to fill the gap.

Battle's Alabamians arrived in time to slow down Thoburn's regiments, which were on Crook's left front. Hayes, without any opposition, soon enveloped Battle's left and the Rebels were forced back. Ramseur, meanwhile, had sent Brigadier General William Cox's brigade toward Battle's left, but Cox, confused in the wooded terrain, obliqued toward the southwest and passed unseen beyond Hayes's charging men. Cox eventually stumbled upon Lomax and some of his men. The cavalrymen ''kindly conducted me by the nearest route to the turnpike,'' the errant officer stated.

Cox's mistake allowed Hayes to penetrate far beyond Battle's left and the Confederates finally broke and fled. The terrain behind Early's line was a series of wooded ridges with intervening bottoms perpendicular

Brigadier General Alfred Thomas Archimedes Torbert.

plained he wanted to claim them. Crook reminded him that his men had already been there and all soldiers were needed for the pursuit.

The Confederate gunners offered the only resistance to the attack of Wright's and Emory's corps. Early stated that they "behaved with great coolness, fighting to the very last." The Confederate commander personally had to order the cannoneers to withdraw. Fourteen pieces were captured by the Federals. Colonel E.M. Atkinson, 26th Georgia, however, personally tried to save one piece, begging retreating soldiers to assist him. One stopped to help but the two could not move it. Finally, with Federals advancing toward them, the Rebel soldier fled, while Atkinson stubbornly held to the wheel until captured.

"The rout of wagons, caissons, limbers, artillery and flying men was fearful as the stream swept down the pike toward Woodstock, as many thought the enemy's cavalry was aiming to get there by the Middle Road and cut us off," campaign veteran Jed Hotchkiss admitted. One Confederate, however, stopped, built a fire by the pike, and crouching and shivering, sang a song. One distinctive line heard by passing officers went:

"Old Jimboden's gone up the spout,
And Old Jube Early's about played out."

The enveloping darkness saved much of Early's

to the Confederate main works. Upon these slight prominences the Confederates managed to offer some resistance. Brigadier General Bryan Grimes posted three North Carolina regiments on the most prominent ridge, the Tarheels valiantly holding until enveloped on their front, flanks and rear. Old Jubal appeared, and seeing his broken army streaming to the rear, ordered the 13th Virginia to fire into Grimes' fleeing soldiers. The Virginians refused and joined the retreating North Carolinians.

While Early vainly tried to stem the Confederate rout, Ricketts' division charged up the hill. In echelon to the left, Getty's, then Wheaton's, and then Dwight's men joined the assault. "The rebel army could have been no more easily held than a whirlwind," a Federal soldier remarked of the combined attack. The Federal assault along the front rapidly became a mad scramble for possession of the crest. Years later the veterans argued who planted their colors first upon the works and which guns they seized. Crook, who had ordered his men not to stop to claim guns, discovered some Federals pulling a piece to the rear. Crook "pitched into them" only to learn they were following Ricketts' orders. At that moment Ricketts rode up, looking "as though he was stealing sheep," as Crook described him, and ex-

Brigadier General William Woods Averell.

army from capture or destruction. Sheridan pushed Devin's cavalry brigade southward in pursuit, followed by elements of Emory's corps. A Rebel rearguard, located a few miles south of Fishers Hill, slowed the Federal pursuit in hand-to-hand combat along a fence. In this melee a Confederate officer, mounted on a white horse, fell with a mortal wound in his abdomen. He was the splendid staff officer Sandie Pendleton. It was another irreparable loss for Early.

The Rebels marched throughout the "intensely dark" night, not halting until passing through Woodstock. Sheridan's army followed, but in "great confusion at times." The Federals finally halted at Woodstock, where Sheridan, who arrived after daylight, waited expectantly to hear gunfire from the south, the signal that Torbert had slammed the door on Early's retreat.

Torbert, however, was far from New Market; in fact, he was retreating down the Luray Valley toward Front Royal, his mission a total failure. The cavalry commander, personally accompanying Merritt's division, had joined Wilson by nightfall of the 21st. The latter officer had spent the day pushing Brigadier General William C. Wickham's Rebel troops up the Valley between the Blue Ridge and Massanutten mountains. Wickham halted Wilson's advance at Gooney Run, where the Valley was "a mere gorge, impracticable for any kind of troops." After dark, Wilson sent Brigadier General George Custer's brigade across the South Fork of the Shenandoah River and up that stream beyond Wickham's flank. Custer only found an abandoned line as Wickham had withdrawn hours earlier to a position on the south bank of Milford Creek.

The combined Federal divisions trotted after Wickham at sunrise and halted on a series of hills across from the Rebel line. Torbert engaged Wickham's pickets throughout the day, but could not discover any weak point. Two Federal regiments, dismounted, charged Wickham's right, but were easily repulsed. "Not knowing that the army had made an attack at Fishers Hill, and thinking that the sacrifice would be too great to attack without that knowledge," Torbert later reported, "I concluded to withdraw." Sheridan's audacious plan had been foiled.

The news of Torbert's withdrawal, which Sheridan received on the morning of the 23d, infuriated the fiery officer. He believed that if Torbert had succeeded in his mission, "we [would] have captured the entire army." Writing years later in his memoirs, Sheridan concluded that "to this day I have been unable to account satisfactorily for Torbert's failure." Though he would not relieve Torbert from command as he did Averell that very day for that officer's feeble pursuit, Sheridan remained extremely disappointed.

The Union commander, nevertheless, had to be pleased. His army had achieved another signal victory—"we have whipped the flower of the Rebel army; they are scattered in all directions," the future President Hayes wrote in a letter. At a cost of 456 casualties, Sheridan had completely routed Early's army, sending it toward the Blue Ridge and clearing the upper Valley for his own troops. The two victories in a space of four days provided Lincoln's reelection campaign with timely, sorely needed military successes. Wright, effusive over the results of the battle, concluded that "the annals of the war present, perhaps, no more glorious victory than this."

Old Jubal, riding toward the security of the mountains, also blamed his cavalry. He failed to recognize, as he often did, his faulty dispositions and the blame he had to bear. John Gordon, a critic of his commander, asserted that "it is the old story of failure to protect flanks." Early suffered casualties totaling 1,235, with 995 listed as missing. Though many of these would return, his army was temporarily "very much shattered, the men very much exhausted."

A soldier finds a moment of rest. (*CWTI* Collection)

Sheridan's Ride (HW)

Cedar Creek
by Joseph P. Cullen

IN THE early morning hours of October 19, 1864, Major General Philip H. Sheridan, commanding the Federal Army of the Shenandoah, was sleeping soundly in the Logan residence in Winchester, Virginia. He had retired at 10 o'clock that night—early for him—with no major worries on his mind. Things had been going well recently for the small (5 foot 5), redheaded Irish general. Just a month ago he had defeated the Confederate forces of Lieutenant General Jubal A. Early, "Old Jube" his men called him, in the Battle of Winchester for the first significant Federal victory of the war in the Shenandoah Valley. A few days later he had defeated him again at Fisher's Hill, and now the Valley, the great granary of the Confederate forces in the East, was devastated from Staunton to Winchester. In grateful recognition, President Lincoln had promoted "Little Phil" to the permanent rank of brigadier general in the Regular Army.

Now he was returning to his army, encamped at Cedar Creek about twenty miles south of Winchester, which he had left several days before for a conference with his superiors in Washington. General Grant, commander in chief of all the Federal armies and presently with the Army of the Potomac which had General Lee's Army of Northern Virginia pinned down at Petersburg, wanted Sheridan to operate against central Virginia from his base in the Valley. He specifically desired that Sheridan destroy the Charlottesville-Lynchburg Railroad, the James River Canal, and the Virginia Central Railroad east to Richmond. Sheridan, however, pointed out that this was impracticable due to the distance he would be operating away from his base of supplies in a country infested with guerrillas, and the "difficulty of transporting this army through the mountain passes on to the railroad at Charlottesville. . . .I think that the best policy will be to let the burning of the crops in the Valley be the end of this campaign, and let some of this army go elsewhere." The Washington officials agreed, and the upshot of the conference was that two engineering officers were returning with Sheridan "for the purpose of reporting on a defensive line in the Valley that could be held while the bulk of my troops were being detached to Petersburg." It was generally recognized that the area at Cedar Creek did not lend itself to a strong, permanent defensive position.

So, all things considered, Sheridan had good reason to feel satisfied with himself. Before he retired that night a courier had reported that all was well at Cedar Creek, and informed him that a brigade (Grover's) would move out early the next morning on a reconnaissance to discover the enemy's exact positions. He went to sleep looking forward to a leisurely morning ride to his headquarters at Belle Grove plantation in the beautiful Virginia autumn weather.

Major General Philip H. Sheridan (KA)

Logan house in Winchester, where Sheridan spent the night before his ride to rally the routed Federal troops at Cedar Creek.

BUT shortly before 6 a.m. the officer in charge of the pickets woke the general to report the sound of artillery fire from the Cedar Creek area. Did it sound like a battle? Sheridan asked. No, the officer replied, it was not a sustained fire. "It's all right," Sheridan then remarked, "Grover has gone out this morning to make a reconnaissance, and he is merely feeling the enemy."

For some reason, however, Sheridan could not get back to sleep. He dressed, ate, and headed out from Winchester shortly after 8:30. At Mill Creek, about half a mile south of the town, his escort fell in behind and then, just as they crested the rise beyond the stream, a shocking scene came in view, "the appalling spectacle of a panic-stricken army—hundreds of slightly wounded men, throngs of others unhurt but utterly demoralized, and baggage-wagons by the score, all pressing to the rear in hopeless confusion, telling only too plainly that a disaster had occurred at the front." Quickly giving orders to form a line across Mill Creek to stop all fugitives and to park the wagons on the north side of Winchester, Sheridan with two aides and a small bodyguard headed for the front. When the road became blocked with retreating men and wagons he took to the fields, stopping every now and then to exhort the soldiers to halt and reform, and ordering all officers he met to spread the word that he was back in command and they would attack. Removing his cap so that the men could more easily recognize his bright red hair, he rode on as many cheered and turned around to follow him.

Just north of Newtown he met "a chaplain digging his heels into the sides of his jaded horse, and making for the rear with all possible speed. I drew up for an instant, and inquired of him how matters were going at the front.

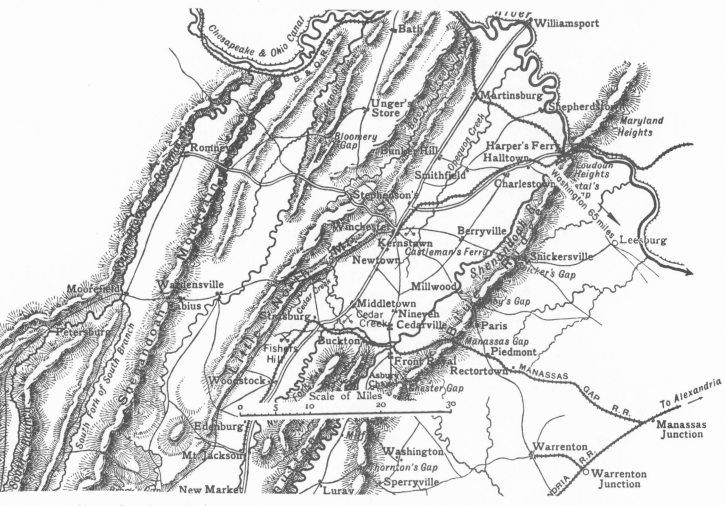

Map 1. *General map of the area of operations.*

He replied, 'Everything is lost; but all will be right when you get there'; yet notwithstanding this expression of confidence in me, the parson at once resumed his breathless pace to the rear."

CONTINUING on, Sheridan noticed Ricketts' and Wheaton's divisions of the VI Corps just west of the Valley Pike, and was informed that the XIX Corps had halted to the right and rear of those divisions. About halfway between Newtown and Middletown he saw Getty's division of the VI Corps and the cavalry, the only forces now actually engaged, although the Confederates did not seem to be pressing any real attack. Establishing his headquarters just in back of Getty, Sheridan ordered the other two divisions and the XIX Corps to be brought up and formed on Getty's right, west of the Pike and north of Middletown. From here he intended to launch his counterattack if possible. It was now about 11 o'clock. Just then General Wright, commander of the VI Corps but commanding the army in Sheridan's absence, rode up, his bushy beard all matted with blood from a chin wound. He reported as best he could the events of the morning. When Sheridan explained his plan of attack, Wright agreed and rode off to get his corps into position.

The question was, what had happened?

WHEN Sheridan left on the 15th for his trip to Washington, his army was in position at Cedar Creek, northwest of the North Fork of the Shenandoah River with Crook's VIII Corps (sometimes referred to as the Army of West Virginia) on the left east of the Valley Pike; Emory's XIX Corps in the center; and Wright's VI Corps in reserve to the right and rear of Emory. General Torbert's cavalry corps covered the flanks. Sheridan had a total effective force of about 35,000, of which about 10,000 were cavalry. As the Confederates by then had withdrawn to Fisher's Hill, Sheridan was not anticipating an attack. Consequently he decided to take the cavalry with him as far as Front Royal, and from there dispatch them on a raid to Gordonsville and vicinity.

Arriving in Front Royal on the 16th Sheridan received a message from Wright enclosing a Confederate dispatch which had been intercepted by Federal signal officers familiar with the enemy code. It read: "To Lieutenant General Early: Be ready to move as soon as my forces join you and we will crush Sheridan.—Longstreet, Lieutenant General." Consequently, Wright was now worried about the right flank of the army with the cavalry gone. "If the enemy should be strongly reinforced in cavalry," he told Sheridan, "he might, by turning our right, give us a great deal of trouble."

However, he would hold on, he stated, fearing only "an attack on my right."

For one reason or another, Wright apparently did not even consider an attack on his left, which, as it developed, was vulnerable. The position at Cedar Creek had not been intended as a permanent defensive position as its defects were obvious. General Merritt, commanding the 1st Division of the cavalry corps, described the left flank: "The approaches from all points of the enemy's stronghold at Fisher's Hill were through wooded ravines in which the growth and undulations concealed the movement of troops, and for this reason and its proximity to Fisher's Hill the pickets protecting its front could not be thrown, without danger of capture, sufficiently far to the front to give ample warning of the advance of the enemy." But Wright apparently believed that the Shenandoah and Three Top Mountain in that front were sufficient protection against an enemy attack there. Nor is there any record that Crook, commanding the corps on the left flank, was unduly worried.

SUSPECTING the Confederate message might be a ruse (Longstreet was actually convalescing from the

Lieutenant General Jubal Anderson Early. (Library of Congress)

wound he received in the Battle of The Wilderness in May), Sheridan nevertheless decided to play it safe and ordered the cavalry back to Cedar Creek. (Whatever Early's objective was in sending the fake message, it certainly backfired on him with the return of the Federal cavalry.) He also cautioned Wright to "Look well to your ground, and be well prepared. Get everything up that can be spared."

When the cavalry reached him, Wright placed Custer's and Merritt's divisions on his right west of the Pike, and Powell's division far out on his left guarding the approaches to Front Royal. When reconnaissances on both flanks on the 18th disclosed no sign of any enemy movement, Wright felt relatively secure, and so did most of the troops, particularly those on the left flank in Crook's VIII Corps.

The situation for the Confederates, however, was now desperate. The Federal destruction of supplies in the Valley was having its intended effect. Reinforced by Kershaw's division of infantry and Rosser's cavalry, Early had a total force of about 18,000 effectives, of whom about 4,000 were cavalry. But the problem was how to sustain this force in order to keep control of at least some part of the Valley. If he withdrew, it would leave the Federals in complete control, and the chances of the Confederates ever regaining it were slim indeed. "I was now compelled to move back for want of provisions and forage," Early reported, "or attack the enemy in his position with the hope of driving him from it, and I determined to attack."

This decision, which on the face of it seemed reckless, was influenced by a strong letter Early had received from General Lee. "I have weakened myself very much to strengthen you," Lee wrote. "It was done with the expectation of enabling you to gain such success that you could return the troops if not rejoin me yourself. I know you have endeavored to gain that success, and believe you have done all in your power to insure it. You must not be discouraged, but continue to try. . . .With your united force it can be accomplished." The trouble here was that Lee consistently underestimated the size of the enemy force Early had to contend with.

WITH the decision made to attack, the next question was where. Because of the Shenandoah (where it flowed nearly east) and Cedar Creek a frontal assault was out of the question; it would have to be a flank attack. Early sent General Pegram to reconnoiter the Federal right, while Gordon and members of his staff, including the brilliant topographical engineer Captain Jed Hotchkiss, climbed to the signal station atop Three Top Mountain to observe the left (Map 2). From here they had a beautiful panoramic view of the whole area. "Strasburg, Middletown, Newtown, and Winchester were in sight visible to the naked eye." But more important, the entire Federal camp was clearly visible. "Not only the general outlines of Sheridan's breastworks," reported Hotchkiss,

Map 2. Battle of Cedar Creek, October 19, 1864—opening phase. This also shows the summit of Three Top Mountain, where the Confederates made their reconnaissance, and the route taken by the Rebels in their approach march. This map was adapted by W.S. Nye from an 1873 map prepared for General Sheridan by Lieutenant Colonel Gillespie.

"but every parapet where his heavy guns were mounted, and every piece of artillery, every wagon and tent and supporting line of troops, were in easy range of our vision." Another staff officer noted, "We were able to locate precisely his cavalry, his artillery, his infantry and his wagon train. Even the house where Sheridan made his headquarters was pointed out. There it all was, with the roads leading to it, the place where he could be best

attacked and how the lines could move, how far to go and what to do."

When Pegram reported that the main cavalry force of the enemy guarded the right flank, Early and Gordon agreed that a surprise attack on the Federal left could be successful, if it should "prove practicable to move a column between the base of the mountain and the river." Gordon and Hotchkiss then discovered a seldom-used, narrow, tree-covered path around the base of the mountain suitable for infantry in single file, but not artillery.

AT 2 P.M. on the 18th Early outlined his plan of attack to his division commanders. Gordon would take three divisions, his own, Pegram's, and Ramseur's, around the base of the mountain, cross the Shenandoah at Bowman's Ford, and proceed to the area of the Cooley house where he would deploy to attack the left and rear of the Federal VIII Corps. Kershaw's division would march through Strasburg, cross Cedar Creek at Bowman's Mill and come up on Gordon's left to strike the front of the Federal corps, Wharton's division would advance up the Pike, secure the bridge over Cedar Creek, and then join in the attack. Rosser, with about half the cavalry, would cover the left flank west of the Pike, while Lomax with the remaining cavalry would proceed from Front Royal and move to Newtown or Winchester as circumstances might dictate, which, in effect, would put half the cavalry out of the main action and beyond Early's control. The artillery would follow Wharton up the Pike to Hupp's Hill, its battle station. The attack was ordered for just before daybreak, about 5 a.m.

With the exception of Lomax's assignment, this was a well-conceived plan of attack that was almost sure to succeed if pushed relentlessly. Probably still sensitive from Lee's criticism that he tried to fight the battle of Winchester by divisions, Early apparently was determined that in this battle he would use almost all his forces at the same time.

AS DARKNESS fell Gordon moved out about 8 p.m. for an all-night march. Swords, canteens, and other cooking utensils that might make noise were left behind. The men marched silently, in single file along the narrow trail. "The long gray line," Gordon reported, "like a great serpent glided noiselessly along the dim pathway above the precipice." At 1 a.m. Kershaw and Wharton moved out, accompanied by Early.

Cedar Creek, Va. Confederates under Early driving back VI, VIII, and XIX Corps under H.G. Wright. From a sketch by J. E. Taylor.

Valley Pike north of Middletown. End of Sheridan's famous ride.

By 3:30 in the chill October morning Gordon had his men resting under cover along the river bank. "In the still starlit night," he noted, "the only sounds heard were the gentle rustle of leaves by the October wind, the low murmur of the Shenandoah flowing swiftly along its rocky bed and dashing against the limestone cliffs that bordered it, the churning of the water by the feet of horses on which sat Sheridan's faithful pickets, and the subdued tones or half-whispers of my men as they thoughtfully

A view from Strasburg, Virginia. Observer is looking south.

communed with each other as to the fate which might
befall each in the next hour." And at 3:30 Kershaw,
on the banks of Cedar Creek, could see the Federal camp
fires. "The moon was now shining and we could see
the camps," Early reported. "The division was halted
under cover . . .and I pointed out to Kershaw and the
commander of his leading brigade the enemy's position
and described the nature of the ground, and directed
them how the attack was to be made and followed up."

AS a soft, white mist crept gently up from the quiet
river, Gordon's gray-clad regiments about 5 a.m.
exploded on the left and rear of Crook's VIII Corps to the
sound of the feared Rebel yell, while Kershaw veered to
his right, east of the Pike, to strike at the front. "The
surprise was complete," General Wright reported later,
"for the pickets did not fire a shot, and the first indication of the enemy's presence was a volley into the main
line where the men of a part of the regiments were at
reveille roll-call without arms." Crook's corps, quickly
shattered into a frightened, disorganized mob, streamed
back toward Middletown, upsetting Emory's XIX Corps
in its flight. "The ground to be passed over," Crook
reported, "was one succession of hills and ravines, so
that it was impossible for troops to make a rapid retreat
in anything like good order."

A soldier in the 61st Georgia in Gordon's division
remembered that he and his comrades "advanced in a run

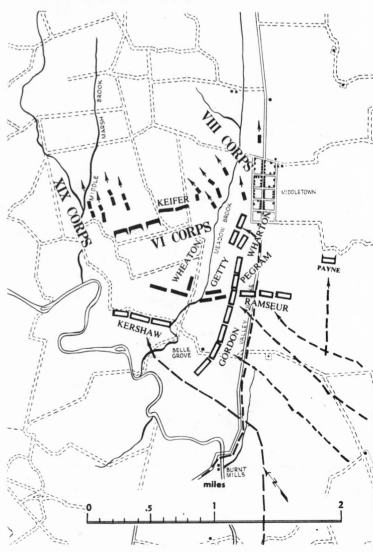

*Map 3.   The situation at about 7:30-8:30 a.m. The Confederate attack
is slowing down as many of the men stop to loot the Union camps.
Crook's VIII Corps is withdrawing in confusion; the XIX Corps is also
retreating, though in somewhat better order. The VI Corps is covering
the withdrawal.*

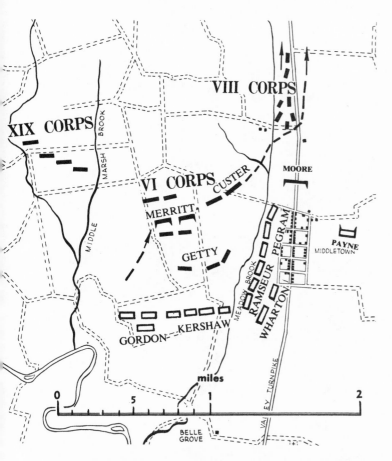

Map 4. *The situation at about 9:30 a.m. The VI Corps continues to cover the withdrawal. Moore's brigade of Powell's cavalry division brought up from Buckton Ford, and Merritt's cavalry division, are supporting the VI corps. Custer has been transferred from the west flank and is moving as shown.*

and raised the Rebel yell. At this signal Kershaw advanced from a different place and raised a terrible yell. The Yankees fired a few cannon shot at Kershaw's men and then fled. We were soon in their camp. The most of them were still in bed when we raised the yell and began firing at them. They jumped up running, and did not take time to put on their clothing, but fled in their night clothes, without their guns, hats or shoes."

SOON the sun was up, but a heavy fog temporarily added to the confusion. By 7:30 the Confederate attack had developed as shown on Map 3. Emory's XIX Corps tried to make a stand but the collapse of Crook's corps allowed Gordon's men to gain their rear and Emory was forced to fall back. Now the only effective force in the path of the Confederates was Wright's veteran VI Corps and the cavalry on the Federal right. By 9:30 the Confederates had formed a line west of the Pike, as shown on Map 4. The VI Corps, which had withdrawn once from its original position, was now forced back again by the pressure from Gordon and Kershaw and the terrific

Early's surprise attack on the VIII Corps at Cedar Creek, Va.

Left to Right: Major Generals Joseph B. Kershaw (Carolina Museum, Lancaster, S. C.), John B. Gordon (LC), and Thomas L. Rosser (Cook Collection, Valentine Museum, Richmond, Va.)

artillery fire from Hupp's Hill and from some of their own guns, now turned against them. On a ridge just west and north of Middletown Getty's division took a position and held, while Torbert moved the cavalry divisions of Custer and Merritt over to the Federal left to support Getty. When Ramseur and Pegram reported to Early that they needed troops to fill a gap on their right, Wharton's division was again ordered into position there. The Confederate line now extended east and west across the Pike, facing north, with Gordon's division on the left, then Kershaw, Ramseur, Pegram, and Wharton.

It was now well past 11 o'clock and a lull in the fighting developed. By now Sheridan had appeared on the field and was in the process of reorganizing for a counterattack. The other two divisions of the VI Corps were ordered to form on Getty's right, and the XIX Corps was ordered up to come into line on the right of the

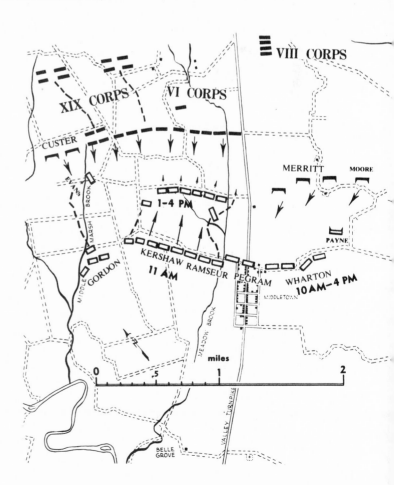

Map 5. Semi-final phase. By 11 a.m. the Confederates had advanced to the line shown, where Early held them idle for several hours. Sheridan had arrived from Winchester and re-formed his line on Getty's division. Custer has been shifted back to the west flank. At about 3:45 Gordon, Kershaw, and Ramseur made a weak attack as shown. This caused a gap between Kershaw and Gordon which was exploited by the Federals during their massive counterattack which was launched at 4 p.m. This attack swept down the field, driving the Confederates south in increasing disorder and giving Sheridan a complete victory.

Battle of Middletown, Oct. 19, 1864. Repulse of General Early by the VI Corps under General Wright. From a sketch by J.E. Taylor.

VI Corps, with the disorganized VIII Corps in the left rear in reserve. Sheridan then sent Custer's division of cavalry back to the right flank, while Merritt's division remained to guard the left (Map 5). All of this would take several hours to complete, of course, but Sheridan noticed that the Confederates were not pressing the attack and Getty assured him he could hold with the assistance of the cavalry.

THE original Confederate assault had naturally resulted in some confusion, and a temporary halt was necessary in order to reform the regiments for another attack. By 11 o'clock, however, this had generally been done and the division commanders, Gordon in particular, waited impatiently for the order to advance. It never came. Writing about it years later, Gordon stated: "My heart went into my boots. Visions of the fatal halt on the first day at Gettysburg, and of the whole day's hesitation to permit an assault on Grant's exposed flank on the 6th of May in The Wilderness rose before me." Wharton on the right flank stated: "I supposed we were arranging for a general movement to the front, and expected every minute orders to advance; but no orders came, and there we stood—no enemy in our front for hours, except some troops moving about in the woodland on a hill nearly a mile in our front." And a private in the ranks recalled, "It seemed that there were no Yankees in our front. Everything was quiet as death. Some of our boys went to sleep while others were plundering the camps."

Captured Confederate guns and wagons pictured at Belle Grove.

In his official report Early told Lee: "So many of our men had stopped in the camp to plunder (in which I am sorry to say that officers participated), the country was so open, and the enemy's cavalry so strong, that I did not deem it prudent to press further, especially as Lomax had not come up." Instead, he decided to try to hold what had been gained and orders were given to carry off the captured "artillery, small-arms, and wagons."

THUS, while Early was counting his booty, Sheridan, unmolested, massed for a counterattack. Shortly after 4 p.m. he threw his divisions forward in a swift,

Federal cavalry spread as the panic-stricken troops streamed back toward Fisher's Hill and New Market. "They would not listen to entreaties, threats, or appeals of any kind," Early reported. "A terror of the enemy's cavalry had seized them, and there was no holding them." Gordon gave a more dramatic description: "As the tumult of battle died away, there came from the north side of the plain a dull, heavy swelling sound like the roaring of a distant cyclone, the omen of additional disaster. It was unmistakable. Sheridan's horsemen were riding furiously across the open fields of grass to intercept the Confederates before they crossed Cedar Creek. Many were cut off and captured. As the sullen roar from horses' hoofs beating the soft turf of the plain told of the near approach of the cavalry, all effort at orderly retreat was abandoned."

By nightfall Early's force was completely routed and totally disorganized. Not until they reached New Market was he able to again establish some semblance of order. Through Early's hesitation and lack of drive, a stunning surprise victory had been turned into a humiliating defeat. Although his casualties were not excessive, about 3,000 to Sheridan's 5,665, he suffered further humiliation by losing all the Federal guns, ordnance, wagons, and supplies he had captured that morning, plus twenty-three of his own cannon. He still had the problem of feeding his army, and in addition he had now lost control of the vital Shenandoah Valley.

coordinated oblique attack by a "left half-wheel of the whole line, with a division of cavalry turning each flank of the enemy, the whole line advancing," and pivoting on Getty's division on the Pike (Map 5). The XIX Corps struck hard at Gordon's division and rolled it up, driving a wedge between that division and Kershaw, while the VI Corps hit Ramseur and Pegram, and Merritt advanced on Wharton. When Gordon's men gave way, Kershaw's and Ramseur's troops also headed for the rear, followed by the remainder of the line.

Panic developed as leaders began to fall. Ramseur was shot, mortally wounded. A great fear of the superb

IN RETROSPECT, it is apparent that Early's original attack was a well-planned and well-executed maneuver that achieved complete surprise and should

Left to right: Major Generals Horatio G. Wright (NA), George W. Getty (KA), and George Crook (KA).

have resulted in a brilliant victory. That it did not was due solely to his own individual hesitation and lack of aggressiveness, due in part, at least, to his apparent fear of the Federal cavalry. But in his dispatches to Lee after the battle the caustic Early blamed everyone but himself. Regarding his troops he stated, "But for their bad conduct I should have defeated Sheridan's whole force," and the "rout was as thorough and disgraceful as ever happened to our army." Even the officers were not immune to his condemnation. "The truth is, we have very few field or company officers worth anything. . . ." Then the perennial excuse for defeated generals: "If I had had but one division of fresh troops I could have made the victory complete and beyond all danger of a reverse." This, of course, was also a tacit admission of failure to press the attack at the crucial moment, but, characteristically, Early placed the blame on factors beyond his control, so therefore the defeat could not possibly be his fault.

It is difficult to believe, however, that a man of Early's intelligence, training, and experience did not know at heart where the real fault lay. That something was bothering him is evident in his statement to Lee: "If you think, however, that the interests of the service would be promoted by a change of commanders, I beg you to have

no hesitation in making the change." More damaging, perhaps, was the journal entry of Jed Hotchkiss, who carried Early's dispatches to Lee: "General Early told me not to tell General Lee that we ought to have advanced in the morning at Middletown, for, said he, we ought to have done so."

Sheridan had now defeated Early decisively three times in little over a month. The Valley was devastated and lost to the Confederates for the remainder of the war. In grateful recognition President Lincoln again promoted Sheridan, making him a major general in the Regular Army. That the dramatic victory was due to his outstanding leadership there can be no question. To be sure, Wright might have held eventually when Early failed to press his advantage, and so prevented complete disaster, but it is not likely that he would have counterattacked as quickly and aggressively as did Sheridan. Yet even the fiery Sheridan admitted in one of his more candid moments that because of the circumstances he would probably get more credit for the victory than he deserved. Sitting at a campfire the evening following the battle, Sheridan stated: "Crook, I am going to get much more credit for this than I deserve, for, had I been here in the morning, the same thing would have taken place."

Sherman Faces Johnston in Georgia

When Grant went to Washington in March 1864 to become general in chief of all Union armies, he left Sherman in charge of the Military Division of the Mississippi, embracing all Union forces from the Appalachians to the Mississippi. In Grant's plan for coordinated offensives in 1864, Sherman's principal field army of 100,000 men, camped around Chattanooga, was to have a role second only to that of the Army of the Potomac. Sherman's force consisted of elements from the three Union armies that had driven Bragg from Missionary Ridge twenty miles into Georgia the previous November: the Army of the Cumberland; the Army of the Tennessee; and the 11th and 12th Corps from the Army of the Potomac, now reorganized as the 20th Corps of the Army of the Cumberland. In addition, a corps known as the Army of the Ohio, which had helped capture Knoxville the previous fall, was part of Sherman's army.

Facing them in strong defensive works along Rocky Face Ridge north of Dalton, Georgia, was the Confederate Army of Tennessee. Its new commander was Joseph E. Johnston, appointed to replace Bragg, who had been discredited by the rout of his troops at Missionary Ridge. Johnston restored the tone and morale of this army. But he faced a formidable task in trying to stop Sherman's confident veterans.

Sherman's strategic purpose derived from Grant's orders "to move against Johnston's army, to break it up and to get into the interior of the enemy's country as far as you can, inflicting all the damage you can against their war resources." In the end Sherman would accomplish all of these goals. But in the initial stages of his campaign—which lasted four months—it became a drive to capture Atlanta, in the

TO THE CITIZENS OF MACON.

HEAD QUARTERS
Macon, July 30, 1864.

The enemy is now in sight of your houses. We lack force. I appeal to every man, Citizen or Refugee, who has a gun of any kind, or can get one, to report at the Court House with the least possible delay, that you may be thrown into Companies and aid in the defense of the city. A prompt response is expected from every patriot.

JOSEPH E. BROWN.

☛ Report to Col. Cary W. Styles, who will forward an organization as rapidly as possible.

Broadside issued by Governor Brown as fighting raged at East Macon. (Special Collection Division, University of Georgia)

General Sherman's troops at Buzzard's Roost Pass, Georgia, moving slowly but inexorably southward toward the city of Atlanta. (Harper's Weekly, May 21, 1864)

same sense that Grant's campaign against Lee became a drive for Richmond and Petersburg.

The campaigns in Virginia and Georgia differed in important ways. Grant and Lee were fighters. Each sought opportunities for battle, hoping to cripple if not destroy the enemy army. Sherman and Johnston preferred a war of maneuver for advantage, fighting only to prevent the enemy from gaining the advantage. Each Union commander carried out frequent flanking maneuvers to force the defending Confederates to retreat to a new defensive position. In Virginia such maneuvers usually took place *after* big battles; in Georgia they generally occurred *without* battles on the Virginia scale. Consequently, the casualties in Georgia were fewer than in Virginia.

During the four months prior to September 2—the day Sherman occupied Atlanta—each side in Georgia suffered about 30,000 casualties. By contrast, Union casualties in Virginia during the same period numbered 75,000 while the Confederates, fighting mostly on the defensive in trenches, lost about 40,000 men killed, wounded, and missing. (In the Civil War most of the "missing" were captured.) The war in Virginia was a slugging match; the war in Georgia was one of thrust and parry while the two adversaries executed fast footwork looking for an opening.

—James M. McPherson

THE CAMPAIGN
FOR ATLANTA

From Dalton to Atlanta by Allen Phelps Julian

The Fighting at Atlanta by Wilbur G. Kurtz, Sr.

From Dalton to Atlanta

by Allen Phelps Julian

Jefferson Davis faced an unhappy prospect in December 1863. His personal friend, the discredited Braxton Bragg, was relieved—at his own request—as commander of the Army of Tennessee, which lay in demoralized condition at Dalton, Georgia. And there was public clamor for him to name as Bragg's successor a man against whom he was intensely prejudiced, Joseph E. Johnston. Davis delayed his decision until the voice of Robert E. Lee was added to others recommending the able Johnston. On December 27 Davis reluctantly appointed "Old Joe" to command the Department and Army of Tennessee.

Johnston accepted, knowing he was taking on a difficult task. After having lost an opportunity to crush Rosecrans' Union Army of the Cumberland the previous September at Chickamauga because of Bragg's ineptitude, the Army of Tennessee was forced to watch the Union army, bottled up in Chattanooga, gain fresh men and supplies day after day until—with U.S. Grant on the scene—the Federals burst out at the Battle of Lookout Mountain (November 24) and routed the Confederates at Missionary Ridge (November 25). Although temporarily safe behind Rocky Face Ridge, the Confederate army was fast losing strength through desertions.

Johnston's job was complicated by the long-stand-

Oliver O. Howard's Corps—part of Sherman's invasion force—crosses a pontoon bridge on the Chattahoochee River on July 12, 1864. Sherman's objectives were to destroy Johnston's army and to capture Atlanta, a large manufacturing city, important railroad junction, and principal arsenal and supply depot for the Confederacy. (Harper's Weekly, July 1864)

ing bad relations between himself and Davis. He felt that Davis had deprived him of his relative rank by an illegal manipulation early in the war. For months, his great military talents had been allowed to lie idle. Davis treated him with curt indifference. On arriving at Dalton, Johnston found a letter from the Confederate President that did little to reassure him. It read, in part:

> The effective condition of your new command, as . . . reported to me is a matter of much congratulation, and I assure you that nothing shall be wanting on the part of the Government to aid you. You will not need to have it suggested that the imperative demand for prompt and vigorous action arises . . . from the necessity of reoccupying (Tennessee) upon the supplies of which the proper subsistence of our armies materially depends.

Johnston replied in detail about the actual conditions, explaining that the army was demoralized and far below fighting strength. Most of the cavalry was with James Longstreet, in East Tennessee. The artillery lacked sufficient horses and was poorly trained. As for moving against the enemy "promptly and vigorously," he pointed out the more obvious difficulties of terrain and manpower: Chattanooga (now a fortress), the Tennessee River, the rugged desert of the Cumberland Mountains, and an army outnumbering his by more than two to one. He summed it up thus:

> I can see no other mode of taking the offensive here, than to beat the enemy when he advances, and then move forward. But, to make victory probable, the army must be strengthened.

Johnston faced grim prospects, but whatever his misgivings they were never reflected in the cheerful energy with which he set about his task. He was a modest, kindly man, but a strict disciplinarian and a clear-headed realist. He visited every camp and outpost. He spoke cordially to officers and men alike, and listened attentively to their views. But he asked searching questions and his keen eyes missed nothing.

Under Bragg furloughs had been rare. Johnston furloughed the entire army, a third at a time. He announced an amnesty for those absent without leave. The response was immediate. Morale rose and, as the news spread, deserters flocked back to the colors.

Johnston worked tirelessly to clothe ragged men, to find shoes for bare feet, and to increase scanty rations. Rewards and punishments, promptly and impartially administered, restored discipline and high standards. Slowly, pride and confidence returned and with them the army's spirit. In a few weeks the Army of Tennessee was a fighting force again and, for the first time in its history, devoted to its commander.

Johnston knew that he was expected to hold Dalton, and that any hint of a retreat would incur disfavor. Yet a realistic analysis of his limited capabilities, and of the advantages which the topography of the region afforded an enemy approach, revealed little hope of remaining there without grave risk.

Dalton was merely the point at which the rout from Missionary Ridge had ended. Although Rocky Face Ridge gave it an appearance of strength, Johnston soon found that the position "had little to recommend it as a defensive one. It neither fully covered its own communications nor threatened those of the enemy."

Rocky Face Ridge is a lofty, sheer rock wall. It begins some seven miles northwest of Dalton and ends in a series of lower ridges 15 miles southwest of the town. Mill Creek Gap (Buzzard's Roost), through which both the highway and the railway to Chattanooga pass, cuts through the ridge three miles from its northern extremity. Five miles below it the old Dalton-La Fayette road passes over Dug Gap, 800 feet above the valley floor.

The lower six miles of the Chattoogata (Rocky Face) Ridges form the east wall of Snake Creek Gap, a narrow valley that opens into Sugar Valley only six miles from Resaca and the Western & Atlantic Railroad—the lifeline of Johnston's army. A parallel ridge, Horn Mountain, forms the west wall of the gap and extends several miles farther to the south. The road from Villanow into Sugar Valley—the most direct road from Chattanooga to Resaca or Calhoun—passes through Snake Creek Gap, affording an easy means of turning Dalton and seizing the railroad.

The railroad paralleled Rocky Face Ridge for 15 miles. Although the ridge sheltered the railroad, it would also mask an enemy approach through Snake Creek Gap. Johnston soon became aware that the topography of the region made Dalton a trap.

He realized, too, the ease with which Grant could send William T. Sherman's Army of the Tennessee across the Tennessee River in Alabama to march via Rome to Kingston, 40 miles south of Dalton, to destroy the railroad. If this move were made, Johnston would have no choice but to abandon Dalton and march swiftly south to interpose between Sherman and Atlanta. Any threat to Atlanta, or to the rails that linked him with Atlanta's warehouses and manufactories, must be met in force. His army's existence depended upon the trainloads of supplies that reached it daily from this arsenal of the South. Without Atlanta's connecting rails between the East and the West, the Confederacy could not long survive.

Late in February Bragg was called to Richmond as Davis' military adviser. At the same time John B. Hood arrived in Dalton to assume command of a corps. Johnston received him cordially, and reorganized his seven divisions into two permanent corps. To William J. Hardee he assigned four divisions: Cheatham's, Cleburne's, Walker's, and Bate's; to Hood, the divisions of Hindman, Stevenson, and Stewart.

Knowing Davis' views, Bragg began pressing for an offensive movement into Tennessee. When the responsibility had been his just after Chickamauga he had rejected a similar plan as "visionary," even though his was then the victorious army.

Johnston patiently pointed out the only practicable course—to gather strength at Dalton, defeat the enemy when he advanced, and then move forward.

Adequately reinforced and supplied, he had no objection to fighting at Dalton and pursuing a beaten enemy into Tennessee. But it must be a beaten foe, not one that could turn on him from secure bases after he had crossed the river and entered a country destitute of supplies. He had neither the men, the means, nor the hope of reinforcement. His opponent had all three. For Grant, close to fortified bases and with reinforcements within call, defeat would be an incident. For Johnston, and for the South, it would be a disaster. But Bragg persisted; and with each refusal to commit his army to a possible disaster, Johnston widened the gulf between Davis and himself.

A new factor—time—had given the Confederacy fresh hope of victory. If Union arms could be denied a major victory until after the November elections, then a war-weary North, persuaded by the powerful "Copperhead" leaders that the war was a failure, might reject President Lincoln's bid for reelection. On the other hand, the fall of Richmond or Atlanta would give Lincoln the great victory to revive the Northern people's will to win. No lesser victory would serve. Lee's army unquestionably could hold Richmond until long past November. And Johnston was confident that the reborn Army of Tennessee could hold the vast fortifications of Atlanta "forever" once it reached there. Shattered in Tennessee, his army could not defend Atlanta.

Time offered another advantage. The three-year enlistments of the Union veteran regiments would expire soon and, as Johnston was well aware, many of them would not be renewed.

In Richmond these factors were ignored.

To Johnston's annoyance Hood also pressed him to assume the offensive. Moreover, unknown to Johnston, in correspondence with Davis, Seddon, and Bragg, Hood was misrepresenting conditions at Dalton.

Hood reported the army "well clothed, well fed," and "anxious for battle." He stated that the army's trains were in the "greatest possible quantity required." Only a few artillery horses were needed to "place this army in fine condition." The enemy, he insisted, was "weak, and we are strong." Although he reported Johnston's aggregate strength accurately as about 40,000 men, he underestimated that of the enemy by 50,000. The addition of Longstreet's corps and Polk's Army of Mississippi would, he stated, give Johnston a force that could "defeat and destroy all the Federals on this side of the Ohio River."

Although the Army of Tennessee was rapidly being restored to effective condition, it was far from ready to fight a superior foe. Yet Hood advised Bragg that only Johnston's unwillingness prevented an advance into Tennessee. Reports rendered by inspectors from Richmond contradicted Hood's assertions. One, with reasonable accuracy, estimated Grant's strength at 103,000. But these reports were ignored.

Grant was made lieutenant general in March and was given command of all the Union armies. Sherman succeeded him as commander of the Military Division of the Mississippi, which covered all the western armies. Grant set May 5 as the date on which Meade's Army of the Potomac, Butler's Army of the James, and Sherman's armies would move upon the enemy. Lee's Army of Northern Virginia and Johnston's Army of Tennessee, "and the cities (Richmond and Atlanta) covered and defended by them, were the main objective points of the campaign." After a final conference with Sherman, Grant departed for Virginia and on March 18 Sherman assumed command of the Military Division of the Mississippi. James B. McPherson succeeded him as commander of the Department and Army of the Tennessee.

Sherman plunged energetically into the tasks of readying his armies and of increasing the capacity of the war-worn, ill-equipped railroad from Nashville to Chattanooga to a minimum of 1,300 tons of freight per day. Although he hoped to trap Johnston's army near Dalton, thus avoiding a long and costly campaign, he respected Johnston's abilities too highly to leave anything to chance.

Johnston was no less busy. Although the defenses of Dalton had already been strengthened, and the Army of Tennessee was ready to defend them, other measures had to be taken. He must be ready to leave Dalton on short notice, either by rail to Kingston or by marching to intercept a closer approach to his rear.

Paralleling Rocky Face Ridge and Horn Mountain lay another barrier—Taylor's Ridge. It extends from Ringgold, on the north, some 30 miles southwestward. Within the area of approach, three roads crossed it. One lay over Nickajack Gap, 10 miles south of Ringgold at Wood Station. Another passed over Gordon Springs Gap, five miles farther south, near the intersection of the Tarvin (Tavern) and Old Alabama roads. The most practicable route for a force moving from Tennessee into Snake Creek Gap lay over Ship's (Maddox) Gap, three miles farther south and eight miles west of Snake Creek Gap. An enemy force marching from the west, with Calhoun or Resaca as its objective, would be forced to use one of these gaps to reach Snake Creek Gap, Dalton's Achilles heel.

Since December elements of Wheeler's cavalry had picketed the gaps and patrolled the country between Rocky Face and Taylor's Ridges. Should a large enemy force approach Taylor's Ridge, Johnston relied upon them to warn him of the danger. He could then evacuate Dalton without loss or confusion, and fall back quickly into selected positions covering the railroad. But to fall back in ample time to frustrate the enemy he must be prepared in minute detail.

Skillfully, Johnston laid his plans. He sent his baggage trains to good grazing areas below the

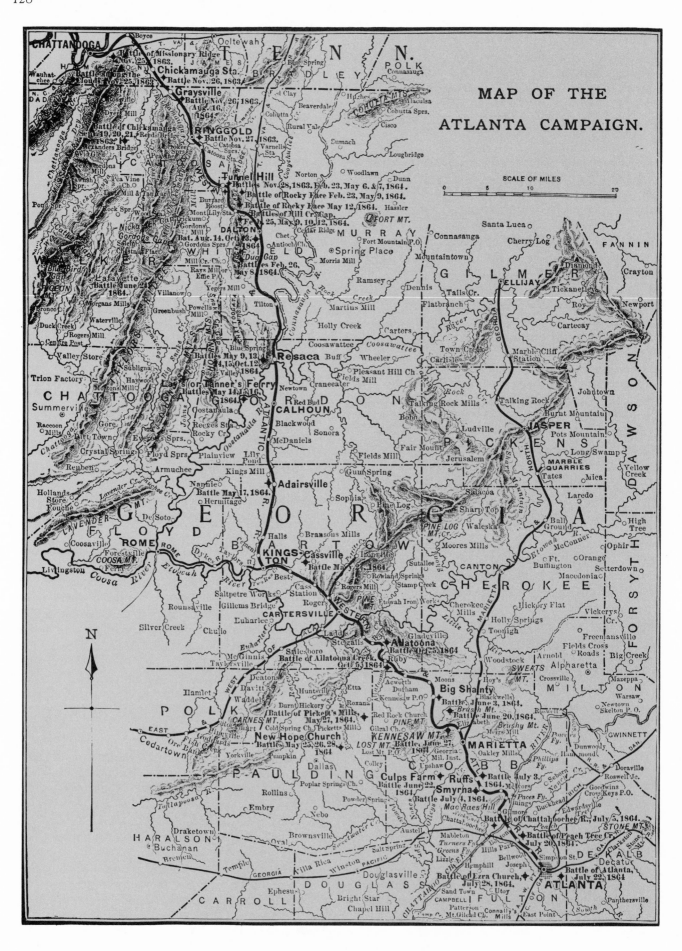

MAP OF THE
ATLANTA CAMPAIGN.

Oostanaula. The roads leading south from Dalton were improved and other roads prepared. Since Resaca with its railroad bridge over the Oostanaula would be a prime objective of a force bent upon destroying the railroad, preparations were made to defend it. A line was staked out on commanding ground in a three-mile arc north and west of Resaca, its right resting on Connesauga Creek and its left on the Oostanaula. With the route of each column designated in advance, and guides provided to conduct them, the whole army could move smoothly into prepared positions.

With his plans laid and their execution well begun, Johnston awaited developments with confidence both in the vigilance of the cavalry pickets on Taylor's Ridge and in the Army of Tennessee. Out of the shattered wreckage of the latter he had recreated an army. It was proud again and ready to fight. A broad trail of Union blood would soon bear witness to its excellence.

On May 1, with the railroad rebuilt and its rolling stock increased to meet his needs, Sherman moved forward from Nashville to open his campaign. The combined strength of his "grand army," after detaching the garrisons for his bases and for the blockhouses that protected the railroad, was 98,797 officers and men and 254 field guns. George H. Thomas' Army of the Cumberland, which had wintered at Chattanooga, Ringgold, and Cleveland, Tennessee, numbered 60,773 and 130 guns. McPherson's Army of the Tennessee had 24,465 and 96 guns. Maj. Gen. John M. Schofield, commanding the Department and Army of the Ohio, furnished only the XXIII Corps, which he chose to command in person, and one division of George Stoneman's four-division cavalry corps, under Stoneman himself. Their total strength was 13,559 and 28 guns. Since the strengths of his armies were far from proportionate, Sherman employed Thomas as the center and the smaller armies on the flanks.

Recruits, small reinforcements, and the return of the cavalry had brought the aggregate strength of Johnston's Army of Tennessee to 63,777 officers and men and 144 guns. Of these, 43,887 were "effectives." More reinforcements were on the way, but Sherman possessed the advantage of far superior numbers.

He enjoyed another advantage. His three senior subordinates—Thomas, McPherson, and Schofield— were fit and loyal leaders. And he could depend upon the loyal support of his superiors.

The movements of Sherman's army and the fighting that led to the Union conquest of Atlanta are shown on the map at left, reprinted by Century *magazine from* The Mountain Campaigns in Georgia: Or, War Scenes on the Western and Atlantic *(1887).*

Johnston was less fortunate. Of his two principal lieutenants, Hardee was both fit and loyal, but Hood was untested. Despite a reputation as a brave division leader, he had faced none of the problems of corps command. And Johnston could expect no loyal support from above.

As Johnston had foreseen, Sherman first intended to send McPherson across Alabama to destroy the railroad at Kingston. But the absence of four of McPherson's divisions decided Sherman against sending him so far from support. Instead, he ordered him to move through Chattanooga to Johnston's immediate rear—via Snake Creek Gap.

Aware that Johnston would anticipate the plan, Sherman issued no warning order. He wanted no flurry of preparations to alert enemy agents to the impending move. McPherson's first orders were to march, and he departed so quickly that Johnston's agents failed him.

On May 1st and 2d, Kilpatrick's Union cavalry, probing toward Tunnel Hill, skirmished with Wheeler's outposts near Ringgold Gap and at Dr. Lee's. As Thomas' army (the IV, XIV, and XX Corps and McCook's, Garrard's and Kilpatrick's cavalry divisions) closed on Dalton from the west, and Schofield from the north, sharper clashes occurred at Catoosa Springs and Red Clay on the 3d, near Varnell's and Tunnel Hill on the 4th and 5th, and at these points and near Nickajack Gap on the 6th and 7th.

By the 7th, Hooker's XX Corps had moved through Nickajack Gap and into positions facing Rocky Face Ridge. Palmer's XIV Corps had moved out from Ringgold and taken position on Hooker's left, on Tunnel Hill Ridge. After slight resistance Wheeler retired within the defenses at Mill Creek Gap. Howard's IV Corps had moved down from Cleveland to Catoosa Springs, on Palmer's left, opposite the north end of Rocky Face Ridge. Schofield's XXIII Corps had moved down from Knoxville and was deployed across Crow Valley on Howard's left. As Stoneman was delayed, McCook's cavalry covered Schofield's left.

Also on the 7th, McPherson's swift columns, Logan's XV and Dodge's XVI Corps, which had passed through Chattanooga the day before, marched from Lee's and Gordon's Mill to Taylor's Ridge, undetected by the Southern cavalry pickets. Sprague's brigade seized Ship's Gap without resistance. Unknown to Johnston, the pickets had been withdrawn.

Unaware of McPherson's approach, Johnston watched the storm gathering in his front. It was obvious that Sherman meant to test the defenses of Dalton. Johnston was confident that the Army of Tennessee would hold them until the attackers staggered back to count their dead. But should it become apparent that Sherman was merely demonstrating strongly, to divert his attention from his rear, an attempt to cling to Dalton with a reduced force while a detachment sought to defend any other point would be folly. He must then break free quickly and retire to Resaca.

Although late reports had indicated that McPherson might be moving toward Rome, Kingston was now in little danger. Cantey's brigade, which had been ordered to Johnston from Mobile, had been stopped at Rome. And President Davis had been persuaded to order Polk there, with Loring's division "and any other available force at your command." Alive to the danger at Dalton, Polk had construed the order literally. Already, Loring's division was en route

to Rome, and Reynolds' brigade would follow him. A few days later French's division would move to join them, as would Jackson's cavalry division. Johnston would have a third corps.

When other troops reached Rome, Cantey was ordered on to Resaca where, with Selden's and Yates's batteries, he detrained on the 7th.

McPherson moved on the 8th to Villanow with his advance in Snake Creek Gap. Thomas and Schofield were pressing hard at Dalton and, to further divert Johnston's attention, Geary's division of Hooker's corps made a spirited but unsuccessful attack on Dug Gap. Although cavalry scouts reported "Yankees in vicinity of Villanow today," they made no mention of a large infantry force. And Kilpatrick's cavalry was in the vicinity covering Geary's flank.

Skirmishing between the two sides occurred frequently as the armies moved toward Atlanta. Here: The Battle of Dug Gap on May 8. The rugged terrain that dominated the landscape between Chattanooga and Atlanta is evident in this drawing by Alfred R. Waud. (Library of Congress)

Early on the 9th the head of McPherson's column debouched from the gap into Sugar Valley. It clashed with Grigsby's cavalry brigade, en route to investigate matters at Villanow. Grigsby retired to Resaca where his dismounted men joined Cantey's in the defenses.

Sherman was overjoyed when he learned that his plan to trap Johnston was so near success.

"I've got Joe Johnston dead!" he exulted. But already the attempt had failed.

A mile west of Resaca, McPherson's skirmishers drove Cantey's outposts from a long range of hills that border Camp Creek on the west. Across the broad valley in his front McPherson saw fortified hills, behind which nestled Resaca. Artillery fire warned him that the town was strongly defended.

McPherson had been ordered to destroy a section of the railroad beyond immediate repair and, that task accomplished, to fall back to Snake Creek Gap, poised to harass Johnston's hasty retreat. But mounted infantry, probing from his left, found that the railroad swung east immediately above Resaca. To reach it, he must pass between Resaca and Dalton; and the sight of Johnston's prepared roads deterred him. Others had learned of Johnston's ability to deliver quick, punishing counter blows, and McPherson was far from support. He retired to the gap and intrenched.

The heavily wooded country masked the size and identity of McPherson's force. Both Geary and Kilpatrick were beyond Johnston's immediate view, and no word had reached him of McPherson's arrival. He had yet to learn that Ship's Gap had been left unguarded.

He sent Hood with three divisions to Resaca to investigate; but though Hood confirmed the presence of the enemy in the gap, he failed to learn their identity. Upon reporting that they were retiring, he was recalled, leaving Cleburne's and Walker's divisions near Tilton, on the railroad north of Dalton.

Although bitterly disappointed at McPherson's failure, Sherman acted quickly. Thomas was ordered to move through the gap, Schofield to follow him. Howard's corps and McCook's cavalry were to remain to hold Johnston's attention. The movement was made as rapidly as the one narrow road through the gap would permit, but the passage was not completed until the morning of the 13th.

Early on the 11th Johnston learned that an enemy corps was "supposed" to be in Snake Creek Gap. Investigation confirmed its presence. Immediately he ordered Polk to Resaca and sent for Wheeler, apparently for explanation of the cavalry's failure. Since Johnston never "threw off" on his subordinates, what was said has never been revealed.

Having detected Sherman's intentions, Johnston began his withdrawal. Even without the warning upon which he had counted his preparations were so complete that, during the night of the 12th, Dalton was completely evacuated without confusion. Next morning Howard's IV Corps followed him through the town. By daylight on the 13th the Army of Tennessee was moving into prepared positions, well before Sherman could deploy and move forward. Polk's left rested on the river, Hardee was in the center, and Hood on the right.

During the day McPherson reoccupied the hills along Camp Creek, his right resting on the river. Hooker formed on his left. Palmer extended the line to meet Schofield, near the head of the valley where the Confederate line turned east to the railroad. Howard deployed facing the latter line but Hood's right division—Stewart's—overlapped his left.

On the 14th an ill-advised assault by Judah's division of Schofield's corps was repulsed with severe loss. Stewart attacked Howard's left; but the arrival of Hooker, who had been shifted to the left, saved it from disaster. Heavy firing continued all along the line until nightfall.

Fighting raged furiously again on the 15th. During the afternoon McPherson launched an attack across Camp Creek which drove Polk from commanding ground south of the Resaca road from which the bridges over the river could be shelled. To relieve this pressure Johnston prepared to launch another blow at Sherman's left. But learning that Sweeney's division of Dodge's corps was crossing the river at Lay's Ferry a few miles downstream, to gain his rear, he recalled the assaulting force and issued orders for a withdrawal.

He withdrew his army skillfully that night, but not until the four guns of Van Den Corput's Georgia battery, unwisely exposed by Hood, had been captured. Sherman had lost his opportunity to trap Johnston north of the Oostanaula and end the campaign at little cost.

Early on the 16th Sherman pressed after Johnston, but the passage of the river with his larger force, encumbered with long trains, was slow. Although McPherson, crossing at Lay's Ferry, forced Hardee to fight near Calhoun for the safety of his trains, the day passed without further incident.

On the 17th Johnston reached Adairsville, 10 miles below Calhoun. Hoping to delude Sherman, he divided his forces temporarily. He sent Hardee, with the entire baggage train, along the main road, which followed the railroad to Kingston. At Kingston the railroad swung to the east. Near Cassville it turned south again toward the Etowah River. A little-used road led over the dry, sparsely settled Gravelly

The Battle of Resaca. Like the drawing on page 130, this was done by Alfred R. Waud after the war for The Mountain Campaigns in Georgia, *a publication by the Western and Atlantic Railroad to promote travel by veterans who had campaigned in the area.* (Century *magazine*)

Plateau directly to Cassville, six miles east of Kingston. He sent Polk and Hood, with a bare minimum of ammunition wagons and ambulances, to Cassville. He accompanied this column.

To gain time to get the trains clear of Adairsville, he had left Cheatham's division on strong ground astride the road, three miles above Adairsville, under orders to delay Sherman. Cheatham did his work nobly. He forced the entire IV Corps, Thomas' leading element, to halt and deploy. Although hard pressed, Cheatham held his ground until the trains were safely on the road to Kingston and Johnston had recalled him.

Next morning Sherman found conflicting evidence at Adairsville. The passage of so many trains created the impression that Johnston's main force had taken the road to Kingston. The few wagons, together with tight march discipline, made it appear that only a small column had marched straight to Cassville, to protect Johnston's left flank. Yet, since he could reach the railroad near Cassville by that road, and destroy it before Johnston could swing over to defend it, logic disputed the evidence—unless Johnston meant to cross the Etowah below Kingston and return to the railroad south of the river.

Sherman's columns were marching abreast of each other on roads which, on the maps, appeared to converge on Kingston. Thomas was in the center, McPherson on the right, and Schofield on the left. Schofield had reached Mosteller's Mill, six miles east of Adairsville. His route would take him close to Cassville.

"All signs continue of Johnston's having retreated on Kingston," Sherman wrote to Schofield, "and why he should lead to Kingston . . . I do not see . . . (unless) his wagons are escaping south of the Etowah by the bridge and fords near Kingston. In any hypothesis our plan is right." He could not afford to ignore the possibility of Johnston's being concentrated at Kingston; yet, in case he was wrong and Schofield was attacked as he passed Cassville, Hooker would be close by to support him. Furthermore, the IV and XIV Corps, on the Kingston road, could move quickly across country to join them. Schofield would continue toward Cassville, Hooker would take the road over the plateau, and Thomas would move on Kingston. McPherson would be close at hand.

At Cassville, Johnston set a trap. Schofield's route would bring him into the road over the plateau, north of Cassville. A little to the east, the road from Spring Place lay parallel to it. Hood was to march out the Spring Place road, and Polk to take position astride the road from Adairsville. When Schofield approached, Polk would engage him in front while Hood struck his left. Before help could reach him, Schofield would be crushed.

Johnston rode out the Spring Place road early on the 19th with Hood, Polk, and Hardee, to show Hood his position. Hood moved into it.

About 10:20 a.m., artillery firing was heard farther up the Adairsville road and, 10 minutes later, from an "easterly direction." As time passed and no other sounds of battle were heard, Johnston learned that Hood had left his assigned position and taken up another astride the Canton Road, facing east, to meet a supposed force of infantry and artillery approaching from that direction. The force proved to be, as Hood later admitted in his report, "the enemy's cavalry." McCook's division, with a battery of guns, was engaging Hood's skirmishers. Whether by accident or design, Hood had denied Johnston his first opportunity to disrupt Sherman's plans with little loss to himself.

General Sherman's wagon train passes through Resaca at night, following the Confederates' skillful withdrawal on May 15. The Confederates destroyed railroad tracks as they retreated but Federal crews soon had them repaired. (Frank Leslie's The Soldier in the Civil War)

Johnston now withdrew Hood and Polk to a semicircular ridge south and east of Cassville. Hood was posted on the right, Polk occupied the center, and Hardee, whose corps was fighting steadily with Thomas' troops as it retired from Kingston, would hold the more exposed left. The trains had passed to the rear of the army, toward the river. Strong positions were prepared and Johnston informed the army that Sherman's further progress would be met by battle.

In the afternoon Hooker appeared opposite Cassville, with Schofield on his left. Posted on hills beyond the town, his artillery shelled Polk's position but inflicted little damage. French's division, which bore the brunt of the shelling, had one officer and nine men wounded, and three horses killed.

Hood brought Polk into conference with Johnston that night. Apparently he had persuaded Polk that the line was endangered by enfilading fire from enemy batteries on their right. Since the Union left was opposite Hood's front, Johnston insisted that this could not be the case. Nevertheless Johnston was dismayed by Hood's insistence—in which Polk concurred—that the line could not be held. Since two of his corps commanders—Hardee was not present—were so sure of defeat, he decided not to risk their fears spreading through their ranks. Reluctantly he gave the order to retire across the Etowah. Hardee was outraged when he learned this. Again Hood had robbed Johnston of an opportunity.

Johnston retired across the Etowah and into the fastnesses of the Allatoona range, where he hoped that Sherman would follow. But Sherman, who had ridden through the area years earlier, remembered its defensive strength. Instead, he rested and refitted his armies for three days while he planned the next move.

Since the railroad ran through Allatoona Pass, Sherman had to resort to his wagons until he could regain it farther south. He made Kingston a strong base, and on the 23d crossed the Etowah beyond Johnston's view, and marched straight for Dallas, 20 miles in Johnston's left rear. If he eluded Johnston, he would be closer to Atlanta than his foe. Davis' division of Palmer's corps, which he had sent from Resaca to capture Rome, was ordered to rejoin Palmer en route.

But the "lynx-eyed watchfulness" with which Sher-

man later credited Johnston detected his purpose, and on the 25th Sherman found Johnston blocking his roads at New Hope Church and Dallas. Thomas was deployed along the New Hope Church line, with Schofield on his left and McPherson in front of Dallas. Heavy fighting developed. At Pickett's Mill northeast of New Hope Church, in a tangled country of deep ravines and easily defended ridges, an attempt by Howard to turn Johnston's right met a costly repulse.

On the 28th Sherman ordered McPherson to withdraw from Dallas and move around to the left of the army. But not until June 1 could McPherson disengage his forces from the vigilant enemy, which attacked him whenever he began to move.

Having forced Johnston to leave Allatoona, Sherman began moving to his left to regain the railroad. He sent Stoneman and Garrard to seize the pass, which they found unoccupied. Sherman ordered the railroad repaired through Allatoona, and a forward base established there.

Detecting Sherman's intention, Johnston withdrew in the night and fell back to a line embracing Lost and Pine Mountains. On June 6 McPherson, now on the left, reached the railroad at Ackworth, where two

Howard's attempt to turn Johnston's right met a costly repulse in the fighting on May 27 at Pickett's Mill northeast of New Hope Church. Following several days of sharp fighting in this area, the armies returned to skirmishing and sniping—"a big Indian war" groused a frustrated Sherman. (CWTI Collection)

days later Blair's XVII Corps rejoined him from veteran furlough.

On the 14th Polk was killed by an artillery projectile on Pine Mountain. A. P. Stewart was promoted to succeed him.

Johnston fell back on the 19th to the Kennesaw line, with Hood on the right, extending to the railroad, Polk's divisions in the center, and Hardee on the left.

Although the railroad below Marietta invited a move around Johnston's left, the incessant rains had made the country in front of his line a vast bog. Sherman was mud-bound. Impatient of delay, he searched for a weak point in the defenses. At an angle in the line, west of the Dallas road, he selected what appeared to be a favorable point. Although Johnston had fortified heavily, his army was stretched thin. If an assaulting force could break it, reserves massed behind them could pour through the break, over-run Johnston's train bivouacs, and split his army in two. Plans made, Sherman issued his orders.

The assault was launched on the 27th. Although the approach was difficult, Col. Daniel McCook's

and Harker's brigades of Thomas' army reached the enemy works. Harker was killed and his men were forced back by a withering fire. McCook's men gained the parapets in their front and success seemed sure. But Mitchell's brigade, on the right, failed to support them and they, too, were forced back. Dan McCook fell mortally wounded. Sherman's second hope of ending the campaign was shattered.

The rain had stopped and the wagons could move again, so a shift around Johnston's left forced him to retire. He fell back on the night of July 2 to prepared works astride the railroad at Smyrna, below Marietta, where Sherman attacked him on the 4th. Again his left was turned, and he withdrew into works of great strength near the Chattahoochee. In each case these works had been prepared solely to gain him time. Under cover of the river line he passed his trains safely across and prepared bridges for his troops. Sherman followed him closely but made no attacks on Johnston's formidable works. Instead, he began to cross the river at other points.

On the 8th, while McPherson feinted at Turner's Ferry on Johnston's left, Schofield crossed the river at the mouth of Soap Creek, upriver from Johnston's right, and occupied a high ridge. The next day Garrard crossed at Roswell, farther up river.

These crossings, which Johnston could not prevent, left him no choice. He crossed his army safely on the night of the 10th and moved toward Atlanta.

Sherman shifted McPherson upriver to Roswell where he crossed the stream and, on the 17th, marched toward Stone Mountain. Upon reaching it he turned toward Atlanta and began destroying the Georgia Railroad from that point to Decatur.

All of Thomas' army had crossed by the 19th at Power's and Pace's Ferries, and had begun moving toward Peachtree Creek. For the first time Sherman's wings were widely separated.

Overlooking the valley of Peachtree Creek, midway between that stream and the city's fortifications, Johnston directed that another line be constructed— his Peachtree Line. Hardee and Stewart were ordered to occupy this line, with Hardee on the right. Hood would be placed east of Atlanta to check McPherson's approach.

From this line Johnston planned to launch Hardee and Stewart at Thomas. Separated from McPherson—and Schofield, who was moving to a position between them—Thomas' forces would be engaged in crossing Peachtree Creek. Thomas' army would be wrecked; if not, the Army of Tennessee had "a near and secure place of refuge in Atlanta." In either case Johnston planned to man the defenses with state troops, move out with his whole army, and crush

The Battle of Kennesaw Mountain on June 27. The Union army assaulted what Sherman—shown in profile on horseback at the right—thought were weakly held Confederate positions. The Union was repulsed with heavy losses. Drawing by Alfred R. Waud. (Library of Congress)

McPherson. He had planned competently, but the sword was about to be struck from his hand.

On the 13th Bragg arrived in Atlanta. Before calling on Johnston he wired Davis that "indications seem to favor an entire evacuation of this place." When he saw Johnston he assured him that he was not there officially, but merely en route to Montgomery. Although the matter was not discussed, and Johnston's preparations spoke for themselves, Bragg wired that he could not learn that Johnston "has any more plan for the future than he has had in the past."

Bragg met secretly with Hood, who gave him a written statement of his views. In it, Hood stated that he had "so often urged that we should force the enemy to give us battle as to almost be regarded reckless." Yet an entry in the journal kept by Lt. T. B. Mackall observes—"Feeling in the army: One lieutenant-general talks about attack and not giving ground, publicly, and quietly urges retreat."

Immediately Davis wired to Johnston requesting his plans. Unfortunately for himself, Johnston did not trust the details to the telegraph and answered in general terms.

Obviously Bragg had been sent to effect Johnston's relief from command. Bragg's wires, together with Johnston's reluctance to explain his intentions in detail, gave Davis an opening. On the night of July 17 Johnston received a wire notifying him that because he had failed both "to arrest the advance of the enemy" and to express confidence in his ability to "defeat or repel him" he was relieved from command. Hood would succeed him.

Next morning Johnston explained his plans to Hood and, at Hood's request, issued orders placing the troops in position. When all was done, Johnston prepared a farewell message to the troops and sorrowfully departed.

Until the news spread through the ranks, the men had been confident of success. Morale was at high pitch. "Old Joe" had brought them safely to Atlanta, at far greater cost to the enemy than to themselves. When they learned that he had gone, "universal gloom seemed cast over the army." Men wept. Many threw away their arms and deserted. The Army of Tennessee had little confidence in his successor.

The Fighting at Atlanta
by Wilbur G. Kurtz, Sr.

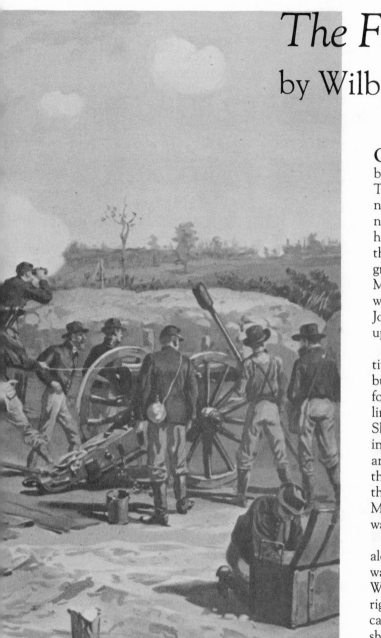

On July 5, 1864, the Federal armies of the Cumberland, the Ohio, and the Tennessee, under William T. Sherman, approached the Chattahoochee River northwest of Atlanta, hoping to find that their opponent, Joseph E. Johnston, had already crossed it with his Confederate Army of Tennessee. But they found their paths blocked by strong fortifications on high ground near the river. A bloody repulse at Kennesaw Mountain, eight days earlier, had made Sherman wary of attacking Confederate forts. To bypass Johnston's "river line" he sent his seven army corps upstream, to cross at points beyond Johnston's right.

Atlanta was protected by almost 12 miles of fortifications into which the Confederates could retire, but Johnston had other plans. Midway between those forts and Peachtree Creek he was building an outer line overlooking the valley of Peachtree Creek. When Sherman's right wing, under Thomas, was busy crossing the creek, Johnston intended to send Hardee's and Stewart's (formerly Polk's) corps forward from this outer line to attack the Cumberlanders before they could get ready to fight. The left wing, under McPherson, was too far away to help, and Schofield was beyond recall.

Northeast of Atlanta the outer line turned south along the present Highland Avenue. Hood's corps was to stop McPherson as he approached there. Wheeler's cavalry would extend the line on Hood's right. Wheeler was to hold a high, bald hill (later called Leggett's Hill) from which Federal guns could shell downtown Atlanta.

But Johnston did not remain to execute his plans. On July 17 he was relieved from command and General John B. Hood replaced him. The change was not popular with the army.

Hardee had crossed the river at Bolton and gone into bivouac to picket the river. On the 18th he marched his corps into Atlanta on the Marietta road,

Sherman (center) inspects Union siege lines before Atlanta. Sherman now faced a new opponent, General John B. Hood, who replaced Johnston's cautious and skillful maneuvering with rash attack. Painting by Thure de Thulstrup. (CWTI Collection)

past Johnston's headquarters. The men had learned that he was leaving, and a feeling of despondency settled down on them. In moody silence they reached today's Five Points and turned north up Peachtree Street (Road). When they reached the outer line, where Peachtree and Spring Streets join, they deployed along it and entrenched. Hardee had three of his four divisions in line: Walker was in the center; Maney was on his left, with his left at Tanyard Branch; Bate's line, on Walker's right, ran to Clear Creek; his fourth division, Cleburne's, was in reserve behind Walker.

Stewart moved from the river into the outer line with his three divisions: Loring on the right, next to Maney, Walthall in the center, and French on the left, west of Howell Mill Road.

Following Johnston's plan, Hood on July 20 made a sortie against the advancing Federals. About 4 p.m., four hours later than Hood had planned, Hardee and

On this page: Three views of the Confederate fortifications that guarded Atlanta. The Confederacy invested a great deal of effort in fortifying and defending Atlanta, which helped make the city a symbol of national independence and resistance second only to Richmond. (Above and left: Library of Congress; Below: Georgia Department of Archives & History)

Hood's delay gave Thomas time to get across the creek and advance to the high ground at Collier Road. Hooker's XX Corps—Williams', Geary's, and Ward's divisions—crossed at Peachtree Road and at the present Northside Drive. Earlier, Newton's division of Howard's IV Corps had crossed at Peachtree Road and moved forward to a high ridge just north of Collier Road. Here Newton deployed his men, with Kimball's brigade west of the road and Blake's

Stewart moved to the attack. Along Hardee's front, Walker was astride the Peachtree (Buckhead) Road, Bate was in the Clear Creek valley, and Maney connected with Stewart's right in the valley of Tanyard Branch. Uncleared forests and dense thickets made it difficult to keep in line.

As Loring's division approached the high ground on which the Collier Road led from Peachtree to Collier's Mill, on Tanyard Branch, and then to the Howell Mill Road at the Embry plantation, it had to cross low, cleared ground. Walthall, on Loring's left, advanced over wooded hills. The right of Scott's brigade, next to Walthall's right, moved from the woods to the low ground where Tanyard Branch flowed placidly to the mill. On Walthall's left, French extended toward the mouth of Peachtree Creek, facing Palmer's XIV Corps across the creek.

(Wagner's) east of it. Goodspeed's battery took position on the road. Bradley's brigade was in reserve, a few hundred yards in the rear. Geary's division moved up to high ground along Collier Road, just west of the mill, with Williams in his right rear; but Ward's division, between Geary and Newton, was slower in getting across the creek and into position. The resulting gap left Newton dangerously exposed, but he had time to erect barricades and do some digging.

Walker's attack met with deadly fire from Newton's barricaded men. Brigadier General C. H. Stevens was killed, and his men strove to avenge him. Although hard pressed, Newton held his ground until Walker was forced to retire to reform his shattered line.

Bate managed to work around the left of Newton's line, over low, swampy ground and through tangles of small growth, and attacked his left rear. But Bradley's brigade quickly formed line of battle along the road, which overlooked Clear Creek. While Bradley's muskets took toll along Bate's front, a storm of canister and case decimated his ranks from guns posted across Peachtree Creek, on his right. He was forced to retire.

On Newton's refused right, Loring's men charged into the gap created by Ward's delay and threatened to engulf Kimball. But Kimball's regiments held firm until Ward could come up and drive Loring back. One of these embattled regiments, the 24th Wisconsin, was commanded by a boy major, Arthur MacArthur, whose son, Douglas, would later win renown.

On Loring's left, a terrible struggle was taking place at Collier's Mill. Scott's brigade, after routing Geary's skirmishers and capturing the 33d New Jersey's state flag, charged into the gap where Tanyard Branch cuts through the ridge by the mill. Colonel Benjamin Harrison's brigade, of Ward's division, occupied the higher ground on each side. A battery was sited to sweep the approach. Scott's men were raked with canister and swept by storms of musket fire from the right and left. Finally they drew back, leaving the ground around the mill thickly carpeted with dead and wounded.

Walthall's men charged across the Embry plantation and into a long, deep ravine to assault Williams' line, posted on the high ground beyond. Although Reynolds' brigade, near the Howell Mill Road, met with some success, enfilading fire from its left forced it back. O'Neal's (Cantey's) brigade, on Reynolds' right, plunged into a section of the ravine between Geary's right and Williams' left, where it suffered heavily from a withering crossfire and was forced to withdraw.

At dark Hardee and Stewart pulled back their beaten men to the outer line. They had lost 4,796 in killed, wounded, and missing. Thomas had lost 1,779. Hood's first sortie had failed. He was not present.

While the Battle of Peachtree Creek raged north of Atlanta, there was also fighting to the east. McPherson's Army of the Tennessee was approaching Atlanta from Decatur. Logan's corps was astride the Georgia Railroad, with Dodge following in reserve. On Logan's left, south of the railroad, Blair moved southwest toward the Bald Hill, which Wheeler was defending, and the Flat Shoals Road. Farther to the north, Cheatham's corps (Hood's) was holding back the advance of Schofield's XXIII Corps and Stanley's and Wood's divisions of Howard's IV Corps. Although Cheatham had no difficulty, the pressure on Wheeler grew too great for his dismounted cavalry force. In the late afternoon, Cleburne's division, Hardee's only reserve, was ordered to march to his relief. After a long, hot march, Cleburne relieved Wheeler at midnight.

On the 21st, fighting was suspended along all but Blair's line fronting the Bald Hill. But Cleburne was attacked by Leggett's division of Blair's corps, supported by Gresham's division under Giles A. Smith, with a fury that Cleburne later described as "the bitterest fighting" of his life. Finally, Cleburne's men were driven from the hill by Leggett, whose name the hill now bears. The intrenchments were at once reversed and Atlanta lay within range of Leggett's guns.

Hood countered with a move that could have spelled disaster to McPherson's forces, whose left flank had no cavalry screen. He decided to send Hardee's corps on a 15-mile night march to McPherson's rear; a well-placed attack there promised better results than the head-on assault at Peachtree Creek. The ensuing conflict, known as the Battle of Atlanta, is dramatically portrayed on the 400-foot canvas of the Atlanta Cyclorama now housed in a special building in the city's Grant Park.

Hood instructed Hardee to move his corps south through Atlanta that night, swing around to the southeast, and then turn north toward Decatur to strike the rear of McPherson's line. Although the route followed strange roads, Hood expected Hardee to be in position by daylight of the 22d to deliver a surprise attack upon the unsuspecting Federals.

Hardee's march began at dark. Cleburne's division, which had been pulled back into Atlanta after fighting all day, joined the column as it passed through the city. The night was hot and the roads ankle deep in dust. The men slogged along wearily, many of them with empty canteens.

At daybreak Hardee was still far from his destination. Since the country was strange to his officers and he had no maps, he secured two guides. Close to East Atlanta the road forked. Hardee sent Walker's and Bate's divisions up the Fayetteville Road toward De-

The contest on Bald Hill, an eminence to the east of the city. The Union XV Corps' 4th Division is in the foreground. Major General Patrick R. Cleburne's Confederates were driven from the hill by troops commanded by Major General Mortimer D. Leggett. The intrenchments were quickly reversed . . . and Atlanta lay within range of Leggett's guns. (Century magazine)

catur, as Hood had planned. But he sent Cleburne's and Maney's divisions straight ahead toward the Federal left flank.

A short distance farther north the road crossed Sugar Creek. Here Walker halted and decided to turn left, up the creek. In vain his guide, Case Turner, argued that he would be blocked by the large pond at Terry's Mill, but Walker was adamant. He turned and, with Bate following, was soon confronted by the pond. The ensuing confusion attracted unwelcome attention. It was now almost noon, and neither wing of Hardee's corps was where Hood wanted it—behind the Federal line.

During the forenoon, McPherson had ridden to Sherman's field headquarters at the Augustus Hurt (Howard) house, east of Atlanta. He asked that Sweeney's division of Dodge's corps, in reserve behind Logan, be sent across Sugar Creek to fill a gap between the refused left of Blair's XVII Corps and Fuller's division of Dodge's corps, on the extreme left, both of which faced south. In the absence of Garrard's cavalry, which had gone eastward to destroy

the rails and bridges near Covington, Sweeney's division would be a welcome addition to that exposed flank. Sherman assented. It was a fortunate decision, for Sweeney's move toward the gap placed his division in position to block Walker and Bate.

Sherman then explained a plan to shift McPherson from the left of the army to the right. On a map, he indicated the line of march. The route would take McPherson behind Schofield's Army of the Ohio and Thomas' Army of the Cumberland, and put him in position to reach for the two railroads that entered Atlanta through East Point—the Macon & Western, and the Atlanta & West Point. With the Georgia Railroad and the Western & Atlantic in Sherman's hands, Hood depended upon these two roads to supply his army, particularly the Macon & Western.

When Sherman had finished, McPherson rode back to inspect his lines—and to meet his death early in the afternoon.

About noon, Sweeney was moving toward the gap when he halted briefly. He was near Fuller, who had pickets out to his front and left and artillery posted

Sherman poses with staff officers alongside one of the large guns that would rain ammunition on the city of Atlanta during the following weeks, slowly pounding it into submission. Sherman, right center, faces Chief of Artillery General W.F. Barry. (U.S. Army Military History Institute)

on a hill near where Sweeney had halted. These pickets had been alerted by the confusion at the millpond, and as Walker got clear of the pond and started to ride farther north he was killed. Brigadier General Hugh W. Mercer took command of his division. Immediately Bate and Mercer hurried into position but only Bate, on Mercer's right, actually reached a point behind McPherson's line. As they moved forward they found Sweeney's men formed to meet them. The Battle of Atlanta had begun.

Near Blair's refused left flank, Cleburne had deployed astride the Flat Shoals Road with his right brigade reaching beyond the gap to Fuller's right. Maney deployed on his left. As Cleburne moved forward to attack Blair and Fuller, Maney swung around and attacked Blair's front. Giles Smith's division was swept back upon Leggett's Hill.

When the firing commenced, McPherson galloped to a hill from which he could see the field. He watched Sweeney—on advantageous ground—repulse Walker and Mercer, then hurried to the sound of Giles Smith's disaster.

As Cleburne's right struck Fuller's left, skirmishers pressing forward through the gap saw a Federal general galloping toward them, accompanied only by an orderly. At their cry to halt, he wheeled his horse and attempted to escape. But a shot toppled McPherson from his saddle.

Cheatham's corps had been shifted to the right to attack McPherson's front. Had Hood launched it as Hardee struck the Federal left and rear, his second sortie might have succeeded in wrecking McPherson's army. But again, Hood was not on the battlefield, so Cheatham's attack was delayed. Blair's men reformed on Leggett's left, facing south, and that flank was secured.

Late in the afternoon Cheatham's attack finally got away. It struck M. L. Smith's division of the XV Corps, astride the railroad on the former Confederate outer line, broke Lightburn's brigade at the Troup Hurt house, and captured DeGress' battery of 20-pounder Parrott guns.

Logan, who had succeeded McPherson temporarily, promptly ordered forward Mersey's brigade of Sweeney's division. Mersey's men double-quicked to the scene and, with Smith's reformed brigades, drove back Cheatham's embattled men and restored the Federal line.

When night finally closed the battle, Hood had lost more than 8,000 men. Sherman had lost 3,722. Again Hood had failed.

On July 26, Major General Oliver O. Howard was assigned to the command of the Army of the Tennessee. Major General D. S. Stanley assumed command of the IV Corps. Already Howard's new command was en route to the right of the army, as Sherman had planned. By the 28th Dodge was in position on Thomas' right, facing Atlanta, and Logan and Blair had moved beyond him to the vicinity of Ezra Church, in the present Mosley Park, southwest of Atlanta toward East Point.

Stung by his failures, Hood watched Howard's movement, which threatened his remaining railroads. Determined to halt it, he sent Stewart's and S. D. Lee's (Cheatham's) corps against the encircling enemy. The resulting Battle of Ezra Church was a third disaster.

Feeling carefully toward East Point, Howard halted on good defensive ground near the church. Increased cavalry resistance in his front warned him that Hood was aware of his movement.

Howard's skirmishers found enemy forces approaching on the Lickskillet (Gordon) Road. He deployed quickly, with Logan on the right and Blair on the left. Blair's line was sharply refused to face southeast, making a sharp angle where the two corps joined in front of Ezra Church. Hasty barricades were erected and Logan and Blair awaited the coming storm.

When S. D. Lee's corps arrived, it was deployed facing the XV Corps line. Brown's (Hindman's) divi-

Confederate soldiers attack General John A. Logan's corps on July 28, during the heated Battle of Ezra Church. Hood failed in this attempt to smash the Union right and pulled his battered army back into the defenses of Atlanta. (The Soldier in the Civil War)

sion was placed on the left opposite the right of Logan's line. Clayton's (Stewart's) division moved to his right. Brown had reached the field ahead of his troops and met Brigadier General William H. Jackson, whose cavalry division had been pressed back by Howard's advance. Jackson offered the opinion, however, that the Federal infantry did not appear to be in great force.

Lee's plan was to strike the Federal right flank and roll it back on its left, at Ezra Church. Moving out to the left, to insure a direct blow on Logan's right flank, Brown advanced with three brigades abreast and one in reserve. About 12:30 p.m., his skirmishers pushed forward through dense undergrowth and engaged Federal skirmishers on the Lickskillet Road. Brown's line moved forward, but fences and thickets disrupted his alignment and slowed his advance. He was forced to halt, under fire from the enemy skirmishers. When he advanced again, he drove the skirmishers back into Logan's line. But as he neared it, a withering fire proved Jackson's opinion wrong. After a desperate struggle, Brown was forced to retire.

Ten minutes after Brown moved forward, Clayton advanced. A misunderstanding caused Gibson's brigade to move unsupported against Logan's left. When the defenders saw but one brigade approaching, they swarmed out of their works and shattered Gibson's regiments. Clayton's attempt to reinforce him was useless. His division, too, was driven back.

It was now 2 o'clock and Lee's attack thus far had failed. But the battle was not over; Stewart's troops were arriving. Walthall's division came first, and deployed in the interval between Brown's and Clayton's shattered remnants. Ordered to retrieve Brown's failure to drive Logan's right from its secure position and back upon his left, Walthall advanced over the same ground that Brown had traversed, his men stumbling over gruesome evidence of the fate of Brown's assault. The dead lay in ominous numbers, and the wounded cried piteously for water. But Walthall, too, failed, and his dead and wounded lay intermingled with Brown's.

Loring was wounded while deploying his division for an assault. Before Stewart could give the order for Walthall to retire, he was struck in the forehead by a spent bullet. Although Stewart had ordered Loring into the fight, Walthall took command when Stewart was wounded and ordered no further assaults. The losses already were appalling—and the men's lives had been spent in vain.

From four o'clock until dark the action was limited to skirmishing. At 10 o'clock, the shattered ranks of

but the results were to shock even the authorities in Richmond, who had been impatient with Johnston's sensible—but less colorful—policy of preserving his men for the task of holding Atlanta so long as it needed to be held. Now, to the humiliation of three failures was added an admonition from President Davis to avoid attacking the enemy in his entrenchments. With his decimated and dispirited army, Hood faced the dull prospect of conducting a defense. But he soon learned that Sherman was not content with besieging the city. Hood found himself forced to fight for the possession of his railroads.

Sherman had found that the fortifications of Atlanta were too strong to assault and too extensive to encircle. Instead of attempting either, he occupied a line facing the city, with his left near the Georgia Railroad and his right probing toward East Point and Hood's vital railroads. His probing forced Hood to extend his own lines to cover East Point.

Meanwhile, Sherman subjected the city to continual shelling. Until August 9, the shelling had been moderate. As his impatience mounted, he had siege guns sent forward. These, together with 50 batteries of field pieces, all emplaced on commanding ground, fired by day and by night. But 30 days of persistent hammering produced no visible results. Hood con-

The Atlanta Union Railroad Depot, or "car shed," before it was destroyed by a Federal demolition team. The baggage belongs to citizens forced to "refugee south." (Library of Congress)

Lee's and Stewart's corps moved back to the shelter of the fortifications.

The burden of the battle now had fallen upon Lee's corps and Walthall's division of Stewart's. Despite their crushing defeat, all had fought with the fury of desperation.

The enemy testified to their valor. Colonel James S. Martin, 111th Illinois Infantry, stated that the battle "for severity is unsurpassed by any of the campaign." Lieutenant Colonel Samuel R. Mott, 57th Ohio Infantry, wrote that "the carnage was fearful and the dead and wounded on the field told a tale that must clothe many hearth stones in mourning and sorrow."

But the words of a tired Confederate soldier were the most eloquent of all. In the early dark, one of the skirmishers whom Logan had sent forward again called out—"Well, Johnny, how many of you are left?" The voice that answered might have been speaking for the dying cause:

"Oh, about enough for another killing."

When the losses at Ezra Church were tallied, Hood had lost approximately 5,000 of his remaining men. Sherman had lost 600. And again, Hood had not appeared on the battlefield. Hood had supplanted Johnston because he was a "fighter." He had fought,

146

tinued to receive supplies, and Federal spies reported no shortages of food or munitions. The citizens went about their affairs with seeming indifference to the bursting shells. Although most of the families had "refugeed," those remaining lived in cellars, and in caves and "bomb proofs" constructed in their yards and gardens. It appeared that Atlanta would, as Johnston had intended, be held "forever."

As August wore on, the opposing lines crept slowly toward East Point, Hood's finally encircling the town. Continual skirmishing, sometimes amounting to sharp engagements, marked each passing day. On the Sandtown (Cascade) Road, near the south fork of Utoy Creek, a repulse by Bate's division of an attempt by Schofield to break his line resulted in the Battle of Utoy Creek. But on the morning of the 26th the defenders found the trenches opposite them empty. Sherman was gone.

In many places the siege lines were plainly visible from the city parapets. As watchers beheld the empty works, rumors flew thick and fast. Although Hood had sent most of his cavalry on a fruitless raid to break Sherman's supply line, Jackson had remained. He reported to Hood that Sherman's columns were moving south. Convinced that his cavalry had interrupted Sherman's supplies and forced him to retreat, Hood concluded that he was crossing the Chattahoochee River at Campbellton ferry. He relaxed his vigilance.

While shelling Atlanta and probing Hood's lines toward East Point, Sherman had been planning a turning movement around Hood's left to break his railroads. Had Johnston remained in command, his watchfulness, together with the striking power of his intact army, would have made the move hazardous. But neither the depleted army that remained, nor its general, now deterred Sherman.

On the night of the 25th the XX Corps moved back to the Chattahoochee River at Bolton, to cover and protect the railroad and Turner's and Pace's ferries. Through the night, the other corps passed to the right and rear, toward Lickskillet (Adamsville) and Mt. Gilead Church. But not until the blue columns had destroyed the Atlanta & West Point Railroad at Red Oak and Fairburn was Hood convinced that a "raid" was directed at Jonesboro, as cavalry reports had indicated. But he still refused to believe that Sherman was moving on Jonesboro in force.

On the 30th Hood was finally satisfied that "two corps" were moving that way. He sent Hardee to Jonesboro, with his own and Lee's corps, to drive them back.

The march began late on the 30th, hence it was noon the next day before the last of the troops reached Jonesboro, hot, tired, and with little stomach for another "killing."

Also on the 30th Howard's three corps marched from Fairburn and Shadnor Church (Union City) to Renfroe's plantation, west of Jonesboro; but finding no water there, Howard moved on to the Flint River, close to the town. Cavalry had disputed his advance, and he had received reports of an enemy force entrenched to protect the railroad, so he moved forward in two columns, with Logan on the left and Ransom's (Dodge's) XVI Corps on his right. Blair and his corps arrived the next morning. Kilpatrick's cavalry preceded both columns.

They advanced so rapidly that upon reaching the river Logan found the bridge intact. Brushing aside cavalry on the east bank, Logan crossed and advanced to the highest ground between the river and the railroad, where he entrenched, with Hazen's division on the left, Harrow's on the right, and Osterhaus' in reserve behind them. Howard placed Ransom in position west of the river, facing south.

The next morning Ransom crossed and took position on Logan's right. When Blair arrived he was held west of the river, behind Logan. Through the night the sounds of trains warned Howard that enemy forces were arriving, so he made his lines strong.

Before abandoning Atlanta, Hood blew up an 81-car train loaded with ammunition, destroying both the railroad and an adjacent rolling mill. (Georgia Department of Archives & History)

At 3 o'clock, Hardee advanced to attack Howard's line, with Lee on the right and his own corps, commanded by Cleburne, on the left. Cleburne was to wheel to the right and attack Ransom's refused right flank, posted behind a wide, swampy ravine, while Lee moved against Logan's front. The sound of Cleburne's firing was to be Lee's signal to advance. But the left of Cleburne's line became engaged with part of Kilpatrick's cavalry and drove it back across the river before Cleburne's actual movement could be effected. Mistaking the small affair with Kilpatrick for Cleburne's assault on Ransom's right, Lee ordered his men forward. Although they charged with a yell and overran the rifle pits of Logan's skirmishers, as they approached his main line they seemed to lack the spirit that had marked their assaults at Ezra Church. Yet, when night fell, an appalling number of dead and wounded lay under the stars.

Although he worked hard to retrieve the blunder on his left, Cleburne was unable to deliver a coordinated attack on Ransom's line. Finally he gave up the effort and withdrew.

Shortly after 3 o'clock, Schofield and Stanley reached the Macon & Western Railroad just below Rough and Ready (Mountain View). Schofield routed a force of dismounted cavalry entrenched to protect the railroad, and captured numerous prisoners. While

Peachtree Street at the Georgia Railroad, after the bombardment. Sherman entered Atlanta on September 2, ending a campaign that had lasted for four months. (National Archives)

this fight was in progress, a train from Atlanta came in sight. The engineer hastily reversed his engine and steamed back to Atlanta to report that Federals were moving north from Rough and Ready.

Bewildered by rumors and unaware of the battle raging at Jonesboro, Hood jumped to the conclusion that Sherman had turned his left and was advancing to attack Atlanta from the south. Without attempting to learn Hardee's situation Hood ordered him, by mounted courier, to return Lee to Atlanta. Lee was to "march by 2 o'clock to-morrow morning."

It was one o'clock when the courier reached Hardee, but Lee assembled the shattered remnants of his corps and began his march. It was a futile move. Atlanta was doomed.

The next morning, September 1, Hardee stretched his corps front to include Lee's position of the day before. His extreme right was sharply refused and, where it crossed the railroad, ran southeast. Cleburne's division was on the right, with Govan's brigade in the salient angle formed by the bend in the line. Granbury's was at the Warren house, and Lewis' between Govan and the railroad. Gist's was east of the railroad; Brown's division, on Cleburne's left, was in line parallel with the railroad, facing Logan's corps.

While Schofield and Stanley were busy destroying the railroad, Stanley nearest to Jonesboro, Davis, accompanied by Sherman and Thomas, arrived near Howard's left with his XIV Corps. Hardee now faced four Federal corps, with two others within easy march.

Learning that Lee had gone, Sherman ordered Thomas to bring Stanley forward quickly and attempt to surround Hardee. Before Stanley could arrive, the attack was launched, the brunt falling on the angle of the works. Bayonets and clubbed muskets sought to stem the tide, but Govan's and Lewis' brigades were swept away. Govan was captured, with 600 of his officers and men and eight guns.

Anxious that Hardee not escape, Thomas himself galloped up the railroad to hurry Stanley's advance. But before Stanley could deploy his corps through the unfamiliar woods, night closed down. Hardee extricated his remaining men and retired down the railroad to Lovejoy's Station, where he halted and again formed an entrenched line of battle. But before leaving Jonesboro he sent a courier to tell Hood that Jonesboro had fallen, and that the railroad was gone.

When Hood received Hardee's message, he had no choice but to evacuate Atlanta. By 5 o'clock his troops began to march south toward McDonough to reunite with Hardee. By midnight only a few cavalry remained in the city. They had a special mission to perform.

Shortly after midnight, heavy explosions from the vicinity of Oakland Cemetery and the rolling mill startled the remaining citizens. Eighty-one cars loaded with ammunition had been set on fire by the cavalry to keep them from being captured.

To Hood, riding despondently down the McDonough Road, the sounds of the explosions were a requiem for his dead hopes. But to Sherman, waiting at Jonesboro among the living and the dead, they were a paean of triumph. They told him as clearly as the notes of a bugle in the night that "Atlanta is ours, and fairly won."

The Final Turning Point

In its impact on both northern and southern opinion, the capture of Atlanta was perhaps the most important single military achievement of 1864. Northern home-front morale had dropped steadily during the summer as both Grant and Sherman seemed stymied before Richmond and Atlanta. The enormous casualties suffered by these two Union armies in the campaigns—100,000 by August—sapped northern will to continue the war. Anti-war activities by the Copperheads revived. Northern Democrats were confident of winning the presidential election in November on a platform branding the war a failure and calling for an armistice and peace negotiations. "Who shall revive the withered hopes that bloomed at the opening of Grant's campaign?" asked a New York Democratic newspaper in July. "All are tired of this damnable tragedy. Each hour is but sinking us deeper into bankruptcy and desolation."

Even Republicans reflected this despair. "Our bleeding, bankrupt, almost dying country . . . longs for peace—shudders at the prospect of . . . further wholesale devastations, and of new rivers of human blood," wrote *New York Tribune* editor Horace Greeley in July. The veteran Republican politician Thurlow Weed predicted flatly in August that "Lincoln's reelection is an impossibility." Lincoln himself agreed with this assessment. "I am going to be beaten," he told a friend in August, "and unless some great change takes place *badly* beaten."

Union soldiers pose at their camp along the Carolina coast. Sherman's army smashed its way through South Carolina to break the South's "unconquerable defiance." (Library of Congress)

Sherman's capture of Atlanta changed all this. "Glorious news this morning—Atlanta taken at last!!!" wrote a New York diarist on September 3. "It is (coming at this political crisis) the greatest event of the war." Southerners reacted with expressions of shock and dismay to the news of Atlanta's fall. The *Richmond Examiner* reflected glumly that "the disaster at Atlanta" came "in the very nick of time" to "save the party of Lincoln from irretrievable ruin. It obscures the prospect of peace, late so bright. It will also diffuse gloom over the South." Diffuse gloom it certainly did. "Since Atlanta I have felt as if all were dead within me, forever," wrote a South Carolina diarist at the end of September. "We are going to be wiped off the earth."

Followed as it soon was by Sheridan's decisive victories in the Shenandoah Valley, which helped insure Lincoln's reelection, the capture of Atlanta was a turning point toward ultimate Union victory comparable with Antietam in 1862 and Gettysburg and Vicksburg in 1863. And in retrospect it became clear that Admiral David Farragut's spectacular achievement at Mobile Bay in August 1864 was the first of what became an unbroken string of Union victories that propelled northern spirits upward from the doldrums of midsummer 1864.

—James M. McPherson

"Long Abraham Lincoln a Little Longer," an elongated caricature of the President commemorating his victory over George B. McClellan at the polls. (Harper's Weekly, *November 26, 1864*)

FARRAGUT
AT MOBILE BAY

by V. C. Jones

Farragut at Mobile Bay
by V. C. Jones

"LACKAWANNA."   "OSSIPEE."   "BROOKLYN."   "ITASCA."   "RICHMOND."
"WINNEBAGO."   "TENNESSEE."

"ARTFORD."   "CHICKASAW."
FORT MORGAN.

THE NAVY of 1864 knew the 63-year-old David Glasgow Farragut as a fighter. At times he seemed gruff and unreasonable and impatient, always fretting for action. But underneath, records old and new show, he was a veteran who went into battle only after every precaution had been taken to protect his vessels and their crews. He loved excitement, but would repress his restlessness and delay for days, weeks, or even months until conditions were favorable: the wind blowing from the right direction, chains lashed over the ships' sides as armor, bags of coal stacked around boilers, unnecessary gear cleared from the decks, and any other steps he could think of to reduce casualties. No gimmicks in the precautions he took, but solid, practical measures.

This officer destined for naval greatness had come up the hard way, at times with the help of fate. Born in Tennessee of Spanish and Scotch parentage, he was residing in New Orleans as a young boy when David Porter, his father's friend of Revolutionary War days, fell ill of yellow fever on a fishing trip and was brought to the Farragut home, where he died. Farragut's mother contracted the disease while nursing her husband's friend and died. Out of this tragedy developed a family tie, because Porter's son of the same name, a prominent naval officer, soon assumed the responsibility of training and educating David Farragut.

A career in the Navy lay ahead. At age 9, under the watchful eye of his foster parent, Farragut was appointed a midshipman. And he was serving in this capacity in 1813, three years later, when a foster brother was born, a third David Porter—David Dixon Porter—who through the years would cite David Farragut as one of the best officers in the Navy.

IT WAS David Dixon Porter who called attention to Farragut when the Navy Department was looking for

CLIMAX AT MOBILE BAY—The Confederate defense of Mobile Bay rested chiefly on the mighty ram, the "Tennessee." Initially this seemed justified as the ironclad fired with effect on several Federal ships while appearing to be invulnerable to return fire. Even 11-inch solid shot bounced off the ram's armor. But the "Hartford" and other U.S. vessels clustered remorselessly around the flailing Confederate champion. "We butted and shot at him," Farragut wrote, "until he surrendered." ("Century" magazine.)

someone to lead an expedition past Forts Jackson and St. Philip on the Mississippi River and capture New Orleans, the South's largest city. Officials at Washington were at first skeptical about Farragut. At the time he was performing quiet and somewhat relaxed duty behind a desk of the Navy Retirement Board in New York, a veteran with 53 years of naval service behind him, all creditable but none particularly outstanding.

He had fought in the War of 1812, while still a boy not yet in his teens, and later in the Mexican War. But except for the tender age at which he started as a seaman, his career throughout had been more or less routine and never spectacular. He had always been somewhat of a plodder, stubborn and efficient but not inspired, and he had performed his duties well, yet without evincing any quality that marked him as an especially great leader.

And then there was the matter of his birth. Could he, a Southerner, be depended on to fight against the South? Farragut's past actions spoke in his favor. During the nullification troubles of 1833 he had been sent as a ship-master to South Carolina to carry out the Presidential mandate that the Union must be preserved, and in 1861 he had moved his wife and son from Norfolk, Va. to New York to get away from the people he charged with trying to break up the Union.

Wisdom in the choice of Farragut to lead the New Orleans expedition soon was evident. He handled the campaign like a father leading his family through unavoidable dangers. Of medium height, leather-skinned, eyes small and sparkling above a nose that curved like the beak of a hawk, he went about the task in a manner that caused his sailors to say he had a bee buzzing in his bonnet. His official papers he filed in his pockets, and orders he wrote on his knee, his foot propped against the ship's rail. His demeanor was solemn, and yet there were times when he became animated, an interesting talker, almost boyish in his enthusiasm. His habits were clean, his speech picturesque, his sense of humor strong. After careful planning, he took New Orleans in such a fashion that Union General Ben Butler commented: "A more gallant exploit it has never fallen to the lot of man to witness."

FOLLOWING the capture of New Orleans, Farragut was ordered with his fleet up the Mississippi River to take the Confederate stronghold at Vicksburg. He went reluctantly, trying all the while to convince officials at Washington that he should be going in the opposite direction, toward Mobile Bay, to take it over before the Southerners could strengthen its fortifications. He had in mind control of the bay rather than capture of the city, for he doubted that his heavy vessels would be able to get up to the wharf at Mobile.

Nearly two years later, six months after Vicksburg had fallen, Farragut was directed to capture Mobile Bay. Down from New York, where he had been on leave, he came in his shot-riddled flagship, the wooden USS *Hartford*. He still favored wood in his ships and iron only in the hearts of his men. In arguing against ironclads, he maintained that shot passed clean through a wooden ship and did less damage than it would rattling around in a mailed ship. But he was beginning to admit, after months of observation, that armored vessels had some advantages. One of his first moves after reaching the

The Story Behind . . .

. . . 'Damn the Torpedoe

Mystery still shrouds many Civil War happenings, while others remain erroneously interpreted. What a thrill, then, comes to the researcher who finds in an overlooked document a clue to, or positive evidence of, the correct explanation of a famous but misunderstood event. V. C. "Pat" Jones had this reward while gathering material for his trilogy The Civil War at Sea. As he tells of his discovery:

Some years ago, while I was working on my trilogy, "The Civil War at Sea," as I mulled through the musty records of that day, battling dust and fretting over difficult handwriting, I suddenly realized that I had turned up evidence indicating that David Glasgow Farragut, called an old fogey because he preferred wooden ships to ironclads, was a man of caution as well as courage, an officer who removed as much peril as possible from his path before facing it.

In a way, I had a feeling of resentment toward this evidence. It seemed to take away some of the glory from his immortal words: "Damn the torpedoes! Full speed ahead!" I thought of the way it would distort in the eyes of school children the vision they had been given of the gallant Farragut hurling defiance in a manner that

Gulf of Mexico was to write the Navy Department for ironclads; he wanted as many as he could get.

In following the main channel into Mobile Bay, his fleet, as at New Orleans, would have to withstand the fire of two forts—Fort Morgan on Mobile Point on the right and Fort Gaines on Dauphin Island on the left, the latter fortunately so far away that it provided no great threat. A third work, Fort Powell in Grant's Pass, a channel open only to vessels of light draft, also was too distant to cause worry.

But in the water ahead of him, he soon learned, would be reposing scores of the Southerners' dreaded water mines—or torpedoes as they were popularly called in that day. Also confronting him would be the ironclad ram *Tennessee*, a warship commanded by his old naval acquaintance, Franklin Buchanan, the same officer who had been at the helm of the CSS *Virginia (Merrimack)* when it first appeared in Hampton Roads on March 8, 1862.

THE "BROOKLYN"—This sketch, made immediately after the engagement, shows the "Brooklyn" after the Mobile Bay battle. In the background (left) are the "Galena," and (right) the "Itasca." ("Century.")

ll Speed Ahead'

would be recalled for centuries by other American warriors as they went into battle.

The more I researched, the more the evidence took definite form. Private journals painstakingly kept by some of the officers who served under this great naval leader, as well as other contemporary records, appeared to show beyond a doubt that for nearly two weeks prior to the battle of Mobile Bay, the engagement in which he uttered his stirring words defying death and destruction, he sent boat crews out at night and even by day to engage in the hazardous task of removing or sinking the water mines it was known the Southerners had placed across the channel. And then there was the additional indication, also disconcerting to hero worshippers, that many of the explosives were duds, having been in the water so long that they had become inert.

I am not one who takes pride in tearing down our vignettes of history, nor do I like to tarnish the names of American heroes whose classic battle cries have come down to us through the ages. So it was quite some time before I bared my discovery to Rear Admiral E. M. Eller, director of naval history for the United States Department of the Navy.

After I told him what I had found, I said, "I hope you won't think that I, as a Southerner, am trying to debunk Farragut."

"Debunk him!" he exclaimed. "You're not debunking him. You're showing he was a smart man."

REFUGEES as early as the end of '63 had brought in reports that the Confederates were placing much of their faith for a successful defense of Mobile in the *Tennessee*, said to be building at Selma, Alabama. She was described as 200 feet long, covered with four inches of iron, and fortified with compressed cotton between her timbers. It was reported she carried eight guns and was considered much more dangerous than the *Merrimack*. But she would be almost alone in defending the bay, and Farragut planned to get together a large enough fleet to overpower her and to offset her mailed strength.

Farragut reached the Gulf in January 1864. By that time, both the North and the South realized that action in the area was long overdue. Mobile was one of the major ports through which the Confederacy was getting supplies and ammunition from abroad.

At just about this time, the last of the *Tennessee's* guns were put into position and a part of her crew was ordered on board. Her immediate problem was to get across the bar at the mouth of Dog River. She was even stronger than the reports leaking to the enemy had made her, for six inches of iron instead of four covered her most vulnerable part. But she had defects that could have been eliminated. One of the most obvious was her port shutters, which opened and closed on a pivot and were subject to jamming in battle. Another was her rudder chains, which were exposed on the afterdeck, and still another was her lack of speed. Her engines had been taken from the old river steamboat *Alonzo Child* and were too weak for the task required of them.

During the next months, Farragut worked diligently on battle preparations, constantly urging Washington to send him more ironclads, maintaining it would "be unwise to take in our wooden vessels without the means of fighting the enemy on an equal footing." This was a sharp reversal of his stand at the time of the New Orleans Campaign.

His impatience over the ironclads grew. "If I had one

ironclad," he wrote in irritation to a fellow officer, "I would go up and destroy the *Tennessee* where she lies."

BY MAY the water mines were becoming a matter of growing concern to him. He wrote Union Navy Secretary Gideon Welles: "Torpedoes are not so agreeable when used on both sides; therefore I have reluctantly brought myself to it. I have always deemed it unworthy of a chivalrous nation; but it does not do to give your enemy such a decided superiority over you."

Records do not reveal that Farragut actually had mines placed in the water as a threat to the Confederates, but they do indicate that he favored attaching one to the bow of each of his ships and that he went along with the idea of placing a torpedo fixture—or a cowcatcher, as the sailors called it—to the bow of one of his largest vessels, the USS *Brooklyn*.

Meanwhile, he knew the Southerners were having trouble in placing the mines and in getting them to stay in position. Before his arrival in the Gulf, he was notified that each of these devices was anchored with manila rope and about a third of a bar of railroad iron, and that some of them had broken adrift and floated up the bay. Reports placed their number at 180. They were of two types, one made of kegs equipped with sensitive primers, and the other of tin in the form of cones fitted with cap and trigger. The keg type were considered more dependable because the caps of the cones were damaged by long exposure to water.

BY JULY, Farragut could see a line of black buoys running eastward from Dauphin Island. At the end, about 160 yards from Fort Morgan, was a red buoy; according to the information that came to him, there were three lines of torpedoes, but none east of this red buoy.

He issued a general order: "There are certain black buoys placed by the enemy from the piles on the west side of the channel across it towards Fort Morgan. It being understood that there are torpedoes and other obstructions between the buoys, the vessels will take care to pass eastward of the easternmost buoy, which is clear of all obstructions." This "easternmost" buoy was the red buoy 160 yards from Fort Morgan. Federal eyes watched it intently.

To run up the channel through the space thus left clear of mines would bring his fleet under the concentrated fire of Fort Morgan at close range. He would have to provide a route farther west. With this in mind, he called to his aid his flag-lieutenant, John Crittenden Watson, grandson of John Crittenden, the eminent statesman and anti-Secessionist from Kentucky. Farragut was especially fond of this young man who, on numerous occasions, sat patiently reading the Bible to him. Watson had been added to his staff in '63, after distinguishing himself repeatedly; and since then, whenever someone had to be sent on a special mission, he was the choice.

On the night of July 25, eleven days before the battle, boats from the Union ships *Hartford*, *Monongahela*, and *Sebago* went out into the channel under Watson's direction in search of torpedoes. They worked for hours, the last of the three returning at 4 a.m.

TWO DAYS LATER Union boats could be seen sounding near the channel abreast of Fort Morgan. It was noticed that they kept constantly clear of the line of torpedoes, indicating knowledge of their location. Directing them was Watson, aided by Martin Freeman, pilot of the USS *Hartford*. They went up toward Little Pelican Pass and placed buoys, and later in the day they buoyed out an anchorage for the four ironclads Farragut had finally managed to obtain. Towing Watson's boats was the little steam tug *Cowslip*.

Again the following morning the *Cowslip* towed them out, and they remained all day, busily sounding and marking with buoys. They did not get back to ship until 7:30 p.m.

They went out toward Pelican Pass once more on July 29. That day the *Hartford's* crew was engaged in getting up starboard sheet chains and hanging them over the side to protect the ship from shells fired from Fort Morgan. Again in daylight on the 30th, Watson's boat crews were out marking locations.

On the 31st Confederate gunboats could be seen moving in behind Fort Morgan. That night Watson led an expedition into the darkness to feel for torpedoes. He was in a large cutter, armed and equipped for action, moving with muffled oars. It was 5:30 in the morning when they returned to their ships.

The following night Watson continued his dangerous task, and repeated it on the 2d, going out so far this time that he was able to return with five deserters from Fort Gaines.

At 8:15 p.m. August 3, Watson started on his final venture after torpedoes. With him went Alexander McKinley, Farragut's secretary, as well as Pilot Freeman. They were transported in two boats from the *Hartford* and the second cutter from the USS *Manhattan*, the latter commanded by Acting Ensign C. W. Snow. At 9:10 signal lights began flashing from the forts. The human mine destroyers wondered if they had been discovered. But no gunfire followed, and they worked on through the hours of darkness, boring holes to deactivate some of the explosives, sinking others. They started toward their ships at daylight and were all back on board by 7:05 a.m.

AUGUST 4 was spent in final preparations for battle. Farragut had issued instructions weeks ahead: "Strip your vessels and prepare for the conflict. Send down all your superfluous spars and rigging. Trice up or remove the whiskers. Put up the splinter nets on the starboard side, and barricade the wheel and steersman with sails and hammocks. Lay chains or sand bags on the deck over the machinery, to resist a plunging fire. Hang the sheet chains over the side, or make any other arrangement for security that your ingenuity may suggest."

For some time Farragut had been working out the battle plans with little wooden blocks shaped like boats that he had had a carpenter trim for him. He experimented with these on a table on which the points of the compass had been traced. As finally decided, he would go in with 14 wooden vessels and four ironclads. The wooden ships would be lashed together in pairs, so that one could float the other in case it became disabled. In advancing, the fleet would be under low steam, on the flood tide of the morning, with a light southwest wind, the ironclads on the east next to Fort Morgan centering their attention on the *Tennessee*, while the wooden gunboats toward the west would be prepared to go after the remainder of the little Confederate fleet as soon as they were past the forts.

At some time during the 4th, Farragut wrote his wife: "I am going into Mobile Bay in the morning, if God is my leader . . . My great mortification is that my vessels, the ironclads, were not ready to have gone in yesterday. The Army landed last night, and are in full view of us this morning, and the *Tecumseh* has not yet arrived from Pensacola . . ." Before sunset the *Tecumseh*, a fairly new, single-turreted monitor, appeared.

AT 3 A.M. ON THE 5TH Farragut stirred his fleet. Hammocks were stowed and breakfast served. A Coston light glowing in the center of the assembly of ships was signal for activity. So were red and green lights on the flagship. As the sailors went about their duties, some of them saw a comet flare up and bear northeast, along the line of their advance, and they wondered if it implied some warning from the Almighty.

Fog delayed an early start, and so did the matter of lashing the vessels together. Farragut had wanted to lead in the *Hartford*, but his officers convinced him—erroneously, he later commented—that the *Brooklyn*, equipped with mine remover, should go in front.

At dawn a light breeze came on, scattering the fog and making for a bright, sunny August day. Later the wind stiffened, blowing from the west, and Farragut and others noted that it would take the smoke from the fleet's guns directly into the eyes of the men in Fort Morgan.

Taking the lead, the *Brooklyn* started moving at a quarter to six. Cheers rang loudly across the water on a day that would make history. Scarcely a man on either side could fail to realize the grave disparity in numbers that marked the impending battle. Farragut's fleet, including the vessels left behind, totaled 30, armed with 252 guns and manned by 3,000 men. The Confederates had a lone ironclad and three little gunboats, armed with 22 guns and manned by 470 men, not counting the guns and the garrisons in the forts. The gunboats were of hasty construction, plated with light iron around their boilers and machinery. The first shot was fired by one of the ironclads, the *Tecumseh*, at 6:22 a.m. It exploded over Fort Morgan. The fort replied at 7:06 a.m. Soon the firing was general.

AS SHE NEARED the fort, the *Brooklyn* stopped, her commander, Captain James Alden, disturbed by the fact that he was getting ahead of the ironclads. He signaled wildly, and Farragut answered: "Go ahead."

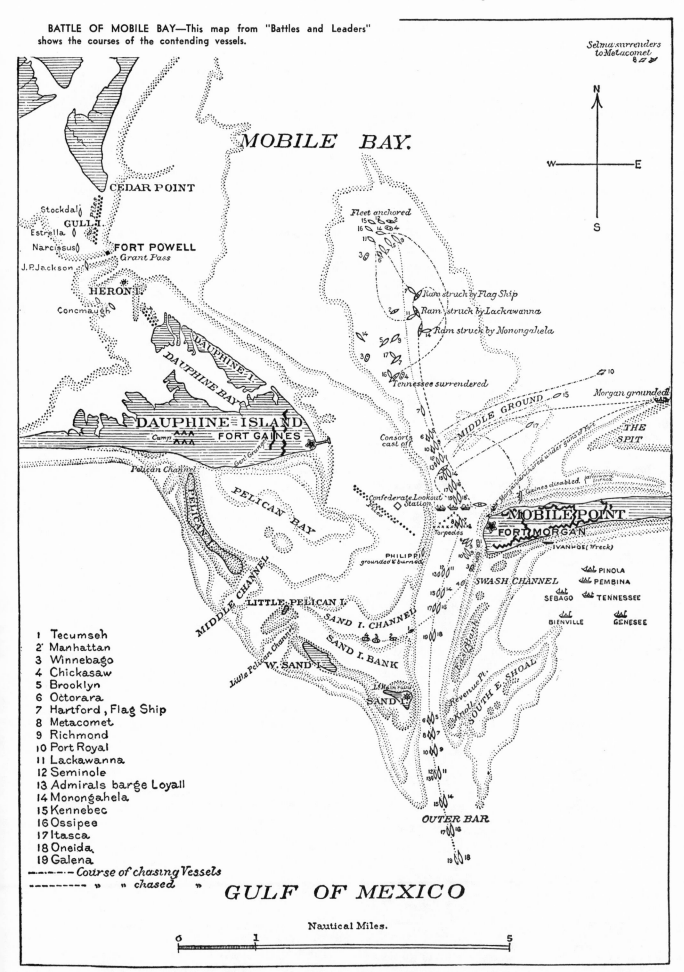

BATTLE OF MOBILE BAY—This map from "Battles and Leaders" shows the courses of the contending vessels.

MOBILE BAY.

Selma surrenders to Metacomet

GULF OF MEXICO

1 Tecumseh
2 Manhattan
3 Winnebago
4 Chickasaw
5 Brooklyn
6 Octorara
7 Hartford, Flag Ship
8 Metacomet
9 Richmond
10 Port Royal
11 Lackawanna
12 Seminole
13 Admirals barge Loyall
14 Monongahela
15 Kennebec
16 Ossipee
17 Itasca
18 Oneida
19 Galena

----·---- Course of chasing Vessels
---------- " " chased "

Nautical Miles.

But Alden began backing: he had seen a suspicious row of buoys in front of him and, not knowing whether they had been placed by friendly or hostile hands, was cautious about proceeding.

All at once there were cries from the men, and they looked off to the right to see the *Tecumseh* rise on end and disappear under the water. Down with her, victim of a mine, went all but a score or so of her crew, as well as her captain, Tunis Augustus M. Craven.

Farragut, his view blocked by the low-hanging smoke from the guns, climbed the rigging of the mainmast as far as the futtock shrouds. While a signal quartermaster ignored his protests and tied a rope around him to keep him from falling, he looked out upon the *Brooklyn*, still backing and starting.

He called to Pilot Freeman in the maintop directly above him: "How deep is the water to the left of the *Brooklyn*?"

"Deep enough for the *Hartford* to pass!" yelled back Freeman.

"I will take the lead," Farragut shouted.

Someone reminded him of the torpedoes.

"Damn the torpedoes!" he cried. "Full speed ahead!"

The *Hartford*, at his signal, swung to the left, to the west of the red buoy, over the ground where boat crews at night had fished so diligently for the water mines. The other ships of the fleet followed him.

As the *Hartford* sped up the bay, the *Tennessee* swung out into the main channel and followed her. Off on the starboard bow, the three little Confederate gunboats, *Gaines, Morgan,* and *Selma,* were demonstrating with the rapidity of their fire that their gunnery crews were well practiced. Of this period of the battle, Farragut later wrote in his log: "Very sharp engagement of the *Hartford* with the *Morgan, Gaines,* and *Selma.* Our men falling rapidly."

CHEERS RANG across the water, some Northern, some Southern. As the Union vessels neared the broader waters of the bay, some of the smaller of them broke away from the line and concentrated their attack on the three gunboats. This action went on for nearly an hour, even continuing during a sudden squall that came up out of the Gulf. But the disparity in numbers was decisive. After

a lively chase, the *Selma* was overtaken and forced to surrender. The *Gaines* was disabled and run ashore, and the *Morgan* was able to make it back under the protection of the fort, where she remained until after dark and then headed for Mobile, keeping close inshore.

The *Tennessee's* chase after the *Hartford* was brief. Easily outrun, the Confederate ironclad turned back toward the *Brooklyn* and the *Richmond.* When a hundred yards away from them, she sheered off and fired two shots at the *Brooklyn,* doing considerable damage. The *Richmond* answered with three broadsides, but they were ineffective.

The next vessel astern was the *Lackawanna,* and the *Tennessee* now headed toward it. The *Monongahela,* expecting this move, was prepared to ram, but the Confederate ship was maneuvered so that the blow was glancing. The *Tennessee* grazed the bow of the *Kennebec,* damaging her planking, after which she continued toward the end of the line and fired two broadsides into the *Oneida.* On past she ran, delivering a raking fire, and then steamed toward Fort Morgan and rounded the point.

The *Hartford* in the meantime continued four miles into the bay and dropped anchor. There she soon was joined by the other vessels of the fleet. It was shortly after 9 o'clock. Cooks began preparing a second breakfast for the men made hungry by battle action. Surgeons worked away over the wounded. Decks were cleared of debris and newly sanded. There was still fighting ahead.

IT WAS Franklin Buchanan, the Confederate officer whose lips curved in an arch around his chin when he was beset in battle, who made the next move. With a remark that "We can't let them off that way," he ordered his ship against the enemy.

A young eyewitness, one of the garrison on Dauphin Island, described the scene that followed:

Here comes the Tennessee! *Yes, here she comes—right for the enemy's fleet—they scatter before her—yes, three ironclads and fourteen wooden vessels mounting 200 guns would run from one—with six guns—did not shame and the scarcity of water prevent them . . . Now comes a fight that throws all others in the shade. I have gazed, as upon a picture, upon the greatest fight that ever took place. Well, they scatter before her. She makes for the flagship. She nearly reaches her, but Farragut glides from in front of her prow . . . The bay for a mile around is boiling with the ricochet of shot and shell. The* Brooklyn *moves past, delivers her broadside, then the* Hartford, *followed by the* Richmond, *but that is nothing. They make no impression.*

The *Tennessee* moved awkwardly. The *Monongahela,* with a false iron prow, struck her amidships, going at full speed, but no damage was done to the ironclad. The *Lackawanna* delivered a similar blow, causing the Confederate ram to lurch to one side.

The two flagships met bow to bow and grated against each other as they passed. The *Hartford* poured a broadside into the *Tennessee,* but the solid shot merely dented her sides and ricocheted into the air. The Confederate vessel, because of defective primers, was able to fire only one gun, powder from which blackened the side of the wooden ship. The shell fired went through her berth deck, killing five men and wounding eight.

MOBILE BAY LIGHTHOUSE—This drawing from "Battles & Leaders" shows ruins of the lighthouse that stood at the entrance to Mobile Bay. The entrance was guarded by Fort Morgan, built of brick and strengthened with sandbags.

" TENNESSEE."   FORT MORGAN.   " HARTFORD."   " BROOKLYN."   SAND ISLAND LIGHT.

BATTLE OF MOBILE—This drawing from "Battles and Leaders" shows the early phase of the attack by the "Hartford," with its accompanying gunboats, on the CS ram "Tennessee."

Farragut leaped from the quarter-deck to the port quarter rail and held to the mizzen rigging. Again a rope was slipped around his waist to keep him from falling.

THE BATTLE was at its peak. The *Tennessee* was fighting the entire fleet beneath an August sun, and the men inside the ironclad were breathing powder smoke in an atmosphere approaching 120 degrees. Wounded were being brought below in increasing numbers.

As the *Hartford* turned to make for the ram, the *Lackawanna* struck the flagship amidships, crushing her planking and causing general confusion. Loosening the rope around his waist, Farragut stared over the side at the damage and, seeing the break was two feet above the water, ordered the ship full speed ahead.

Over on the *Tennessee* a shell struck the cover of a stern port, jamming it against the shield. While a machinist worked to remove the bolt of the cover, a shell struck directly above him and tore him into bits. One fragment of the shell struck Buchanan below the knee, breaking his leg.

No ship of that day could withstand for long the pounding the *Tennessee* was taking. Her flagstaff was shot away, and most of her smokestack was missing. The Union ships were firing 15-inch solid shot at her. The two quarter ports from which were fired the aftergun were jammed. Her gun primers repeatedly failed. And then a shot cut her rudder chains, so that she no longer could mind her helm.

When told of the condition of his ship, Buchanan, who had been taken below, gritted his teeth with pain and instructed: "Do the best you can, and when all is done, surrender."

The ship's captain, James D. Johnston, quickly hoisted a white flag. In answer, as if by general signal, the terrific cannonading ceased, and cheers burst over the water from the Federal fleet. The first shot that morning had been fired at 6:22 a.m. It was now 10 o'clock.

THE SURRENDER was quickly over. It made possible a reunion of old friends as Northerners and Southerners who had not seen one another for years shook hands over ships' rails. On the Union vessels, 172 had been killed and 170 wounded. The South's losses totaled 12 killed, 20 wounded, and 243 captured.

That night Farragut wrote his wife: "The Almighty has smiled upon me once more . . . It was a hard fight, but Buck met his fate manfully. After we passed the forts, he came up in the ram to attack me. I made at him, and ran him down, making all the others do the same. We butted and shot at him until he surrendered."

There were certain members of Farragut's crews, Lieutenant John Crittenden Watson among them, who knew that the Almighty had been smiling upon them for days. This was impressed upon them even more indelibly later that month when seamen continued to drag the bay for water mines. On one day in particular, they took out five, four of which were found to be harmless. This encouraged carelessness in handling the lethal obstructions, and on August 25 the inevitable happened. One of the mines exploded, killing five men and wounding nine others.

Mobile Bay--A Gallery of Photographs

TOP PHOTOGRAPH—Admiral Farragut with Captain Percival Drayton on the deck of the frigate USS "Hartford."

LOWER LEFT—Farragut's flagship, the "Hartford," at West Point during the coaling of his ships.

NEXT PAGE—Rear Admiral David G. Farragut, USN. (All three photos from Library of Congress.)

UPPER RIGHT—Admiral Franklin Buchanan, CSN, who formerly commanded the "Merrimack" (CSS "Virginia"). At Mobile Bay he commanded the Confederate naval forces. He was wounded aboard the "Tennessee." (U.S. Navy.)

LOWER RIGHT—CSS "Tennessee." This dreaded ram, built near Selma, Alabama, was 209 feet long, 48 feet wide, and had two 7-inch rifles and four 6.4 rifles. It was formidable because of its six-inch armor, and long, underwater ram. Vital defects were its poorly engineered port shutters, weak engines, and exposed steering chains. (Library of Congress.)

162

From Atlanta to the Sea

Farragut's occupation of Mobile Bay shut blockade runners out of the Confederacy's last major port in the Gulf. Along the Atlantic coast the South's principal blockade-running port was Wilmington, North Carolina, where the multiple entrances and treacherous shoals at the mouth of the Cape Fear River made the task of blockade ships difficult. A few blockade runners also still managed to slip in and out of Charleston and Savannah. But Sherman would soon close down the latter port by capturing it from the rear as part of his famous march from Atlanta to the sea.

Savannah as such was not the primary goal of Sherman's campaign. Rather it was the point where he intended to establish contact with the Union fleet and obtain supplies after his army of 62,000 men cut loose from its base and smashed its way through the interior of Georgia. After capturing Atlanta, Sherman expelled the civilian population and turned the city into a military base. Knowing that it would be impossible to dislodge the Yankees by attacking them, Confederate General John B. Hood decided to take his army north toward Chattanooga, breaking up the single-track railroad that supplied Union forces in Atlanta. It was an effective strategy because it forced Sherman to send most of his army after Hood. During October the two armies skirmished and maneuvered back over much of the territory they had fought over from May to July. The Yankees finally drove Hood into Alabama. Sherman was content to leave him there, or even to let him invade Tennessee. For Sherman had sent George Thomas to take command of 60,000 Union troops in Tennessee, more than enough to deal with anything that Hood's 40,000 might try.

Sherman was frustrated by having to remain inactive or go on the defensive after capturing Atlanta. This was no way to win a war, he believed. He pleaded with Grant to turn him loose for a mobile campaign through Georgia. Though this would mean cutting loose from his base of supplies, it was better than skirmishing all over north Georgia to protect his precarious supply line. If there was enough food in Georgia to feed the state's population of almost a million, Sherman anticipated no difficulty in finding and taking enough to feed his army. "If I turn back now, the whole effect of my campaign will be lost," Sherman wired Grant. "It will be a physical impossibility to protect the [rail]roads, now that Hood, Forrest, Wheeler, and the whole batch of devils, are turned loose. . . . By attempting to hold the roads, we will lose a thousand men monthly and will gain no result." But if he could "move through Georgia, smashing things to the sea," said Sherman, "instead of being on the defensive, I would be on the offensive. . . . I can make the march, and make Georgia howl!"

Sherman's proposal rested not only on his conception of military strategy, but also on a grasp of what in the twentieth century would be called psychological warfare. Sherman had a more realistic—and ruthless—perception of the kind of total war the Civil War had become than did any of his contemporaries. "We are not only fighting hostile armies, but a hostile people," he wrote. Defeat of southern armies was not enough; the railroads, factories, and farms that fed them must be destroyed; the will of the civilian population that sustained the armies must be crushed. "If we can march a well-appointed army right through [Jefferson Davis's] territory, it is a demonstration that we have a power which Davis cannot resist. . . . We cannot change the hearts and minds of those people of the South, but we can make war so terrible that generations would pass away before they would again appeal to it."

Troops such as Judson Kilpatrick's cavalry earned the hatred of Georgians by their destructive foraging during Sherman's march to the sea. (Battles and Leaders of the Civil War)

Sherman convinced Grant and Lincoln. They turned him loose to make Georgia howl. Sherman's hard-handed veterans marched out of Atlanta on November 15 after burning everything of military value—and much else—in the city. Through Georgia they cut a swath fifty miles wide on their trek of 285 miles to Savannah and the sea. Behind them they left precious little in the way of material or psychological resources to sustain any further Confederate war effort. And, yes, they pillaged a great deal of private property as well—though not as much as southern myth has recorded. Nevertheless, Sherman's march did make Georgia howl. And it demonstrated to the world that the North had a power the South could no longer resist.

—James M. McPherson

SHERMAN'S SAVANNAH CAMPAIGN

by Richard McMurry

A view of the Savannah River as Sherman's troops saw it. The photographer, George N. Barnard, followed Sherman's army from Tennessee to Atlanta, and from Atlanta to the sea. (Library of Congress)

Eighteen miles above its mouth, the Savannah River bends gracefully from southeast to east, flowing past high bluffs. On those bluffs, in 1733 English humanitarian James Oglethorpe proclaimed the founding of Georgia, Britain's thirteenth North American colony. And for almost a century and a half Oglethorpe's settlement there, Savannah, remained the most important city in it.

It became a magnet for merchants, manufacturers, seafaring traders, and railroads that buffered gentle Georgia plantation life from the sea. It also became a city familiar with war. Built first by English convicts and debtors, its men left to follow Oglethorpe and defend their land against the Spanish in the 1740s. In the American Revolution, while British troops occupied the city, its men left to fight for independence. And with the spark of civil war in 1861, embracing its third government in less than 100 years, its men enthusiastically marched away to another appointment with martial destiny. A community of 22,000 souls, its 14,000 white citizens were firm in their support of Confederate independence. Their support was put to the test just in time for the Christmas season, 1864.

With secession, spring 1861 found many of Savannah's men trotting off to fight in Virginia or Tennessee; it also found others turning to the defense of their city. Savannah's location made it vulnerable to attack from the sea and its importance ensured that capture or neutralization would be an objective of Federal military operations. In these early, optimistic days thought and effort were directed toward defending Tybee Roads and Wassaw and Ossabaw sounds—three routes east and south of the city by which an enemy thrust from the sea could reach Savannah. Confident, city Confederates quickly established a series of forts, batteries, and marine obstructions to close this "lacework of rivers and creeks." It would be their last act of self-assurance.

Later that year Federals established a base at Port Royal on the South Carolina coast, thirty miles to the northeast. In April 1862, they captured Georgia's unassailable Fort Pulaski at the mouth of the Savannah River. Impervious to shells, built under the talented hands of engineers like Robert E. Lee, it was to have been the city's salvation.

The collapse of Pulaski fanned Southern fears for Savannah's safety. And with Federals hovering at the river's mouth, its importance as a haven for the blockade-runners who kept the Confederacy supplied was in jeopardy. As long as Union warships lurked outside the city's port, ships could only occasionally slip in with goods. Capture seemed imminent. But this soon degenerated into a war of wills. Unionists overestimated Rebel strength and lacked the nerve to attack the city directly. For two and a half years they only stirred up occasional skirmishes on nearby islands, creeks, and rivers. And for two and a half years the city's defenders kept a close watch on the southern approaches.

It was not until late 1864 that Savannah became a definite Federal target, just one in a series of cities in the path of Major General William T. Sherman's planned scourge through the South. From Atlanta, he and 62,000 men readied themselves for a march to Savannah to establish a secure supply base from which they could later conduct operations against Rebel forces in Virginia. All their telegraphic communication with their own lines would be purposely severed; they would campaign on to their objective without aid. And they would converge on the target city from the northwest, not from the south as the Confederates had anticipated.

Sherman divided his troops into two "wings." Major General Oliver O. Howard took command of two corps that would make up the Right Wing, while Sherman appointed Major General Henry W. Slocum in the same capacity to head two corps as the Federal Left Wing. Howard's corps commanders were Major General Peter J. Osterhaus, in charge of the XV Corps, and Major General Frank P. Blair, commanding the XVII Corps. Brigadier General Jefferson C. Davis of the XIV Corps and the XX Corps' Brigadier General Alpheus S. Williams served as Slocum's subordinates in the Left Wing. A pontoon train and a force of engineers joined each wing, but artillery was reduced to a minimum. Sherman entrusted control of his all-important cavalry division to Brigadier General Judson Kilpatrick.

The opposing Confederate force was not as well-manned. The strong army that had opposed Sherman earlier in 1864 moved west and north, carrying the war into Tennessee. With that army gone, the Southerners could deploy little opposition to Sherman. A few thousand Georgia militia under Major General Gustavus W. Smith, along with some local defense troops and a few brigades of cavalry under Major General Joseph Wheeler remained at Lovejoy's Station below Atlanta to observe Sherman's actions. That was the extent of the Confederate force—perhaps 8,000 men.

In mid-November Sherman began his "March to the Sea." Kilpatrick's cavalry and Howard's infantry started south toward Macon, while Slocum's wing headed east toward Augusta. Sherman's immediate objective was Milledgeville, southeast of Atlanta, and the general's methods confused his opponents and divided their efforts. The Rebels were fooled by Sherman's apparent movements against different objectives.

Smith's militia fell back to Macon. But on November 20, the Federals abandoned the feint on Macon and turned east toward Milledgeville. Confederate Lieutenant General William J. Hardee, commanding at Savannah, whose authority had been extended to central Georgia, realized by November 21 that Macon was in no danger and ordered the militia east to stand between Sherman and Augusta. Hardee's order brought on the only serious fight during the March to the Sea. On November 22, Brigadier General Pleasant J. Phillips' militia (three brigades plus several miscellaneous units) marched east from Macon and collided with Brigadier General Charles C. Walcutt's brigade, the rear guard of the XV Corps, near Griswoldville. Phillips, "with more courage than discretion," attacked Walcutt, whose brigade lurked behind rail and log works on a strong hill, its flanks protected by swamps. The battle was, as one writer noted, "unnecessary, unexpected, and utterly unproductive of any good." Phillips lost 51 killed and 472 wounded; Federal losses

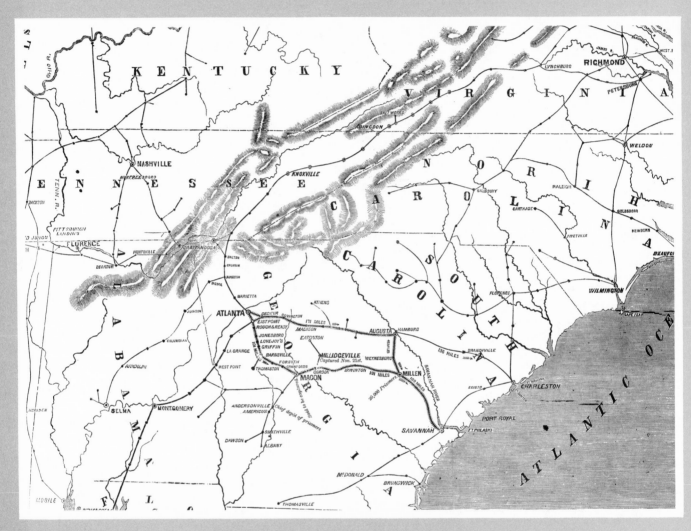

Map depicting "Sherman's advance across the Southern states." (Frank Leslie's
Illustrated Newspaper)

were fewer than 100. The militia fell back to Macon; the Yankees concentrated in the vicinity of Milledgeville.

On November 24, Sherman moved eastward toward the Ogeechee River, skirmishing occasionally with Wheeler's cavalry. On November 29, the Yankees were in Louisville, a few miles east of the Ogeechee. And by December 3, Sherman had reached Millen, seventy miles northwest of Savannah and sixty-five miles from the Union base at Port Royal. There the Charleston *Mercury* reported Port Royal Yankees were "throwing up signal rockets, and balloons with calcium lights attached" to signal the approaching army.

While Sherman's "Promenade militaire," as General Williams called it, was under way, the Confederates intensified their efforts to hold Savannah. Work began on fortifications west of the city, and reinforcements came in from Georgia and the Carolinas. G. W. Smith's Georgia militia had to make the most arduous journey to join the defenses. On November 25, the militia, still at Macon licking its wounds after the clash at Griswoldville, was ordered to move on Savannah through Albany and Thomasville. The long trek involved a train trip south to Albany, a sixty-mile march overland to Thomasville, and another slow train ride to Savannah.

Even as Smith's men rode from Thomasville, the actual struggle for Savannah had already started. On November 11, while he still communicated with the North, Sherman requested that the Federal troops on the South Carolina coast break the railroad between Charleston and Savannah in early December. On November 29, Major General John G. Foster, commander of the Department of the South, sent Brigadier General John P. Hatch with 5,500 troops to Boyd's Neck on the Broad River, some thirty-five miles northeast of Savannah. Once established on Boyd's Neck, Hatch would be only ten miles from the railroad at Grahamville. A Yankee seizure of that railroad would make it impossible for Hardee to hold Savannah and might make his escape more difficult.

Overly cautious, Hatch spent the day fortifying his position on Boyd's Neck. Only a few companies of the 3d South Carolina Cavalry were in the area to oppose him. But when he moved forward at 7:30 a.m. the next day, he found his way blocked by a much larger group of Rebels.

The leading elements of Smith's militia had reached Savannah at 2:00 a.m. that morning. Before the men could get off the train, Hardee ordered them on to Grahamville to meet Hatch's force. To take the militiamen out of the state was against Georgia law, and Smith had authority to withdraw them from Confederate service if they were ordered out of Georgia. However, after conferring with Hardee, Smith was convinced that "for the purposes intended it was right and proper" that the movement be undertaken. He thereupon ordered his "jaded" troops on into South Carolina. There was some grumbling, but the order was obeyed.

By 8:00 a.m., Smith's lead brigade was pouring off the train at Grahamville and a second train was not far behind. Other rein-

Brigadier General John P. Hatch. An outnumbered Confederate force frustrated his efforts to destroy the railroad link between Savannah and Charleston (U.S. Army Military History Institute)

Camp near Vining Station, Ga.
Nov. 8th, 1864

As the mail is going out soon, thought I would write you a few lines to let you
know that I am well and expecting to get our little greenbacks soon. Have been on a long [trip]
for the last month chasing up Mr. [General John Bell] Hood. [Major General George] Thomas
has got an army up there now that will take care of him and we came back near Atlanta.
Expect will have to trikie [sic] out for Savannah or some other sea port far in the South. Have
been living on the country for the last month and it suits me first rate. It is my best hotel.

The weather is quite cool now. [It] rains pretty often and is very chilly. If we start out
on another campaign[,] it will be cold for [we] cannot carry clothes enough to keep warm.
But where there is plenty of rail fences there is no trouble in keeping warm. The first thing
after going into camp and stacking arms is to pile . . . rails for a fire, and boards to sleep
on. We make the houses and barns suffer. When we are on the march there is a guard at every
house while the column is passing. No one is allowed to go inside of any house. [If caught
he] will be put under arrest and made to march in front of the general's headquarters [Brigadier
General Joseph A.J. Lightburn] six hours with knapsacks on after going to camp. He is an
old tyrant. The boys all hate him worse than a Reb.

It is said that the 20th A.C. is attached to the Army of the Tennessee, and Thomas has
got another corps of conscripts. Bully for the conscripts.

It is reported that the Army of the Tenn. is going to Savannah, and going to start
as soon as the troops can be payed off and get clothed. It will be a gay trip when we get down
there. [We] can get all the fresh oysters we want.

Our orderly sergeant is at home, and George Wilcox. If you see any of them[,]
see if they will not bring down me a pair of boots, some tobacco, and a pair of suspenders. [I]
don't know how it will be about sending money home. Am afraid it will not be safe to
express it on account of the Rebs cutting the railroad.

Wellwood, John Dougherty, and Captain are well and stand the storms first rate. John
D. came to the company about a month ago, [he] is all right again.

I must bring my letter to a close. It is [al]most supper time and I must go and make
hoecake or a pone as the Southern ladies call it. Stir up a little meal, cold water, and a little salt,
then bake it on an old-fashioned bake kettle. What then? (Eat it, of course).

From
Andrew Mc

*Sergeant Andrew McCornack of Company I of the 127 Illinois, winner of the
Medal of Honor, wrote about his experiences during Sherman's march to the sea
(above). Sergeant Eugene A. "Casey" McWayne, also of the 127th Illinois, wrote
home about his arrival at Savannah (opposite). (Both courtesy of Wiley Sword)*

Near Savannah, Ga.
Dec. 19th, 1864

Dear Mother & Sisters:

    . . . We arrived here safe & sound. We had a pleasant trip, leaving Atlanta the 15th of Nov., arriving here the 8th of Dec. (that is the troops). We did not cross the river until the 11th. We had plenty of yams, molasses, fresh pork & mutton, corn meal, chickens, turkeys & geese. We lacked for nothing. It was a march of plenty. The people along the road would tie their horses and mules in swamps, drive their cattle, sheep & hogs onto islands in the swamp. Buried all of their clothes, corn, salt pork, jewelery [*sic*], money (the most of it Confederate money)—well, in fact, everything they had in the house except themselves. But they were found by the D-- Yankees, after all. You would ask how the Yankees knew where it was. Well, in the first place, there was about 60,000 Yankees. They occupied a tract of land about 40 miles in width on the whole march. Well, they would come across a pretty soft piece of ground. The first thing they would do would be to pull the ramrod out of their guns and run it down into the ground until it struck something that sounded like a board, or iron. Then they would commence digging for it. I dug up a valise on a plantation where we stopped overnight, and found $16,300.00 in Confederate money. I will [send] a $5 bill home. Well, I almost forgot one thing that will be amusing. The boys were hunting around a plantation to see what they could find. Well, they came across some fresh dirt, so they pushed their ramrods down. It struck a board so they commenced digging. Well, to their surprise someone beneath the board yells out, "Hold on, let me *out*, I will surrender." Well, they dug on till they could get hold of the board and pulled it out. And there was a *Johnny*. He had dug a hole in the ground, placed a board over it with a hole in it, so he could get air. Then [he] covered it over with dirt, but was careful to keep the hole open to get a supply of fresh air. This was done by the aid of the women folks, I suppose. You may bet he was a scared *Johnny*. We are having oysters & fish a plenty. Oysters in the shell, of course, for we have to rake them out of their beds ourselves. We are camped on a plantation owned by Dr. Chevers. He had about 2,000 acres of rice in the shock when we came here, but we are gathering [it] as fast as 2 or 3 hundred 6 mule teams can draw it. We have 4 teams drawing to feed our cattle. We have about 800 head now, so you can't say but what I have walked in the rice field, or raked up the oyster beds, and have seen salt water. Just think of having an oyster supper at anytime you please, and just as many as you please. [Major General William T.] Sherman advances his lines today. I suppose I will spend the holidays in or near Savannah. . . . I have seen a full blooded African on this march. We have a dance here on this plantation [al]most every night. There is between 40 & 50 little Negroes . . . , they pat, dance, & sing at the same time. It is worth more to see them than all [of] your theatres or circuses, or prayer meetings in the whole North.

                              My respects to all
                                 Eugene [A. McWayne]
                                 [127th Illinois Volunteers]

Our regt. has about 200 cows to milk. Whenever that [we] want our milk—Don't go good in oyster soup, oh no, I guess not, or a little corn bread & milk is bad to eat too, ain't it.

forcements from Charleston were on hand and more were on the way from North Carolina. Skirmishing had already begun between Hatch's advance and the Rebel cavalry. Smith put his men into some light works on Honey Hill three miles south of the town. The road on which the Federals would come was a causeway that turned to the west (the right as seen from Smith's line), crossed a creek bordered by a marsh, and then ran for 150 yards across a cleared area to pass through the Confederate position. The underbrush was dense. Smith's men could not see the approaching Yankees until they rounded the bend in the road. Before the battle ended, Smith had about 1,400 men and five pieces of artillery to hold this position.

Hatch's advance—part of Brigadier General Edward E. Potter's brigade with the 127th New York—pushed forward along the causeway with "a thick jungle, almost impassable for infantry" on the left and a ditch-scarred field on the right. Southerners set fire to the broomsedge in the field to confine the Unionists to the road. Rebel cavalry delayed Potter's march, and it was late morning before the Federal advance rounded the bend in the road and found Smith's fortified men waiting for them.

The battle that followed was simple. Hatch managed to get Potter's brigade into line and later advanced Colonel Alfred S. Hartwell's brigade in another line. The Federals, however, could make no progress. Potter reported that "the dense undergrowth and deep swamps" hampered the advance of his right and "the deep swamp and abatis in front of the enemy's works" stopped his left. Hartwell reported that the Confederate grape and canister fired down the road "became insupportable." It was not a good day for the Federals. Hartwell, especially, had a bad time. Early in the battle he took a musket ball in the hand. Soon, his voice had "nearly given out." As he rounded the bend in the road, an exploding shell killed his horse and the beast fell on top of him. When Hartwell was pulled from beneath the horse, he was struck in the heel by a "shot that burned my ankle," he said. Next, a spent grape shot knocked him down and stunned him. And finally, a musket ball struck him in the back. "I regret extremely to say," he wrote later, "[that] I was unable to give further orders or superintendence and was taken to the rear."

About 4:00 p.m., Hatch abandoned the fight and began to pull back. By 7:30, the Yankees had retreated from the field and were falling back to Boyd's Neck. Hatch reported a loss of almost 750 killed, wounded, and missing. Smith's casualties were fewer than fifty.

More Confederate reinforcements soon reached the Honey Hill area, and on December 1 Smith's militiamen started back to Georgia to defend Savannah. Protection of the railroad as far to the north as Pocotaligo was entrusted to Major General Samuel Jones. In effect, Jones' line became a second front of the Savannah defenses where the two sides struggled for possession of the railroad. Skirmishing and small unit actions continued on this front as long as Hardee held Savannah. Although the Northerners gained several positions from which they could shell the railroad, they were never able to sever the Rebels' communications with Charleston.

Savannah's waterfront during Sherman's occupation. Photograph by George N. Barnard. (National Archives)

Failure to cut the railroad was a lost opportunity to trap Hardee. And responsibility for the failure rested clearly on the Northern commanders in the Department of the South. Though Foster was then suffering from an old injury and was unable to exercise effective leadership in the field, his troop's timid conduct of operations was inexcusable.

Meanwhile, work continued on the Savannah defenses. The Southerners had no real expectation that their 18,000 troops could save the city from an assault or even withstand a long siege. Instead they seem to have hoped that resistance would compel Sherman to bypass Savannah as a supply base on the coast. But Hardee's defense plans were complicated by the hope of keeping the railroad intact. The tracks swung to the northwest from Savannah and crossed the river about twenty miles upstream. The Confederate commander therefore chose an "outer defense" designed to cover the railroad. The line began at the river above the railroad bridge and ran southwest to the Great Ogeechee, passing behind a swamp. The Rebels built detached works along this line, placed light artillery in position, and felled trees across the roads.

Sherman left Millen on December 4, advancing with three of his corps along the tongue of land between the Savannah and Ogeechee rivers and skirmishing occasionally with troops sent out by Hardee to delay the Northerners. The area was flat and interlaced with sluggish streams; the soil was sandy. The XV Corps moved down the right bank of the Ogeechee.

The advance of the XV Corps outflanked Hardee's "outer defense" and forced the Rebels back to the "inner line." The right of this line rested on the Savannah River at Williamson's Plantation north of the city, near the upper end of Hutchinson's Island. The position stretched southwest across higher ground to the impassable Little Ogeechee. Creeks, swamps, and flooded rice fields covered much of its front. The causeways leading across these low areas into the city were cut so that several feet of water covered the entire area. Fortifications had been built to command the approaches to the city, and the Rebels occupied the lower end of Hutchinson's Island to protect their right flank.

G. W. Smith's Georgia militiamen held the right of this line from the river around to the Central Railroad. Troops under Major General Lafayette McLaws held the center, and the right was held by the men under Major General Ambrose R. Wright. Wright's left rested upon the Little Ogeechee near the Atlantic & Gulf Railroad bridge. The line was about ten miles long. The Confederates had to man the defenses below the city as well as Fort McAllister, a small earth work at Genesis Point on the south bank of the Great Ogeechee that Hardee had decided to hold.

The decision to fight for McAllister was a desperate one. The little fort, completely isolated after Hardee abandoned the outer defense line, had several times demonstrated its ability to hold off the Federal navy. As long as it was in Confederate hands the

Federals would be denied use of the Ogeechee. To abandon McAllister would be to hand Sherman a perfect line of supply for an attack on or siege of Savannah. Hardee really had no choice; he probably hoped McAllister could hold out long enough for Sherman to abandon the effort against Savannah and go elsewhere to reach the sea.

The Savannah River Squadron of the Confederate navy was also active in the defense of the city. After abandoning his "outer line," Hardee sent Commodore W. W. Hunter upriver with part of the squadron to destroy the railroad bridge. Hunter accomplished this mission, but upon returning, found the river closed by Sherman's artillery. In the ensuing fight, Hunter's ship *Ida* was disabled, captured, and destroyed, and the other vessels were compelled to retire upriver to Augusta. The remainder of the squadron, including the heavy gunboat *Savannah*, was in the river at and below Savannah.

On December 10, the day *Ida* was captured, Sherman's infantry closed on the Savannah defenses. Rifle and artillery fire broke out along the line as the Northerners sought to envelop Hardee's position. Within a day or two Sherman had his men deployed on a line parallel to Hardee's with the XX Corps on his left, then the XIV, the XVII, and the XV which had been brought to the north side of the Great Ogeechee.

Sherman, realizing that the area could not long supply his army, decided against an immediate assault on the city and turned his attention to opening communication with the fleet and establishing a line of supply. For the next several days, while small unit actions flared along the lines, the most important developments were those that took place at Fort McAllister.

On December 9, the Northerners built a pontoon bridge across Ogeechee, and on the 10th they began rebuilding King's Bridge, the major highway crossing about a mile above the Atlantic & Gulf Railroad the Confederates had destroyed. While

Sherman's objective at the end of the road, Savannah and its Oglethorpe Barracks. (U.S. Military History Institute)

On arrival, Sherman made himself comfortable in some of Savannah's finest homes. He is shown here in the entrance hall of one of them. Drawing by William Waud. (Library of Congress)

work was under way, Sherman swung Kilpatrick's cavalry to his right. The blue horsemen crossed the Ogeechee and reconnoitered the area around Fort McAllister on December 12, reporting that only about 200 Southerners defended the work. Kilpatrick then moved south to scout along the coast and attempt to contact the fleet.

King's Bridge was completed on December 12, and Sherman ordered a heavy force of infantry across the river to deal with McAllister. Brigadier General William B. Hazen's division of the XV Corps was sent to capture the fort. At dawn the next day, Hazen crossed King's Bridge and turned eastward, marching down Bryan Neck to approach the fort from the rear. About noon Hazen halted some two miles from the fort and sent forward a party of scouts who surprised and captured a Rebel outpost. From the prisoners Hazen learned details of the fort's defenses and the fact that a field of "land torpedoes" was buried across the road on which he was marching.

Removal of the torpedoes delayed Hazen's advance, and it was several hours before his men were close enough to the fort for the assault. But then Hazen threw out sharpshooters to annoy the Rebels. Northern artillery across the Ogeechee shelled the fort, and he prepared to begin the attack. Three regiments from Hazen's second brigade, the 47th and 54th Ohio and 111th Illinois, deployed on his left; three from his third brigade, the 48th and 90th Illinois and 70th Ohio, were in the center; and three from his first brigade, the 30th Ohio, 6th Missouri, and 116th Illinois, were on the right. The completed line stretched from the river above the fort to the river below, about 600 yards from the Confederate defenses.

The general began his assault about 4:45 p.m. But the struggle was a short one, as the Northerners forced their way through the obstructions around the fort and climbed over the parapet. The garrison, commanded by Major George W. Anderson, put up a good fight but was simply overwhelmed. The battle was over within a few minutes. Southern casualties were 14 killed, 21 wounded, and 195 captured. The Federals lost 24 killed and 110 wounded. Most Union casualties came from the explosion of the dread unfound torpedoes—shells that had been buried along the direct approaches to the fort. Eleven heavy guns, a 10-inch mortar, twelve field guns, and sixty tons of ammunition were captured.

Sherman and Howard had been impatiently watching McAllister from the roof of a shed several miles upstream and on the opposite side of the river. A signal station at the mill was in communication with Hazen. Just as the assault began, the station also opened communication with a Federal vessel in the river below the fort. After McAllister fell, Sherman and Howard climbed into a skiff and made their way to the captured fort, where they dined with Hazen and the captured Major Anderson. They then continued downstream to a boat that proved to be the tug *Dandelion*. From the tug, Sherman sent off messages to the North and returned to the fort for the night.

Captain James H. Polk of Wheeler's 6th Tennessee Cavalry (above). His unit harassed Sherman's marching army in Georgia. (CWTI Collection) Private John Rigby, Company D, 35th Georgia Infantry. He represents one of the many Georgians who fought with Lee's Army of Northern Virginia on "foreign soil." (Patricia Mullinax Collection)

The Federal commander had not slept long when he was awakened by a messenger who brought word that Foster had arrived on a steamboat anchored below the fort and was extremely anxious to confer with Sherman. Foster's old wound prevented his leaving the vessel, so the weary Sherman made a second trip downriver to meet Foster and Rear Admiral John A. Dahlgren. From those officers Sherman learned on December 14 of the situation along the Charleston-Savannah Railroad. Plans were made to bring heavy siege guns from Port Royal to use against the Savannah defenses, and Sherman went back to his army.

The capture of Fort McAllister solved the Federals' supply problem. A wharf and warehouse were soon built at King's Bridge, the obstructions were removed from the river, and by December 16 ships arrived from Port Royal with supplies to be moved by wagon up the Ogeechee Road for the troops before Savannah. The city's capture was only a matter of time. The question was whether Sherman would also conquer Hardee's troops.

After December 13, the center of action shifted to the extreme left of the Northern line. There, late on December 11, three companies of the 3d Wisconsin reached Argyle Island, between Hutchinson's Island and the railroad bridge, and reinforcements soon joined them. Other Federals moved onto the northern end of Hutchinson's Island.

A week later, Colonel E. A. Carman's brigade of the XX Corps crossed from Argyle to the South Carolina bank and established a a strong position at Izard's Mill. However, the fields in South Carolina were flooded, and Carman soon found himself facing a strong line of Rebels, but unable to advance.

The importance of these maneuvers lay in the possibility that Sherman's left might be stretched from the river eastward to the Union Causeway that connected Savannah with Hardeeville, South Carolina. After the evacuation of the "outer line," this causeway was the Confederates' sole connection with South Carolina. At Hardeeville it connected with the railroad and the rest of the Confederacy.

While these maneuvers started, the Federals were preparing to attack Hardee's line. They built earthworks for the heavy guns that Sherman ordered shipped in from Port Royal, and Federal engineers worked to drain the rice fields before the Confederate line.

On December 17, Sherman sent Hardee a letter, promising to "grant liberal terms to the inhabitants and garrison" if they would surrender. If they would not, Sherman wrote, "I shall then feel justified in resorting to the harshest measures, and shall make little effort to restrain my army." Hardee replied the same day, refusing to surrender and mildly threatening to retaliate for any violation of the "rules of civilized warfare" that Sherman's men might commit.

Well aware of the danger to his only line of retreat and knowing that he could expect no reinforcements, Hardee began preparations to evacuate the city. The Confederates had to construct a crossing within the limits of their lines. So it was decided to build a pontoon bridge to Hutchinson's Island, a second bridge to Pennyworth Island, and a third to the South Carolina mainland. Finding themselves short of boats, the Confederates, working under the supervision of Lieutenant Colonel B. W. Frobel, used "rice-field flats," shallow skiffs each 75 to 80 feet long. Collected from plantations along the river, they were lashed end to end to serve as floats for the bridges. Railroad car wheels were used to anchor the flats into position, stringers were put across the flats, and planks from waterfront buildings were used to floor the structure. Rice straw was scattered on the crossing to deaden the sound.

Fog delayed the work, but by the evening of December 17 the bridge to Hutchinson's Island was completed. Three days later the other crossings were finished. Escape appeared possible.

The Confederates evacuated the city during the night of December 20-21. By 3:00 a.m. the rear guard was on Hutchinson's Island, and soon all the garrison was across. Rebel engineers cut the bridges loose and punched holes in the flats to prevent the Yankees from using them. And the ships of the Rebel Savannah Squadron were blown up to prevent their capture.

Sherman's men discovered the evacuation during the night and occupied the city early in the morning. But Sherman himself was not present for the victorious entry. He had gone to confer with Foster and did not get back to his army until that evening, when he found his men in possession of the city. As well as real estate, they had come into much of the heavy ordnance that had been collected for the city's defense, stores of all kinds, steamboats, railroad equipment, and thousands of bales of cotton. It had been a resounding coup.

Critics faulted Sherman for being overcautious and allowing Hardee to escape. However, in defense of his conduct, Sherman maintained that Grant was planning to order his troops shuffled from Savannah to Virginia by sea. Until logistic problems were resolved, he had to be in position to move rapidly to the coast for embarkation. It would have been unwise to commit too much strength on operations on the South Carolina end of his line. Furthermore, he asserted, Rebel gunboats in the river made an extension of his left "extra hazardous."

Despite the failure to capture the garrison, Sherman's Savannah Campaign resulted in severe damage to the Confederacy. Railroads and other property in Georgia had been wrecked, and Lee's army in Virginia was cut off from one of its major sources of supply. Sherman clearly demonstrated that the Federal government was able to march its armies at will through the heart of the dying Confederacy. And strategically, Sherman had placed a large, powerful army in a position from which it could move northward through the Carolinas and, if necessary, Virginia to help bring the war there to an end. Sherman was fulfiling a prophecy he had made some months earlier: "From the west, when our task (here) is done, we will make short work of Charleston and Richmond, and the impoverished coast of the Atlantic."

HOOD'S NASHVILLE CAMPAIGN

To Rescue the Confederacy by Campbell H. Brown
Bloody Franklin by Hugh F. Walker
The Battle of Nashville by Stanley F. Horn

To Rescue the Confederacy

by Campbell H. Brown

The Campaign for Atlanta, which resulted in General William T. Sherman's capture of the city from General John Bell Hood's Army of Tennessee, spawned two separate campaigns.

After some maneuvering in pursuit of Hood, Sherman moved back to Atlanta, burned it, and started his army south and east "to move through the bowels [of the Confederacy] and make a trail that would be visible for fifty years."

Hood, whether the idea was his own or Jefferson Davis', had an equally ambitious plan. It was to cross the Tennessee River, advance rapidly, overwhelm or bypass the scattered Federal garrisons in Tennessee, move through lightly held Kentucky, cross the Ohio River and go even as far as the Great Lakes, splitting off the Middle West from the rest of the United States and making the Yankees agree to a negotiated peace. As an alternative, he might swing east up the Ohio Valley and effect a junction with General Lee's Army of Northern Virginia. Together, the two armies would crush Grant and then turn and ruin the exhausted Sherman, then emerging from the swamps of inland Georgia.

Either of Hood's plans had a remote chance of success. But as things worked out, he had no opportunity to develop either.

After the final attempt at Jonesboro to drive Sherman from Atlanta, Hood moved to Lovejoy Station, 20 miles southwest. Here the army reorganized, then moved west and north to Palmetto where President

Nighttime march: General John Bell Hood leads his Confederate troops through a burning Georgia wood on the way to Tennessee in late 1864. (The Confederate Soldier in the Civil War)

Major General George H. Thomas was chosen to protect Nashville against Hood. (Battles and Leaders of the Civil War)

General John Bell Hood, who at age 33 was the youngest army commander of either side during the war. (CWTI Collection)

Jefferson Davis and Brigadier General Howell Cobb, ex-Governor of Georgia, visited it. Davis addressed the army on September 26. This speech was published in a Macon newspaper; Sherman had the entire speech telegraphed to the War Department. Davis promised the Army of Tennessee that it was not only going home, but it would plant its banners on the banks of the Ohio. Sherman was grateful for the information; now he could go about his own plans.

He left the defense of Tennessee in the capable hands of Major General George Henry Thomas. A Virginia-born officer of the Old Army, he had been major of the cavalry regiment whose lieutenant colonel was Robert E. Lee. At secession he remained loyal; thereafter his sisters, at mention of his name, would draw themselves up primly and announce, "We have no brother." He had never failed in an operation, beginning with his victory at Fishing Creek in January 1862, and in 1864 he commanded Sherman's largest army in the Atlanta Campaign.

To help Thomas, Sherman sent the IV Corps, under David S. Stanley, the XVI Corps, under Andrew Jackson Smith, and the XXIII Corps, under John McAllister Schofield. The IV Corps had been

part of Thomas' Army of the Cumberland; Schofield's XXIII had been practically an army in itself— The Army of the Ohio. There would be a delay, though, before the XVI could come to Tennessee. General Sterling Price was making things unhappy for the Federal command in the Trans-Mississippi Department, and Smith was to go there before coming to Tennessee to help Thomas.

To begin his new campaign, Hood moved northward toward Chattanooga; Sherman moved with him. Soon the two armies were back where they had been a hundred days before. Stevenson's division stormed Corse's Union blockhouse position at Allatoona and was repulsed; somebody wrote a song about the action, "Hold the fort, for I am coming"; a sort of "Praise the Lord and pass the ammunition" thing. Hood continued to move toward the Alabama line, apparently seeking a crossing over the Tennessee, and at the same time arranging for stores to make his move north. Hood, unlike Sherman, had no efficient supply line, and no stockpiles. He had to accumulate a backlog the hard way, mostly from Mississippi, using that part of the Memphis &

Charleston Railroad still in Confederate hands, and supplementing this with slow and costly wagon hauls. So the Army of Tennessee moved toward its railhead at Cherokee, Alabama, a good day's march from Decatur.

While this was going on, the Confederate regional command system was rearranged to put Hood under a higher commander. Davis created a new department, the Military Division of the West, and placed Pierre Gustave Toutant Beauregard in command. He was to have command over Hood's army, and the forces around Mobile and in Mississippi under Lieutenant General Richard Taylor. Beauregard actually did very little commanding. His last prominence in command had been at Shiloh in April 1862, after the death of Albert Sidney Johnston. Following the withdrawal to Corinth and thence to Tupelo, for reasons of health he had turned over command to Braxton Bragg. His subsequent service had been somewhat static, barring a very able defense of Charleston, and recently distinguished action against Butler near Richmond.

So now he turned up with Hood's army, and apparently learned of Hood's plans for the first time. He seemed not to have been impressed by the scheme; however, after telegraphic exchanges with Richmond, he established headquarters at Selma and moved over to the Gadsden area to be in closer touch with Hood.

Neither commander seemed to have relished this arrangement. Hood soon moved his army, without notifying Beauregard, to the Florence area, to be nearer his railhead. He could better cross the Tennessee here, since upriver gunboats could not get at him. Sherman, tired of chasing the Army of Tennessee, began moving back to Atlanta. Hood put down a pontoon bridge across the Tennessee and began crossing his army. Beauregard, who had by that time moved his command post to Florence, remained there.

In Tennessee the Federal command had followed closely Hood's movements. Stanley's IV Corps had moved to Chattanooga, then to Pulaski. (Smith's XVI Corps was still in Arkansas.) Schofield's XXIII Corps had moved first to Chattanooga, then had been hurriedly trundled up to Johnsonville as a result of Forrest's brilliant raid. Finding at Johnsonville only a discomfited garrison, a large acreage of smoking ruins, and sunken ships in the river, Schofield began returning his corps to Pulaski. It was there, except for most of Ruger's division, when Hood crossed the Tennessee.

Once across the river, Hood waited for Forrest, who arrived on November 17 in miserable weather with the jaded veterans of the Johnsonville and earlier Middle Tennessee and North Alabama raids.

On November 22, Hood started north. Alexander P. Stewart's corps headed for Lawrenceburg, Benjamin F. Cheatham's corps toward Waynesboro, while Stephen D. Lee took his corps toward a point between those two towns. Hood himself was with Stewart.

Thomas continued to build up his force. He was heartened to learn of the impending return of the XVI Corps from Arkansas. He had a new cavalry commander, the remarkable young James Harrison Wilson, who had served under Grant. As the invasion became imminent, Wilson moved to Pulaski to take personal charge of the cavalry operations there. His corps was not completely ready but it had greatly improved, even in the short time since Forrest's raid.

The orders originally given Schofield, at Pulaski, gave him the option of moving north and entrenching at Columbia. But with Hood approaching, Thomas ordered him to Columbia, leapfrogging his units as a precaution against an attack along his line of march.

Brisk cavalry action marked the Confederate advance from the Alabama line to the Columbia area. On the right, the divisions of Buford and Jackson drove Hatch's cavalry division through Lawrenceburg and Campbellsville and back on Pulaski.

On the left, Rucker's brigade of Chalmers' division, with Forrest himself present, chased Horace Capron's brigade through Henryville and Mt. Pleasant to the southern outskirts of Columbia, where the cavalry slammed up against intrenched infantry.

Schofield, thanks to the alertness of Major General Jacob D. Cox, 3d Division, XXIII Corps, had Columbia safe. Cox, by forced marches from the Pulaski Pike (US 31) along a road that ran east and west about three miles south of Columbia, had moved his people at the double to positions astride the Mt. Pleasant Pike (US 43) just north of Bigby Creek, and had them lightly fortified by 7:30 on the morning of the 24th, when Forrest drove Capron's harried troopers into his lines. The remainder of the XXIII Corps and the IV Corps followed the Pulaski Pike into the town, taking up positions prolonging Cox's line eastward; this line, after crossing the Pulaski Pike bent northward to Duck River. Cox's sector bent northward and westward to the river below the town.

While Cox was beating off attacks by Forrest, Schofield established an interior defensive line. This crossed the Mt. Pleasant Pike near the intersection of that pike with the present city street system (it was then the Hampshire Pike), and bent generally parallel to the initial defensive line. This line encompassed the then residential area of Columbia. There was only open farmland in the valley of Bigby Creek and

On October 5, Hood's troops assault a Federal position at Allatoona, Georgia, that protects Sherman's supply line to Atlanta. (Harper's History of the Great Rebellion)

to the south. During that day and the 25th, the new interior line was completely occupied, although Cox's division retained its original advanced position across the Mt. Pleasant Pike. There was violent artillery action by the Confederates and considerable skirmishing, during which some Federal units fell back short distances; but General T. J. Wood, whose 3d Division, IV Corps had been placed to cover the entire IV Corps sector as other units withdrew to the interior line, noted that by 2 p.m. on the 25th the Confederates had deployed only a single infantry division, doing most of the skirmishing with dismounted cavalry, a clear indication that Hood was merely demonstrating, with the intention of crossing Duck River elsewhere, or of side-slipping toward the Nashville & Chattanooga Railroad, about 50 miles to the east.

On the morning of the 26th, Schofield received Thomas' orders to hold the north bank of Duck River, keeping Hood south of the river until the Union forces could be concentrated to take the offensive, the orders indicating that A. J. Smith's force was arriving or about to arrive at Nashville. It had been raining all day, but Schofield now had a pontoon bridge across the river. That afternoon, he ordered

the bulk of his trains to the north bank, using this and the railroad bridge, and prepared to move infantry and artillery over after dark. However, the all-day rain had rendered the approaches to the two bridges practically impassable, so the crossing was postponed.

By evening of the 26th, leading infantry elements of the Army of Tennessee had deployed in front of Columbia, taking over from the cavalry. These were from Lee's corps. The next day they completed their deployment, with the right lapping over the Mt. Pleasant Pike. Cheatham's corps camped between the Mt. Pleasant and Pulaski Pikes, but near army headquarters, which was at Ashwood Hall, the residence of Colonel Andrew Polk. This stood a few hundred yards north of and across the Pulaski Pike from St. John's Church, at the intersection of the road to Ashwood.

Major General Patrick Ronayne Cleburne, the Irish-born commander of one of Cheatham's divisions, noted the beauty of the little church in its quiet grove. "If I should happen to die in battle," he said to his aide, "I should like nothing better than to be buried there." He was, after Franklin, along with Granbury and Strahl.

Stewart's corps was camped along the pike with its rear elements about two miles north of Mt. Pleasant.

Hood had lost the race to Columbia. He was disappointed but, he said later, he had a chance to use one of the maneuvers favored by Stonewall Jackson. He moved quickly, for he noted that Schofield had pulled his troops out of Columbia, across the river, following his trains, which were then moving north toward Franklin. He conferred with Forrest, who was familiar with the country between Columbia and Brentwood. Forrest needed little direction. Laying his plans carefully, on Monday morning, November 28 he moved his divisions across the river and to the east.

Hood assigned all the artillery with his army except two batteries to Lee's corps, which kept up pressure against the Federal positions south of Columbia. To anticipate: later, as Schofield withdrew from the town, Lee moved in behind him, halting only when he came to the bridges that Schofield had destroyed. Cheatham posted his division on Lee's right, his right resting on Duck River and his left on the Pulaski Pike. Stewart brought his corps into echelon behind Cheatham and Lee, his right on the Pulaski Pike.

On the 28th, none of Schofield's troops had yet left Columbia, except part of Wagner's division, detailed as train guard. The trains had moved north and the head of the wagon column was now approaching Rutherford Creek, about six miles from Columbia. Thomas had counted prematurely on A. J. Smith's arrival and he wired Schofield, the evening of the 28th, to be prepared to defend the line of the Harpeth River at Franklin, rather than try to hold Hood beyond the Duck.

On the morning of the 29th, Schofield advised Thomas that Confederate cavalry had crossed in force on the Columbia-Lewisburg Pike, and that their infantry was crossing above Huey's Mill, four miles from Columbia. He promptly got under way for Franklin. He sent Stanley with two divisions of his IV Corps to Spring Hill, initially to protect the trains, later to hold the place until the rest of the Army of the Ohio could pass north. He issued detailed orders to each corps for the passage, going into meticulous detail on provisions for the passage of the Rutherford Creek bridge and Spring Hill. Cox's division was to be the last to leave Columbia; his pickets were to be withdrawn at midnight on the 29th.

The impetus for this action came mainly from a dispatch from Wilson, at Hurt's Cross Roads, dated 3 a.m., bearing the outside address, "Major General Schofield by Courier from Spring Hill. Important! Trot!" In this, Wilson advised that all of Forrest's corps had crossed Duck River above Huey's Mill, Forrest himself leaving Columbia at 4:30 p.m. on the 28th. Included in the message was the caution, "Get back to Franklin without delay." A subsequent message from Wilson to Thomas advised that Forrest appeared to be heading for Nashville, and that he, Wilson, would retire toward Nolensville. However, by 10 p.m., after being driven rapidly north through Hurt's Cross Roads and Mt. Carmel, Wilson, with Hatch's division plus Hammond's brigade, was on the Franklin-Triune Road about 2½ miles east of Franklin. He was by this time out of communication with Schofield, but was in touch with Nashville, and had advised Thomas that the Confederates, using three pontoon bridges, had crossed the Duck River, driven Capron and Garrard away from Rally Hill, and were apparently heading for Franklin.

Hood had crossed most of his infantry at Davis' Ford around daylight of the 29th, sideslipping his two corps from Columbia along the same road by which Cox had moved from the Pulaski Pike to the Mt. Pleasant Pike, thence by country roads to the river. Cheatham's corps led the march from Duck River, with Stewart's following and Edward ("Allegheny") Johnson's division from Lee's corps bringing up the rear. As they marched along country roads toward the Rally Hill Pike, they could hear Lee's bombardment of Columbia. Forrest, having pushed Wilson out of the action by 10 a.m., had turned west, toward Spring Hill. Seizing this place, Hood would have Schofield in a vise between his own force and Lee's corps, following from Columbia.

But as Forrest approached Spring Hill along the road from Duplex and Mt. Carmel, he ran into infantry pickets of the Federal IV Corps. Stanley, taking Wagner's and Kimball's divisions, had moved north rapidly. He had left Kimball at Rutherford Creek to cover that crossing. En route to Spring Hill with Wagner's people, he learned of the approach of Forrest and moved his infantry at the double into the tiny village. He put them in a hastily prepared position enclosing the village on three sides. Within the enclosure thus formed Stanley completed the parking of Schofield's enormous wagon train in a 50-acre open field south of the road between Spring Hill and the railroad station, and just east of the railroad.

Along its northeastern extent, Wagner's position, held by the brigade of Colonel Emerson Opdycke, with Colonel John Q. Lane's Brigade on his right, and to the south of the Duplex (or Mt. Carmel) Road, overlooked one of the junctions of the Rally Hill Pike with the Franklin Pike. In its southeastern sector, skirmishers from Bradley's brigade covered the Rally Hill Pike, along which the Army of Tennessee was approaching Spring Hill. It was these skirmishers whom Forrest first encountered about 11:30 a.m. While pushing them back toward Spring Hill, Forrest received a message to hold his position at all hazards, until Hood could bring his infantry into the action.

This Forrest did, although it was midafternoon before Cleburne's division came up on the left of the dismounted cavalrymen. These, being nearly out of ammunition, were pulled out of the line and moved north, to cover further the advance of the army, or to deter the Federal advance.

Hood at this time was at the crossing of Rutherford Creek. Having dispatched Cleburne, he took Bate's division, next in column, which was moving along the Rally Hill Pike a short distance north of the Absalom Thompson house (where Hood had established his command post), and personally directed its commander to deploy and move west to the Franklin Pike. On reaching that pike, Bate *was to sweep toward Columbia.* With these orders, Hood countermanded orders which Cheatham, his corps commander, had already given Bate; these were to form and move on Cleburne's left, against the enemy near Spring Hill. Bate apparently said nothing about receipt of Cheatham's orders to Hood, nor did Hood tell Cheatham that he had been giving orders to one of his divisions. Although there is not always time for the niceties of command when an action impends, this silence by all concerned was inexcusable.

Bate advanced nearly 3,000 yards in line of battle before reaching the pike. On arriving, his leading element—Caswell's battalion of sharpshooters— promptly fired on a Federal column approaching from their left, a little south of the Cheairs house, which faces the highway from the east. At about the same time, a staff officer from Cheatham caught up with Bate and directed him to halt and move to join his right with Cleburne's left. It was now almost dark and Granbury, with Cleburne's left brigade, was about 500 yards north along the pike. Procuring a guide, Bate made the contact. He also reported his contact with the Federal force to his left front, but Cheatham seemed not to have been impressed. As a matter of fact, these people were from Ruger's division, and the leading element of Schofield's main body, advancing north from Columbia.

Following Bate's division was that of John C. Brown. By 4 p.m., it had cleared the crossing of Rutherford Creek. Cheatham moved it forward along the Rally Hill Pike, with orders to deploy on the right of Cleburne's division in the area vacated by Forrest's dismounted cavalrymen.

Cleburne, by 4:30 p.m., had fought a sharp little engagement in the southeastern outskirts of Spring Hill, in which he had pushed the Federal brigades of Bradley and Lane back into the village. He had sustained some casualties, one of which was his bay horse, Red Pepper, scored in the hip by a shell fragment, and thus deprived of the privilege of dying under his master at Franklin the next day. Just before sunset, the leading elements of Brown's division commenced arriving to take position on Cleburne's right.

About this time Stewart's corps, which had been following Cheatham's at a short distance, came into the picture. It had been held for a time south of Rutherford Creek to meet some fancied threat from the south, but was now marching north along the Rally Hill Pike, to pass behind the battle positions of Bate, Cleburne, and Brown, having left Edward Johnson's division south of the creek under orders from Hood. While his corps was marching north, Stewart had met Hood, who was then "about a half mile north of Rutherford Creek and about the same distance west of the Rally Hill Pike"; this would place him about 300 yards west of the Thompson house, Hood's command post. Hood gave him a guide, a young man from the neighborhood, and directed him to move ahead and place his right across the pike beyond Spring Hill, his left to extend "down this way." This might have put his line behind Cheatham's to some extent, but it would not have been masked at the place where it mattered.

As they moved north, his guide told Stewart that, at a certain point, the road made a sudden turn to the left, that is, toward Spring Hill, and that at this point there was a little-used road that continued north, meeting the Franklin Pike "at the tollgate some mile and a half beyond Spring Hill." This was the junction that lay in front of but outside the Federal defensive line by about 400 yards. They reached the fork of the road; here they found a road, apparently little used, passing through a large gateway. Mistaking this for the right-hand road, they moved up it a short distance until they ran into the Caldwell house, Forrest's command post.

While they talked with Forrest, a staff officer from Cheatham's corps rode up and halted the column. He told Stewart that he had just come from Hood with orders that Stewart was to go into position on the right of Brown's division, and that the officer would act as guide. The head of Stewart's column then retraced its route and took the road to the left, leading into Spring Hill. Arrived at General Brown's command post, and being oriented as to his new orders, Stewart was still unsatisfied and rode back to Hood's command post, two miles south of the town. There he asked Hood if he had really sent the officer from Cheatham's staff to place his corps in position; he had, Hood said. Had he changed his mind as to what he wanted Stewart to do? He had not. Stewart then explained that, uncertain by reason of the change of orders, he had put his people in bivouac, since they had been on the move since daylight and it was now 11 p.m. For answer, according to Stewart's report, "Hood remarked, in substance, that it was not

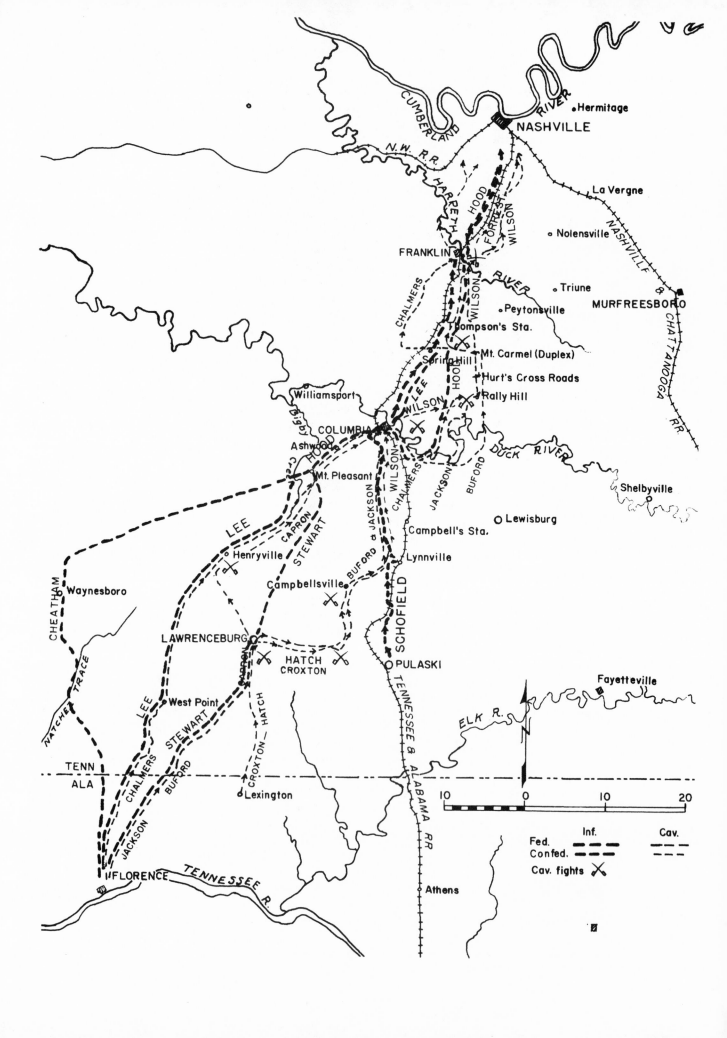

material; to let the men rest, and directed me to move in the morning, taking the advance toward Franklin."

But in the morning Schofield was gone. In the darkness between midnight and dawn he had moved his army out on the road to Franklin past the jaws of Hood's trap, imperfectly set with the withdrawal of Stewart's corps from the position where it could have blocked the retreat. Creaking wagons and marching men passed unchallenged the campfires of Confederates sleeping within a few hundred yards of the road. Only as the column neared Thompson Station was there brief cavalry harassment by some of Forrest's men stationed there. The wagon train and most of the IV Corps moved first, then the XXIII Corps, and finally, near dawn, Wagner's division fell in as rearguard. It was a clean escape from what should have been a foolproof trap.

There had been a straggling Confederate private who, lost from his unit, reported to Hood that he had been on the Columbia Pike; that it had been full of Yankees, moving in both directions, and that somebody ought to do something about it. Hood awakened Pen Mason, his adjutant general, and directed him to order Cheatham to get somebody across the pike to stop that northward movement, then went back to sleep. So, apparently, did Mason, for Cheatham never received the order, although at one time he said that he had. But this last incident was all of a piece with the fumbling, indecision, and misunderstanding that beset the Army of the Tennessee.

Who was responsible? Not Cheatham, although Hood tried to pin the blame on him, but recanted. However, Cheatham might have been a little more aggressive and intelligent in gathering information in his front. Not Cleburne, on whom Hood, after that general had died on the field of Franklin, laid halfhearted hints of accusation. Not Bate, who tried to carry out conflicting orders from two commanders. Not Brown, who did as he was told. Certainly not Stewart, who in his perplexity finally got from Hood the decision that left the Franklin Pike wide open for Schofield. Not Forrest, nor any of his cavalrymen, who did all they could to keep the initiative.

The culprit can have been none other than the army commander. In his final report, and in his book, *Advance and Retreat*, Hood comes up with a self-glorifying story that is so shot full of inaccuracies

that it should not be considered in an analysis of the action. He, the commanding general, was officially responsible. If the operation had succeeded, his would have been the credit.

How does one explain the series of foggy decisions and conflicting orders that characterized Hood's conduct? The people around Spring Hill, and some well-educated students of the present generation say simply, "Hood was drunk." Stories of a bibulous celebration at the Thompson house, over the prospect of gobbling up Schofield in the morning, have been invented and embellished. There is no foundation for them.

But there is a theory propounded by a professional gentleman with military experience, who spent the greater part of his life in Spring Hill. He had the education, experience, and imagination to offer an hypothesis worthy of consideration.

Hood was a man in constant pain. The stump of his leg had hardly healed from Chickamauga. In his useless arm he had what the doctors now call "central pain." He had had at least one fall with his horse during the march from Columbia that day. It is entirely conceivable that his staff doctor may have given him a small vial of brownish liquid, with an explanation something like this, "General, here's some laudanum. Too much of it'll put you to sleep, but if the pain gets too bad, just take a couple of small swallows. It'll help you."

Laudanum, derived from opium, produces within the consumer a state of euphoria, a certainty that everything is going to turn out right, that the user has the key to all problems, and has only to push a button, or turn a crank, or give an order, and the world's confusion and despair will vanish in a rosy cloud. It is not impossible that this is what happened to poor Hood, pain-racked and irritable. It can explain, also, the senseless waste of his army at Franklin the next day.

There is another theory, propounded by an old Negro preacher who had been one of the Thompson servants around the very house where Hood had spent the night of November 29. (Incidentally, he pooh-poohed the idea that Hood and his staff had been drunk that night.) This writer's father had occasion to ask him once for his theory on the collapse of the Confederate hopes at Spring Hill. "I'll tell y'u, Mist' Lucius," he said, earnestly, "God just didn't want 'at war to go on no longer."

Left: Map by Colonel Wilbur S. Nye showing troop movements. Schofield, aware that Hood was about to move against him, left Pulaski on November 22 to join Thomas at Nashville. Hatch's cavalry division plus Capron's and Croxton's brigades screened his left flank. On the 21st, as soon as Forrest's cavalry joined him, Hood hastened toward Columbia to cut off Schofield.

Bloody Franklin
by Hugh F. Walker

The Battle of Franklin is a "compact" among Civil War battles. In number of men and the time and space covered, it was fought upon a small scale. Yet Franklin ranks as one of the great spectaculars of the war in the West.

Years afterward survivors of Franklin recalled the battle with a sort of painful revulsion, as though the very memory evoked agony. "My flesh trembles and creeps and crawls when I think of it today," wrote Sam Watkins of Columbia, Tennessee. "My heart almost ceases to beat at the horrid recollection. Would to God that I had never witnessed such a scene!"

General Jacob D. Cox, commander of the Federal battle line, put his finger on the thing that made men, especially Confederates, want to forget the battle.

"Hood had more men killed at Franklin, than died on one side in some of the great conflicts of the war," he noted. "His killed were more than Grant's at Shiloh, McClellan's in the Seven-Days Battle, Burnside's at Fredericksburg, Rosecrans' at Stone's River or at Chickamauga, Hooker's at Chancellorsville, and almost as many as Grant's at Cold Harbor."

Captain Robert Banks of the 37th Mississippi, marching across the field on the morning after the

Hood and the Army of Tennesse caught up with Schofield and his two Federal corps at Franklin, 19 miles south of Nashville. Below: A highly unrealistic vision of the Battle of Franklin on November 30, 1864, from a Kurz & Allison print. (CWTI Collection)

battle, wrote of "that sickening, blood-curdling, fear-kindling sight. . . . The hell of war was depicted cruelly in the ghastly upturned faces of the dead."

The long, narrow, iron-fenced Confederate cemetery at Franklin is a reminder of that tragic November 30, 1864. Here the fallen sleep under chaste lines of silent stones and sighing cedar trees—424 dead from Mississippi alone.

The stage for battle was set at dawn of that autumn day when Major General John M. Schofield, with two Federal corps, the IV and XXIII, arrived in Franklin with the advance of Hood's Confederate Army of Tennessee hard on his heels.

Concerned for his seven-mile-long wagon train, Schofield two days before had requested pontoons and bridging equipment from General George H. Thomas at Nashville. But the equipment had not arrived; moreover, of the two bridges across the Harpeth River one was destroyed and the other damaged.

The tired Federal commander considered his situation. The river could not be crossed by the wagon train without many hours of preparation. His men had marched all night, having started on the afternoon of the 29th from Columbia, and were exhausted. Schofield made a quick decision. He would throw up a line of fieldworks south of Franklin and fight, if he must, with his back to the Harpeth River. At the same time he would find means to pass his wagon train across the stream to the Federal fortifications at Nashville, 20 miles to the north.

The town of Franklin, then merely a village, lies in a curve of the Harpeth with the opening to the south. From the river the land rises gently southward for a mile, where it reaches an elevation 40 feet above the square at a point marked then and now by the Carter house, chief landmark of the battle. Through what were then open fields and meadows, so slightly rolling as to appear almost flat, the plain continues another mile and a half to the Winstead Hills. This open field upon which the battle was fought has been likened to the left hand, held palm up and pointed south. The palm represents the village, the little finger and thumb the Harpeth River. The three fingers, from the left, represent the Lewisburg, Columbia, and Carter's Creek Pikes entering the town from the south. The Tennessee & Alabama Railroad also came up from the south, east of the Columbia Pike, and crossed the Harpeth just east of the town and the turnpike bridge.

Schofield's works at Franklin were constructed so as to protect his river crossing and line of retreat to Brentwood and Nashville. He directed Cox to throw up a line of fieldworks extending from the river and railroad cut on the left, across the three pikes and bending northward toward the river on the right, the whole about two miles long. Cox's own division was the first to take position in this line, with Brigadier General James W. Reilly temporarily in command. Its three brigades extended from a knoll at the railroad cut westward to the Carter cotton gin and the Columbia Pike. Cox set up his headquarters in the Carter house dooryard.

The Federal line was extended westward to the Carter's Creek Pike by two brigades of Brigadier General Thomas H. Ruger's division under Colonels S. A. Strickland and O. H. Moore, and northwest toward the river by a broken line of light works held by Brigadier General Nathan Kimball's three-brigade division from the IV Corps. As they took position along this line the Federals threw up an earthwork with a ditch in front, topped by headlogs with a three-inch space for rifles. On the left a light abatis of bois d'arc, or osage orange, was cut from a hedge in front and added to the defenses.

West of the Columbia Pike Ruger's line was strengthened by light logs cut from a locust thicket growing in his front. Except for this grove and the bois d'arc hedge, the ground in front was open and almost level.

Upstream and to the left of Schofield's line the Harpeth was fordable at several places, and the Federal commander expected Hood to launch a flanking attack from that direction. He therefore placed two brigades of Brigadier General George D. Wagner's division, IV Corps, three-quarters of a mile south of the main line to observe Hood's advance. In event of a frontal assault it was to fall back within the main works, but if a flanking movement developed, it would swing eastward and check Hood until a new line of battle could be formed.

To guard further against the expected flanking movement, Schofield moved a battery of 3-inch rifled guns into Fort Granger, on Figuers' Hill, north of the river near the railroad crossing. This old earthwork, built by Federals earlier in the war, commanded the railroad cut and the ground in front of Cox's division. To its immediate protection was assigned Brigadier General Thomas J. Wood's division of the IV Corps.

Having arranged protection of front and flank, Schofield began work on the bridges, and by midmorning his train began moving slowly across the Harpeth. With this concern eased, the general went to the village home of a Union sympathizer and slept briefly. The exhausted troops, having thrown up the works and eaten their breakfast, dozed on the line in the autumn sun. And it was upon this quiet scene that the head of Hood's army came into view, shortly after noon.

Bitter after his failure at Spring Hill and spoiling for a fight, Hood came over and through the Winstead Hills with two corps, Lieutenant General Alexander P. Stewart's and Major General Benjamin F. Cheatham's, to which was soon added Major General Edward Johnson's division of Lieutenant General Stephen D. Lee's corps. His artillery, except for a battery for each corps, was still in the rear. His cavalry, under the redoubtable Major General Nathan B. Forrest, consisted of three divisions under Brigadier Generals James R. Chalmers, Abraham Buford, and William H. Jackson, numbering perhaps 6,000 men. And historian Stanley F. Horn states that Hood had about 20,000 infantry up for the battle—roughly the same number as the Federals had waiting to receive the attack.

Hood's enemies had said the year before in Richmond that he had "the heart of a lion and a head of wood," and his biographer, John Percy Dyer, remarked that the general "never was able to think of battle except in terms of long lines of men charging to glory across an open field." These caustic comments,

though perhaps exaggerated, nevertheless seem to fit Hood at Franklin. He was to spend the rest of his life explaining away his mistakes on that battlefield.

His first error was the decision to form his two corps in line of battle immediately, and charge the Federal works. Cheatham "did not like the looks of the fight," and Forrest strongly advised a flanking movement to the right across the Harpeth. Given a supporting infantry column, the cavalryman asserted, he could "flank the Federals out in 15 minutes." And despite Hood's denial, there is evidence that Major General Patrick R. Cleburne, his ablest division commander, did not favor the head-on assault. But Hood was adamant. "No, no," he said. "Charge them out!"

Hood's attitude in this situation is usually ascribed to his crippled physical condition and his bitter disappointment at Spring Hill, where Schofield had escaped him the day before. But the reasons for it go deeper than this, and deserve study. They emerge from the pages of his *Advance and Retreat*, written after the war.

The Franklin battlefield, from the headquarters of Confederate Major General Benjamin Cheatham. In mid-afternoon on November 30, eighteen Confederate brigades advanced on both sides of the Columbia Pike to attack the Federals. (Battles and Leaders of the Civil War)

CARTER HOUSE (UNDER STEEPLE).   GIN-HOUSE.   ROPER'S KNOB.

In the first place, on the morning of the 30th there was bitter feeling between Hood and his officers. Furthermore, the commanding general entertained a poor opinion of his soldiers—the kind words he later lavished on them came after the battle. He felt, and said so, that this army was a cut below Lee's Army of Northern Virginia, where Hood had first won fame as a brigade commander. He conceded that the western troops had the potential to fight as well as Lee's men. But they had been ruined by the leadership of Joe Johnston from Dalton to Atlanta, fighting behind breastworks and falling back. And at Spring Hill he had been irked to see that after a forward march of 180 miles his men were still "seemingly unwilling to accept battle unless under the protection of breastworks."

Hood could see the Federal works at Franklin. He knew they were strong, that the ground was open before them, and that his losses would be heavy. But he did not hesitate to order the charge. He thought, among other things, that it would improve the morale of his army. No other conclusion can be reached from reading his account.

Another reason for Hood's love of the charge is less substantial, but does provoke speculation. He was, he said, a member of the "Lee and Jackson" school which sought to strike the enemy, and despised breastworks except under special circumstances.

As a young man Hood had served on the frontier under Robert E. Lee, and was a devoted admirer of the great Confederate. Lee had earnestly advised the young officer not to marry until he could marry well, and Hood took his advice to heart. "He perhaps thought I might form an attachment for some of the country lasses," Hood wrote, "and therefore imparted to me his correct and at the same time aristocratic views."

While convalescing from wounds in Richmond, Hood became a social lion. Dyer wrote that he was received in the best society; his crutch thumped in almost every drawing room of the city and he courted four girls. It was not until after the war, however, that he "married well" and settled in New Orleans.

Hood's ideas of aristocracy and the "school of Lee and Jackson" may have had little to do with the charge at Franklin, but Wintringham in his *Weapons and Tactics* has some interesting remarks on this. A myth of cold steel, he wrote, was a shock weapon that conservative commanders could understand, and this "social myth included the proposition that courage, discipline, and will power of peculiar and exclusive sorts had to be possessed by officers leading troops in modern battle. The need to cultivate these qualities

during a whole lifetime was the justification for maintaining an exclusive caste of professional officers."

Be this as it may, Hood ordered the charge. And he did it without artillery preparation to soften up Federal defenses, having no more than two batteries available as his two corps formed in line of battle.

Hood's next error was to divide his cavalry into two equal parts, ordering Chalmers' division and Colonel Jacob B. Biffle's brigade to the left flank, beyond Major General William B. Bate's infantry. Forrest himself, with Buford's and Jackson's divisions, took position on the right flank, covering the right of Stewart's corps, and facing the fords on the Harpeth.

Cox suggests that Hood threw Chalmers to the left because he was concerned by the possible approach of a Federal brigade under Brigadier General Joseph Cooper, which had been ordered to march to Franklin from Centerville. But we can nowhere find that Hood even knew of this brigade—which never got near the battlefield—much less took precautions against it. Hood's orders indicate that he did not expect the cavalry to take a major offensive role, but merely to follow up the successes of the infantry and harass Schofield as he fled across the Harpeth.

The Confederate charge came just before four o'clock. It was one of the great spectacles of the war. Eighteen brigades of infantry moved forward in line of battle across the gently rolling plain, the line converging and moving in on itself as the field narrowed in front of the five Union brigades behind their works.

Horn mentions that a long line of rabbits scurried across the field before Hood's lines, kicked from their burrows by hurrying feet. Coveys of quail were flushed from their coverts. Federal soldiers, watching behind cocked guns, were impressed by the grand array moving on their defenses, battle flags waving in the late afternoon sun.

The detached brigades of Colonels Joseph Conrad and John Q. Lane, of Wagner's division, were hit first. The day before, this division had held off half the Confederate army at Spring Hill, and its commander rashly decided they could do it again. Wagner did not retreat as ordered, and his two brigades remained in line to fire into the charging divisions of Cleburne and Major General John C. Brown.

The Confederates, checked momentarily, fell back to reorganize. During this interval both Stewart on the right and Bate on the left reached the main Federal defense line.

Now Cleburne and Brown came on again, harder than ever, and on their flanks Wagner's men could see

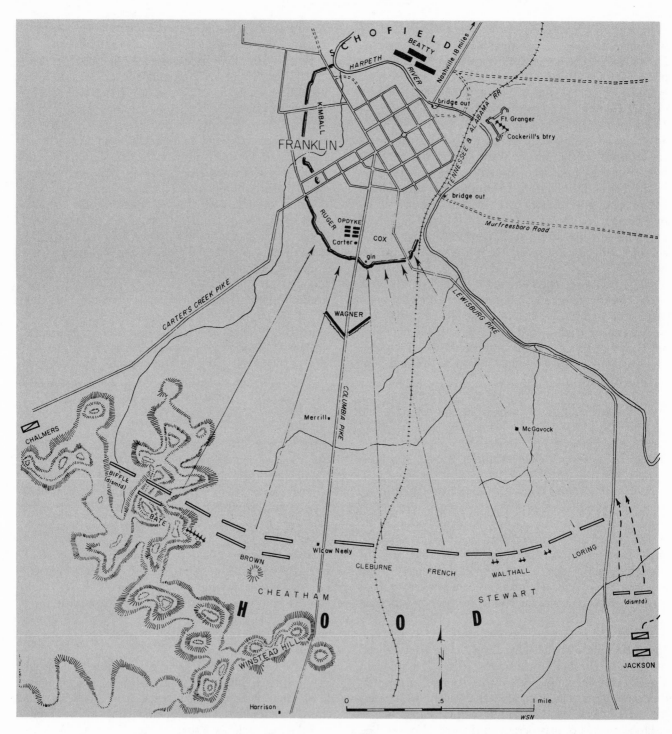

The Battle of Franklin, where Hood demonstrated again the folly of moving across level, open ground to attack steady troops protected by fieldworks. Stewart's corps, shown ready for the charge, had approached north along the Columbia Pike to Henpeck Lane (not shown) .6 mile below the Harrison house, turned right to the Lewisburg Pike, then north to deployment on the line shown. Cheatham's corps deployed to the left of the pike and moved up abreast. Lee's corps (not shown) was in reserve. Parts of Chalmers' cavalry division, on the left, and Jackson's, on the right, participated dismounted. The remainder of the cavalry on the right crossed the river to the right of Stewart's position and confronted Wilson's Federal cavalry. The chief Federal defense was effected by Cox's and Ruger's divisions and, to a lesser extent, Kimball's. Wood's division, then under Beatty, was in general reserve and guarding the river crossings north of the town. The Harrison house was where, before the battle, Hood held his last conference with his chief subordinates, and where he issued his order for the attack. Forrest then roughly told Hood that he lacked good sense. (CWTI Collection)

long lines of Confederates hurrying by. Too late, the Federals turned and ran.

Now it was a footrace to the Federal main line. One writer remarked that the old soldiers in Wagner's brigade got away but the recruits were captured, being afraid to run under enemy fire. No such technicality deterred the veterans, however, and they ran straight down the pike, through the main line at the Carter house, and on into Franklin, where they finally paused on the river bank. Wagner, furious, tried hard to rally them, but was swept backward by the mass of men.

Federal artillery on the Columbia Pike had been unable to fire at the charging Confederates without blasting Wagner's fleeing fugitives, and the same was true of Reilly's and Strickland's brigades near the pike. As a result, the Federals held their fire until the pursuing troops were almost on top of them before they opened up. "It seemed to me," a charging Confederate officer wrote after the battle, "that hell itself had exploded in our faces."

Some of the men in Reilly's and Strickland's brigades, caught up in Wagner's disaster and misunderstanding their orders, joined in the pell-mell rush to the rear, and Cleburne's and Brown's men poured through the gap on the pike near the Carter house. They took the guns just to the left of the road, but providentially for the Federals they could find no primers and the guns remained silent.

Suddenly the crucial point of the battle was at hand, with Confederates 50 yards inside the Federal works. For a few minutes Hood was on the verge of victory.

But the break did not spread. Instead, it was plugged up by the third brigade of Wagner's division, commanded by Colonel Emerson Opdycke, which had been held in reserve 200 yards behind the main line north of the Carter house. Opdycke's men, needing no orders, charged into the break and fought hand-to-hand with the exhausted, outnumbered Confederates. In a few minutes Confederates inside the works were dead or prisoners and the lines had been restored, though in some places to the rear of the original line of works.

The desperate character of the fighting from the cotton gin to the Carter house has been well described by participants who survived the battle. Writers on both sides noted that men charging into the holocaust of fire walked bent forward, like men breasting a strong wind, heads bent down and caps shielding their eyes from the leaden hail of death.

Of the many brief descriptions of the fighting the following, taken by Crownover from Thatcher's *Hundred Battles*, are the best.

Colonel Wolf, a Federal officer:

> I saw a Confederate soldier, close to me, thrust one of our men through with the bayonet, and before he could draw his weapon from the ghastly wound his brains were scattered on all of us that stood near, by the butt of a musket swung with terrible force by some big fellow whom I could not recognize in the grim dirt and smoke that enveloped us.

A member of the 100th Ohio Infantry:

> I saw three Confederates standing within our lines, as if they had dropped down unseen from the sky. They stood there for an instant, guns in hand, neither offering to shoot nor surrender—dazed as in a dream. I raised my gun, but instinctively I felt as if about to commit murder—they were hopeless, and I turned my fact to the foe trying to clamber over our abatis. When I looked again the three were down—apparently dead; whether shot by their own men or ours, who could tell?

Again and again, as daylight faded into twilight and darkness, the divisions of Cheatham and Stewart renewed their charges. But the high tide of battle, for them, had been reached. They met a solid sheet of flame and lead where the Federal lines, massed four deep behind their works, stood to their guns. As one writer put it, irresistible Confederates came up against immovable Federals.

In some places Hood's men collected in the ditches in front of the works, where they were unable to advance or retreat in the face of certain death. Men held inverted muskets over the parapet and fired blindly into the ditch, exposing only the hand that held the gun.

The Carter cotton gin on the Columbia Turnpike, a prominent feature of the battlefield. The Union line ran just in front of the building. (U.S. Army Military History Institute)

The railroad through Franklin to Nashville crossed the Harpeth River on this covered bridge. Fort Granger was built by the Federals (on the right of this view) to protect this important crossing. (U.S. Army Military History Institute)

in the ditches before the works, where the dead were piled three and four deep.

West of the Columbia Pike Bate's division charged somewhat later than Brown and Cleburne, his right striking Ruger's right and Kimball's left. The left of his line never reached the Federal works. Chalmers' attacks on Kimball's light works were not long sustained, and are described as a "reconnaissance-in-force." To the rear of the Carter buildings Bate's men did effect lodgment in the "outer works" of the Federal line, and remained there until nightfall.

At 7 o'clock, long after dark, Hood sent Johnson's division of Lee's corps stumbling through the grove west of the pike in a last-gasp assault upon the works west of the Carter house. But the battle was already lost, and this last charge was another waste of men.

Until 9 o'clock the fighting continued, attackers and defenders firing at the flashes of guns. And then, at last, the weary Confederates drew back, and the front was quiet.

At 11 o'clock, while most of Hood's army slept on its arms, Schofield began his withdrawal. A house caught fire as Federal soldiers filed out of the works, and for a moment the lines of marching men were darkly outlined against the reddened sky. The fire was soon put out and the silent retreat continued.

At the crack of dawn Hood's artillery was blazing away at the works as Confederate officers prepared for a new assault. And then the army commander got the news—his stubborn foe had abandoned the field, and the road was open to Nashville.

Wagner's delayed retreat, which shielded the charging Confederates and caused the break in the Federal line, is generally regarded as the blunder that almost gave Hood the victory. It is interesting, however, to note another point of view. James Barr had been a member of Co. E, 65th Illinois Volunteers, stationed across the pike and just south and east of the Carter house. For a few minutes he had been held prisoner by charging Confederates who reached the works, and was released by a Federal countercharge. Barr had an excellent view of the flight of Wagner's men and the Confederate charge into the gap at the Carter house. He wrote:

> General Cox censures General Wagner for holding to his advanced position too long, calls his action a gross blunder, etc., but as one of Cox's men I looked upon the matter in a different light.

The battle was by no means confined to the Federal center. On the left and right things had gone even less well for the Confederates. Forrest's two divisions on Stewart's right pushed back the Federal cavalry early in the fight and crossed the Harpeth. Here, upstream from Figuers' Hill, the dismounted cavalry of both armies fought a pitched battle. The Federals had the advantage of Wood's infantry in support, but this IV Corps division was not engaged. Details of the fight are lacking, but the upshot of it was that Brigadier General James H. Wilson's cavalry could not be dislodged from Schofield's flank, and Forrest's two divisions, having expended most of their ammunition, pulled back across the Harpeth.

Forrest's failure to break up Wilson's units has generally been blamed on his being outnumbered in not having the services of Chalmers' division and Biffle's brigade. But actually he had as many men as on the day of his great victory at Brice's Cross Roads, and Wilson had 2,500 fewer men than Federal Brigadier General Samuel D. Sturgis had on that occasion. One may conclude that Forrest fought better when campaigning under his own independent command—and so did his soldiers.

On the right of the Confederate infantry Stewart's divisions were crowded to the left by the in-curving river and the high ground near the railroad, with the additional disadvantage of running into the hedge of osage orange, which broke their formations. From a knoll near the railroad track a Federal battery opened on them at almost point-blank range, and from across the river the guns in Fort Granger poured enfilading shells into their lines. From Colonel John S. Casement's brigade Stewart's men received the fire of two companies of the 65th Indiana armed with repeating rifles (probably Spencers) along with a storm of musketry fire. The men in the divisions of Major Generals William W. Loring, Edward C. Walthall, and Samuel G. French were either driven back or pinned

I think if Cleburne had not struck Wagner's two brigades as he did that his brave lads would have broken our line successfully; but, as it was, his brave men were badly winded with his work with Wagner, which gave Opdyke's and White's men a better chance to check him at the cotton gin.

The way I saw it was this: I was acting as orderly and standing a few paces east of the cotton gin. The first Confederate troops that came in view were Stewart's corps on our left, with Cheatham's corps to the left of Stewart. The Confederate line moved easily and steadily on, until Cleburne was checked for the time by Wagner. The short time lost by Cleburne threw Stewart's line too far in advance. Stewart was the first to receive the fire from our main line, and was unable to carry our works, his men who were not killed or wounded being compelled to retire. Now Cleburne, who had been delayed by Wagner, came up just in time to receive a heavy right oblique fire from the men who had repulsed Stewart's corps. I never saw men put in such a terrible position as Cleburne's division was in for a few minutes. The wonder is that any of them escaped death or capture.

Other writers have spoken of the fury of this oblique fire from the Federal left. Under it Confederate lines are said to have "withered away." In this connection it should be recalled that in addition to the repeaters in Casement's brigade, Cox mentions that two companies in the 12th Kentucky of Reilly's brigade were armed with "revolving rifles," and other troops are mentioned as having breechloading rifles—weapons that could be fired much faster than the standard muzzleloaders.

According to one source (H. M. Field), much the same thing happened on the Confederate left. Field, writing in 1890, toured the field with S. A. Cunningham, Major Joe Vaulx of Nashville, Moscow B. Carter, and Sam Ewing of Franklin, all of whom had seen the battle. These men said Bate's division was the first to strike the Federal line, where it had to take the whole defensive fire, and had to withdraw. When it is considered that Brown, on Bate's left, had been slowed by Wagner, as had Cleburne, and that Bate could not see Stewart's brigades from his position, all this seems possible. It is also hard to see how such men as Vaulx and Cunningham could have been mistaken as to Bate's premature attack. Carter repeats it, and Field sets it down as a matter of fact. But nowhere else do we find it reported. If it occurred, it explains how Ruger's men, between Bate's first and second attacks, also had time to direct an oblique fire eastward across the field.

The Confederate loss in general officers is a notable feature of the battle. Adams, Granbury, Gist, Strahl, and Cleburne were killed outright, and Car-

Confederate Major General Patrick R. Cleburne, killed during the Battle of Franklin. The Confederates lost over 6,000 in dead and wounded during the battle. (CWTI Collection)

ter mortally wounded. Gordon was captured, and Brown, Manigault, Quarles, Cockrell, and Scott were wounded. Included in the casualties were 53 regimental commanders.

By way of comparison it is notable that Pickett's total loss at Gettysburg was 2,882, while at Franklin the Army of Tennessee lost over 6,000 in dead and wounded. Pickett's men had the advantage of artillery preparation, Hood's did not; Pickett's charge was totally repulsed, while the charge of Brown and Cleburne penetrated deep into the breastworks; Pickett, once repelled, retired from the field, while the Army of Tennessee renewed its charge time after time.

Though it failed to crush Schofield, the Army of Tennessee convinced its commander, that November 30th, that it would fight without protection of breastworks. "Never," Hood reported, "did troops fight more gallantly." They had shown that the men, as well as their commander, belonged to "the school of Lee and Jackson"—an aristocracy of valor in the best tradition of the American fighting men.

Brigadier General O. F. Strahl, soon to die, summed up the Battle of Franklin when he said, just before the charge: "Boys, this will be short, but desperate." And so it was.

The city of Nashville, where on December 15-16, 1864, the Confederate Army of Tennesse under General John B. Hood was effectively destroyed by Union troops under Major General George Thomas, in a battle well planned by both sides. (CWTI Collection)

The Battle of Nashville

by Stanley F. Horn

One distinguishing feature of the Battle of Nashville was that it was thoughtfully planned by both sides, and was fought in accordance with those plans. It was not an accidental collision of opposing armies, as at Gettysburg, nor was it the climax of complicated pre-battle military maneuvers as at Chancellorsville or Chickamauga. Neither was there the element of surprise, as at Shiloh. Thomas had decided to leave his fortifications and attack the Confederates in theirs at the first opportunity, and had worked out and explained to his subordinates his

detailed plans and tactics for the action when it was launched.

Whatever the other reasons for Hood's failure to win the battle, surprise was not among them. When he advanced his army from Franklin to the environs of Nashville he had no idea of attacking Thomas in his fortified position. His declared plan, fatuous though it proved to be, was to place his army in defensive entrenchments to await attack by Thomas in the hope that such an attack could be repulsed and Nashville captured by a counter-charge. The only question in his mind was as to just when and where Thomas' attack would be made. That he was not at all surprised when Thomas did move is shown by the fact that at 2 a.m. on the morning of December 15 he sent a message to General J. R. Chalmers, commanding the cavalry on his left, warning him that the Federal attack would fall on him in a few hours—a warning that also indicated that Hood had some remarkably accurate information.

Thomas, always careful in his planning, several days before the battle had issued to his corps commanders detailed orders for an attack at daylight on December 10. With the abrupt change in the weather, with snow, sleet, and freezing temperatures making this movement impossible on that date, he notified the corps leaders on the 9th that "it is found necessary to postpone the operations designed for tomorrow morning until the breaking of the storm." Thomas, however, specifically instructed that everything be prepared to carry out the attack as planned as soon as the weather would permit.

On the morning of the 14th, when a welcome rise in the temperature and a warm sun rapidly melted the ice and frozen ground, Thomas completed his plans to attack the next morning. At 3 p.m. he called his corps commanders into a council of war at his headquarters to discuss these plans. They were the same as those for the previously postponed attack. But to make sure that there could be no misunderstanding, Thomas handed to each commander his Special Field Orders No. 342, outlining precisely what each of the units was expected to do.

Overlooking nothing, Thomas had also been closely in touch with Commander Fitch, in charge of the naval forces guarding the river approaches to the city. Thomas wanted to make sure that the Confederates would not cross the Cumberland, bypassing Nashville (which they had no intention of doing), but it was characteristic that he proceeded with such caution.

Hood, too, had not been idle during the two weeks preceding the battle. Acutely aware of the disparity in numbers between his 23,000 men and the 55,000 combat troops of the Federal commander, he tried desperately but fruitlessly to increase his strength. Hood was actually destined to fight the Battle of Nashville with fewer men than he had at the close of the action at Franklin. In a move that has been characterized by military critics as one of Hood's greatest blunders, he had detached two brigades of infantry and two divisions of cavalry (nearly a quarter of his total force) under General Forrest to operate against the Nashville & Chattanooga Railroad and the Federal garrison at Murfreesboro. From Hood's standpoint, containing the Murfreesboro garrison doubtless was a military necessity, but it now appears that this might have been done with fewer men. Certainly Hood could have better guarded his flanks if he had retained his full cavalry force at Nashville, especially if that cavalry had been under the magnetic leadership of Forrest.

In addition to his vigorous though unsuccessful efforts to increase his strength, Hood was alert in taking all possible steps to have his command at the peak of its efficiency and preparedness. Regular and frequent rollcalls were employed to discourage straggling, and commanding officers were instructed to have their entire lines examined late each evening and early each morning to observe the enemy and ascertain if any changes in their own positions should be made.

On December 10, Hood issued a circular order stating that it was "highly probable that we will fight a battle before the close of the present year," and urging that the troops be "kept well in hand at all times." When the battle began, the order said, the corps commanders were to park all their wagons, except the artillery, ordnance, and ambulances, in the vicinity of Brentwood. In addition to these precautions, corps commanders were to fortify their flanks "with strong, self-supporting detached works" to facilitate defense.

Hood, in taking his position before Nashville, placed Stephen D. Lee's corps in the center, A.P. Stewart's on the left, and Cheatham's on the right. The Confederate entrenched line, hastily constructed under adverse weather conditions, was about four miles long, much shorter than the Federal defensive fortifications. The Confederate right wing rested on a deep cut on the Nashville & Chattanooga railroad between the Nolensville and Murfreesboro Turnpikes. Slightly in advance of the main line at this point was a small lunette occupied by the 300 survivors of the brigade of General Granbury, who had been killed at Franklin. The main Confederate line extended westward across the Nolensville Pike to the principal stronghold of the right flank on Rain's Hill.

Extending on to the west, Hood's line ran across high ground, crossing the Franklin Pike. Thence the line continued back of Brown's Creek, crossing the Granny White Pike at a sharp angle with the road, then on to Hood's main salient, known as Redoubt No. 1, which crowned the high hill just east of the Hillsboro Pike and north of the present Woodmont Avenue. Here Hood's line turned sharply back southward at almost a right angle to Redoubt No. 2, east of the pike, and on to Redoubt No. 3 across the pike to the west. Further support for Hood's left was supplied by two more detached works west of the pike—

A railroad bridge over the Cumberland River at Nashville. The bridge was fortified and flooring was installed to enable the passage of troops. Note the loopholes and the sentry. In the foreground, a small boy on his steed. (Library of Congress)

lin, and Nolensville Turnpikes. General John F. Miller's garrison troops occupied the works to the Lebanon Pike on the left. A little later Colonel James L. Donaldson's armed quartermaster's force, and others under his command, were placed in the works from the right of Cruft to the river on the right, covering approaches to the city by the Hillsboro and Harding Pikes. This rearrangement of Thomas' force provided a continuing defensive line all around the city, manned by troops not taking part in the actual fighting, thus relieving for combat the approximately 55,000 men who were moving out to the attack.

General Steedman, after looking to the establishment of the reserve defensive line in his rear, marched out at 6:30 a.m. with his three brigades under Colonels T. J. Morgan, C. R. Thompson, and C. H. Grosvenor, to make his scheduled attack on the Confederate right. Delayed by the fog, it was 8 o'clock before his 7,600 men made contact with the enemy. Cheatham's advanced skirmish line fell back but the main Confederate line and the lunette occupied by the 300 men of Granbury's brigade held firm. The assault by Morgan's 3,200 men failed.

Later in the day some of Morgan's men took over a brick house at a safe distance and cut loopholes in the house and brick outhouses from which their sharpshooters kept up a desultory fire on the Confederate line. Colonel Thompson's report shows that after his

Redoubts No. 4 and No. 5—work on which had been delayed by the bad weather and which were incomplete on December 15 when the battle started. Hood's engineers had originally placed his main line in a somewhat more advanced location, but it was considered too close to the Federal works on the left; therefore the engineers established the stronger line to the rear, with its redoubts. This line was occupied as the main line on December 10, the abandoned entrenchment in front of the main salient on the left being lightly occupied as a skirmish line.

At 4 a.m. on December 15 the brassy blare of reveille bugles was heard all along the Federal lines, and the movements preliminary to the day's action began. A heavy blanket of fog hung over the city and its environs, and there was a spectral quality to the pre-dawn activities as the troops started to move.

As scheduled, the first movements were on the left, where General J. B. Steedman commanded. Shortly after 4 o'clock Wood's IV Corps and Schofield's XXIII Corps marched out of the works into their battle positions. As soon as they were out of the line, General Charles Cruft's provisional division of recruits and others was placed in the works commanding the approaches to the city by the Granny White, Frank-

Louisville & Nashville passenger depot looking northeast, with the State Capitol in the background. The merging of river, rail, and road connections made Nashville important to the Federals, who had captured it in 1862. (Library of Congress)

brigade's preliminary skirmish his men "retired to our position in line," where they were content to remain the rest of the day.

The Federal officers who took part in this action against the Confederate right asserted that they had led Hood to think this the principal point of attack, and even alleged that by their attack they had pinned down Cheatham's corps in its breastworks until the day's fighting was ended. Actually, Hood recognized Steedman's attack as a feint, and during the afternoon withdrew most of Cheatham's force from that flank to strengthen his strongly assailed left; apparently Steedman was unaware that the troops he attacked in the morning had left his front.

During this more-or-less sham battle on the Federal left, the main purposeful movement of Thomas' force was developing on the right. There was some confusion in the initial movements of the infantry and cavalry, and it was nearly 10 a.m. before the infantry corps of Smith (about 15,000 men) and the cavalry corps of Wilson (something over 12,000, of whom 9,000 were mounted) were able to start their big sweep against the Confederate left. But when this movement did get under way it was irresistible.

Wilson, whose cavalry on the right was to provide the deciding force in the battle, handled his part of the assignment with efficiency and a thorough attention to detail. A young West Pointer who had graduated into the Engineers, he was quick to learn from experience and was rapidly developing into a first-rate cavalry commander. When he returned from the final conference with Thomas on the afternoon of the 14th, he assembled his division and brigade commanders and explained that the plan of battle called for them to advance on the right of the infantry, turn and envelop the Confederates' left flank and, if possible, strike their rear. To avoid misunderstanding, Wilson personally showed each officer on a map, exactly the ground over which he was to advance, orally reiterated his instructions, and then supplied each with a written copy of the orders.

As a final touch, Wilson conferred with General A. J. Smith (with whose corps he was to cooperate) to correlate their activities so as to avoid any confusion in the initial movements. There was confusion nevertheless. Wilson, in his subsequently published recollections, elaborates on the delay caused by what he considered Smith's (or McArthur's) bungling, as McArthur's division, contrary to what Wilson thought was the arrangement, crossed Wilson's front instead of his rear in getting into position to move out the Charlotte Pike. In spite of this delay, the movement, once started, proceeded like well-oiled clockwork.

The Confederates, to meet this attack, had only a token force between their solid left wing on the Hillsboro Pike and the river—a distance of about three miles. Chalmers, in command of the single division of Forrest's cavalry left with Hood, had one brigade patrolling the distant right wing of the Confederate line. The remaining brigade, Rucker's, was placed on high ground behind Richland Creek near the Charlotte Pike, and Colonel David C. Kelley, with Forrest's "Old Regiment" and a battery of four guns, was to Rucker's left on the high banks of the river. As a sort of outpost of observance between the actual left wing of his line and Rucker's cavalry, Hood had put Ector's depleted infantry brigade (about 700 men) on a ridge west of Richland Creek, north of the Harding Pike, with pickets out front.

Rucker's brigade, where Chalmers was in person, first tasted fighting early in the morning when they were shelled by Fitch's gunboats. The gunboats were soon driven off by Kelley's artillery, however, and Rucker was not molested further until about 11 a.m., when R. W. Johnson's division of Wilson's cavalry came sweeping out the Charlotte Pike. Rucker's resistance was sufficiently tenacious to give his cannoneers time to limber up and displace to the rear. But when the guns had been withdrawn, Chalmers ordered the brigade to fall back farther out the Charlotte Pike, where until nightfall he resisted Johnson's efforts to dislodge him.

Meanwhile, General Kenner Garrard's division of Smith's infantry corps had moved out from the works on the Harding Pike, and passed by the left flank to connect with the right of Wood's corps, which was to serve as the pivot of the big turning movement as the right wing wheeled to the left. McArthur's division, after shaking off the few skirmishers in front of Ector's position, formed on Garrard's right; and Smith's third division, under Colonel J. B. Moore, moved out the Harding Pike and formed in rear of Smith's center to act as a reserve to either flank. Once in position outside the breastworks, Smith's veteran infantry swung forward, carrying out their instructions to "touch the left and guide right." Thus advancing and wheeling gradually, the corps was soon in a position south of the Harding Pike and almost parallel to it. Obviously, Ector's skeleton brigade could offer only a show of resistance to this powerhouse drive. In fact, Ector had orders to fall back to the Confederate main line along the Hillsboro Pike when attacked, and this he had done with alacrity.

General Thomas J. Wood, who commanded the Federal center at Nashville, had the largest corps in Thomas' army—13,256 "present for duty equipped." Wood was an old Regular Army officer, having graduated from West Point in 1845, and served in the Mexican War. He had served with the Army of the Ohio and the Army of the Cumberland since October 1861, and was regarded as a sound and competent, though not especially brilliant, general officer. When Stanley was wounded at Franklin, Wood succeeded to the command of the IV Corps.

With characteristic efficiency and care for details, Wood on the evening of the 14th had briefed his division commanders, explaining to them the next day's intended movements, and had handed to each of them a copy of the orders for the 15th: Reveille was to sound at 4 a.m.; the troops were to breakfast, break camp, pack up everything, and be ready to move at 6 a.m. The orders are interesting as an indication of just how an army corps prepared to move into battle. The exact movement and position of each division were detailed; and, leaving nothing to chance or guesswork, the orders specified:

> The pickets on post will advance as a line of skirmishers to cover the movement. The formation of the troops will be in two lines—the front line deployed, the second line in close column by division, massed opposite the interval in the front line. Each division commander will, so far as possible, hold one brigade in reserve. Five wagon-loads of ammunition, ten ambulances, and the wagons loaded with the intrenching tools will, as nearly as possible, follow immediately after each division; the remaining ammunition wagons, ambulances, and all other wagons will remain inside of our present lines until further orders. One rifle battery will accompany the Second Division, and one battery of light 12-pounders will accompany each of the other divisions; the rest of the artillery of the corps will maintain its present positions in the lines.

With only minor fog-induced delay, Wood's men had gone into their designated positions when they moved out of the works early in the morning. From then until shortly after noon the main body of the corps remained inactive, waiting for the adjustment and advance of Smith's and Wilson's forces on their right. Wood's skirmishers, however, had been pushed forward and soon became sharply engaged with the Confederate skirmish line, keeping up a brisk but inconclusive action. Since early morning the guns in Fort Negley and the other forts, as well as the batteries in position along the whole Federal line, had been thundering their salvos, arousing a replying artillery fire from the Confederate positions. This booming of the big guns, Wood commented in a conservative understatement in his official report, "added interest to the scene."

The battle of Nashville was fought before an exceptionally large "gallery" of civilian as well as mili-

tary spectators. A participant recalled that "citizens of Nashville, nearly all of whom were in sympathy with the Confederacy, came out of the city in droves. All the hills in our rear were black with human beings watching the battle, but silent. No army on the continent ever played on any field to so large and so sullen an audience."

Shortly after noon, when Smith's wheeling line of infantry had been brought around to a point where it served as a continuation of the right of Wood's line, Wood ordered his men forward. The great sweep of some 40,000 men got under way, and Stewart's men holding Hood's left flank knew that their hour of trial had arrived, as they heard what one of them described as "the sharp rattle of fifty-calibre rifles, sounding like a cane-brake on fire." In somewhat more poetic language, Wood said in his report:

> "When the grand array of the troops began to move forward in unison, the pageant was magnificently grand and imposing. Far as the eye could reach, the lines and masses of blue, over which the nation's emblem flaunted proudly, moved forward in such perfect order that the heart of the patriot might easily draw from it the happy presage of the coming glorious victory."

Wood's third division (Beatty), as it swung forward on the shortest arc of the big wheel, was confronted with the works on Montgomery Hill, salient of the advanced skirmish line which had been Hood's main line before that line was moved back on the 10th. From the viewpoint of the attacking Federals, the position looked formidable, but it was actually

Left: The strongly fortified Fort Negley, with a view to the northeast. Nashville's fortifications were so formidable that even Hood would not attack the city. (National Archives)

manned by only a few skirmishers placed there before the battle.

Wood, of course, had no idea how strongly Montgomery Hill was defended. He did know, however, that it barred the further advance of his men in this sector and would have to be reduced. So, after ordering a thorough pounding of the position by artillery, Colonel Sidney Post of Beatty's division was ordered to lead his brigade in an assault on this position. They swept up the wooded slope, over the enemy's intrenchments, and the hill was won.

Meanwhile, Schofield's corps had remained idle

Below: Both days of the Battle of Nashville are depicted on this map, drawn after the war and based on an official Federal military map. (CWTI Collection)

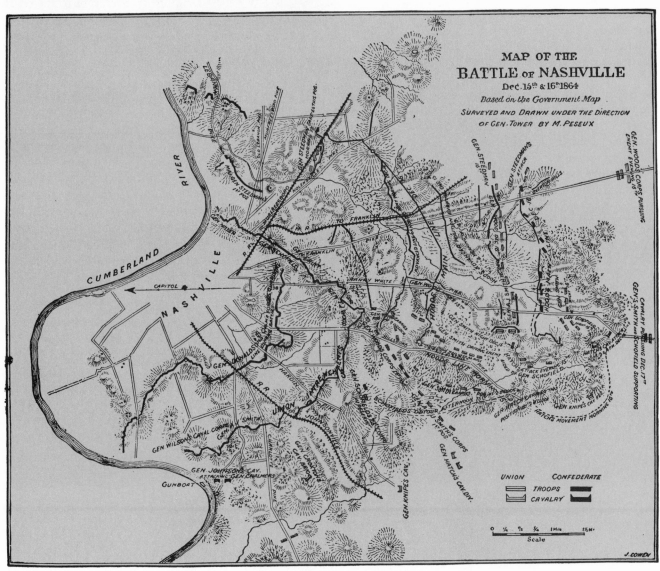

just outside the works where it had moved at daylight. General Darius N. Couch's division had formed in the rear of General Smith's left near the Harding Pike, and while Smith was maneuvering into an advanced position during the morning, Couch moved forward behind his left, within supporting distance. The division commanded by General Jacob D. Cox had remained practically stationary to the left of Couch.

Couch was an 1846 West Point graduate, and had served as a corps commander and second in command to General Hooker at Chancellorsville in May 1863. After that battle Couch, refusing to serve further under Hooker, had been given a noncombat assignment. Then in December 1864, he volunteered to serve as a division commander under Thomas, and was assigned to Schofield's corps. Cox was an Ohio lawyer and politician, without prewar military training or experience, but was regarded as able. In active command of the battle line at Franklin, he conducted that operation efficiently. Couch was 42 and Cox, 36.

As Smith's corps advanced, with Hatch's and Croxton's divisions of Wilson's cavalry on his right, his advance drove the Confederate skirmishers before them like a covey of quail. Smith's forward movement bore more to the left than Thomas had expected, so about 1 p.m., Schofield was ordered to swing his corps far around the rear of the advancing line and form on Smith's right, thus allowing the cavalry to operate still more widely and effectively against the extreme Confederate left with its isolated and lightly manned redoubts.

Early in the afternoon, the advancing Federal infantry, cavalry, and dismounted cavalry confronted and overlapped the Confederate line along the Hillsboro Pike. The zero hour had come.

As the blue juggernaut rolled across the fields between the Harding and Hillsboro Pikes, General Hood had not been idle. When he saw that he was confronted with the overtures to a full-scale assault on his lines, he moved up his headquarters from Travelers' Rest on the Franklin Pike to Lealand, the home of Judge John M. Lea, just east of the Granny White Pike. Here he began to do everything he could —which was not much—to meet the formidable assault he could see rolling up on Stewart in his weakly defended left wing.

General Alexander Peter Stewart was a native Tennessean, born in 1821, who had graduated from West Point in 1845 but served only three years in the Army. He was given a brigadier general's commission in the Confederate Army in 1861, and had served in the Army of Tennessee since then. He was promoted to major general in 1863, and when General Leonidas Polk was killed in June 1864, was given command of Polk's corps, with the temporary rank of lieutenant general. His men called him "Old Straight."

Stewart, that misty morning of December 15, soon perceived that his position was the immediate objective of the Federal attack, and he began promptly to make the best possible disposition of his inadequate manpower. When he had moved back on December 10 from the Montgomery Hill line to the solid works he now held, based on his main salient at Redoubt No. 1, General Walthall's division was not placed in the line but was put in bivouac, protecting the extreme left of the Confederate infantry line. Walthall was Hood's youngest division commander, only 33 years old, but he was a dogged fighter of great ability. His division had suffered severely at Franklin, one of his brigades having 432 casualties out of the 1,100 who went into battle. When General Samuel G. French, in failing health, left Hood's army before Nashville, his two brigades (Ector's and Sears's) were assigned to Walthall. Ector had been sent to the relief of Chalmers on the far left, and Sears was placed in the main line, to the left of Loring, holding the salient embracing Redoubts No. 1 and No. 2 to the east of the Hillsboro Pike.

As soon as Stewart learned that the Federals were advancing in full strength west of the Hillsboro Pike, he ordered Walthall to prepare for action. Walthall placed a company of infantry and a battery of artillery in each of the redoubts in his immediate front (No. 4 and No. 5), although they were still incomplete. The remainder of his command was put in position behind a stone wall along the eastern side of the pike, extending for the distance between Redoubts No. 3 and No. 4. Ector's retreating brigade reached the Confederate main line in the early afternoon and Walthall placed it on his left. Even with this extension, however, Stewart's line on his extreme left flank was still not long enough to cover Redoubt No. 5; he expressed it mildly when he said in his report, "My line was stretched to its utmost tension."

Stewart appealed to Hood for reinforcements. In response, Hood about noon ordered General Edward Johnson, commanding the left division of Lee's corps, to send Manigault's and Deas's brigades to Stewart's immediate assistance, later sending also the other two brigades of the division, Sharp's and Brantley's—a shift that could be safely made, as Lee's corps was experiencing hardly more than a token attack. Hood also ordered two of Cheatham's divisions on the extreme right to support Stewart, and they started promptly on the march of nearly three miles across country.

Union defenders of Nashville, looking west from Fort Casino. Note the long breastworks thrown up in front of the tents and the long line of stacked muskets. (Library of Congress)

The first collision of the enveloping Federals and the defending Confederates came when Colonel Datus E. Coon, with his hard-riding brigade of Hatch's cavalry division, swinging around the right of McArthur's infantry division, found himself on the exposed flank of Redoubt No. 5, the detached and unsupported outermost outpost of the Confederate left. Coon's men quickly dismounted and with their deadly Spencer repeating rifles moved to the attack. They were supported by the first brigade of McArthur's division and a battery of artillery that immediately opened on the Confederate position.

The Confederate guns replied and there was an artillery duel for about an hour, during which Coon's dismounted troopers and McArthur's infantrymen edged closer to the Confederate works. When they eventually got close enough to charge the redoubt they were met with a burst of canister from the four Napoleon guns on the hill, accompanied by as heavy a musketry fire as a hundred defenders with their single-shot muskets could develop. The result, however, was never in doubt. The fast-shooting Federals swarmed up the hill, over the breastworks and through the embrasures, and literally overpowered the defending force, capturing the guns and practically all the men in the redoubt.

As was not unusual during the war, there was some dispute among the victors as to who got there first. Smith said in his report that Coon's men scaled the fortifications "simultaneously with our skirmishers"; but the cavalrymen denied this, saying that the infantry did not get there until after they had the situation well in hand.

Whoever got there first, the Federals had hardly reached the inside of the captured works when they received a salvo from the guns in Redoubt No. 4, and

they then turned their attention to this Confederate strong point, which was being invested by the rest of Hatch's and McArthur's divisions.

Redoubt no. 4 proved to be not quite so easy a nut to crack as No. 5, although held by no larger a force. It also had a battery of four smoothbore Napoleon guns, manned by 48 men under Captain Charles L. Lumsden, supported by 100 infantry in shallow breastworks stretching a short distance on both sides of the redoubt. Lumsden, a graduate of Virginia Military Institute and, when the war started, commandant of cadets at the University of Alabama, had been ordered to hold the position "at all hazards," and he took his orders literally. Hammered by three batteries of rifled guns from a ridge 600 yards to the west, and almost encompassed by 12 regiments of infantry and two brigades of dismounted cavalry, the Confederate defenders by some miracle of valor clung to their beleaguered position for three hours, banging away with their smoothbores as fast as they could be served. Not until the swarming Federals were actually within the works did Captain Lumsden give the "Take care of yourselves, boys" order, as he and the surviving defenders made off for Walthall's rock wall along the pike.

Meanwhile Schofield had swung his corps around as ordered and was forming on Smith's right, thus making it possible for Wilson to remount his men and move out on a wider arc across the Hillsboro Pike to the left and rear of Walthall's infantry line, commanding both the Hillsboro and Granny White Pikes. Chalmers was still miles away on the Charlotte Pike, pinned down by Johnson's cavalry division, so Wilson was unopposed as he placed his force in position to take a decisive part in the action the next day, although he took no further active part in the fighting on December 15.

With the two defending redoubts in his front lost, Walthall's line was now subjected to a blistering bombardment of heavy shellfire from Smith's big guns. Lacking artillery, Walthall was unable to reply. But there was no immediate effort to charge Walthall's thin line as Smith regrouped his divisions on the western side of the pike. During this breathing spell, Walthall tried to strengthen his precarious position by moving Ector's brigade "down near Compton's house" to hold the pike for the protection of the left flank. But after Redoubt No. 5 had fallen and the victorious Federals came streaming down across the pike, Ector's men were driven back to the east and a spearhead of advancing Federals drove in between them and Cantey's brigade, thus isolating Ector's brigade from the ensuing action of Walthall's division.

The Federals driving across the pike into the woods near the Compton house placed a battery on the high hill southwest of the house. Walthall attempted to meet this threat by detaching Reynolds and his brigade from the right of his line to his left, and Reynolds had some temporary success in stemming the Blue tide. But soon the Federals had occupied also the hill west of the Compton house and, shelling Reynolds with the guns on both hills, and threatening both flanks of his brigade with their advancing infantry, drove him back through the woods toward the Granny White Pike.

The reinforcing brigades of Deas and Manigault had meanwhile arrived on the left flank, and were placed in support of Walthall. They were of little or no help. Walthall, to save his men from capture, went into precipitate retreat and the flanking Federals swept northward east of the pike.

Stewart, witnessing the impending debacle on his left, hastily withdrew a battery from his not yet hard-pressed salient at Redoubt No. 1 and placed it on a hill east of the pike where it could sweep the flanking Federals. He ordered the brigades of Deas and Manigault to rally to its support; but says in his report, "they again fled, however, abandoning the battery, which was captured. . . . The other brigades of Johnson's division had come up, but were unable to check the progress of the enemy, who had passed the Hillsboro Pike a full half-mile, completely turning our flank and gaining the rear of both Walthall and Loring, whose situation was becoming perilous in the extreme." Seeing that his position was untenable, Stewart immediately ordered both Walthall and Loring to withdraw, an order that Walthall's men had already anticipated. Loring promptly evacuated his men from the line, leaving Redoubts No. 1 and No. 2 unoccupied and undefended.

Meanwhile, the third brigade of McArthur's division had been coming up in front of that portion of Stewart's line defended by Redoubt No. 3, west of the pike. As the brigade approached the Confederate position, it came under direct and vigorous artillery fire, which inflicted considerable damage but did not slow the advance. When the men got within striking distance of Redoubt No. 3 they were ordered to storm it, and thus they reduced the last pocket of resistance on the Confederate line of defense.

McArthur's men, having captured Redoubt No. 3, turned their attention to No. 2 and No. 1, the guns of which had been playing on them as they advanced on No. 3. They were unaware that during the afternoon General Wood had been cautiously approaching Redoubt No. 1. Wood recognized it as the key to the Confederate position, but realized that it would be

difficult to carry by frontal attack. He therefore attempted to prepare for a successful infantry attack by a prolonged bombardment of the position by two batteries of his artillery, which almost demolished the Confederate works. He still experienced difficulty in getting his infantry to charge the position; but about 4:30 p.m., Kimball's division did move to the attack and, as Wood says in his report, "rushed forward up the steep ascent and over the intrenchments."

Kimball's and McArthur's men each claimed they reached the top first. Neither Wood nor Smith mentions that whichever attacking force had that distinction, it was somewhat of an empty honor, as Loring's defending force was already in retreat, having been ordered by Stewart to withdraw and form along the Granny White Pike.

When the early December nightfall ended the day's action, the elements of the two contending armies were scattered in bewildering confusion. Thomas' units had to a great extent lost their cohesion. On his left Steedman's men were still holding on to the position they had taken early in the day, apparently unaware that Cheatham's forces had been withdrawing from their front all afternoon. Wood, after sweeping over Stewart's salient, had been ordered by Thomas to move east toward the Franklin Pike, reach it if possible before dark, and form his troops across it

Nashville looking north from the roof of the Literary Department of the University of Nashville. On the Cumberland River may be seen a pontoon bridge and beyond it, the foundation of a destroyed bridge. Still further in the distance, a railroad bridge crosses the river. (CWTI Collection)

facing south. Darkness, however, caused Wood to halt his corps shortly after crossing the Granny White Pike to wait until morning. Smith, after driving the Confederate left wing out of its position, had halted for the night in a line between the Hillsboro and Granny White Pikes, and roughly parallel with them. Schofield, on the right, was east of the Hillsboro Pike, with Couch's division entrenched across the hill he had occupied late in the afternoon; and Cox's division, on Couch's right, was roughly perpendicular to him, facing east. Wilson's cavalry divisions were bivouacked on the extreme right, from the Hillsboro to the Granny White Pikes, where they had taken a strong position on the ridge where the road passes through a gap just beyond the old site of Granny White's tavern.

The Confederate forces were also disorganized and scattered. Cheatham's divisions at nightfall, in the process of being moved to the left, were widely scattered. Bate was already in position on the left, though he arrived too late to take part in the action. Cleburne's division, now under J. A. Smith, was on its way to the left, but bivouacked on the Granny White Pike near Lealand when stopped by darkness. Lowrey's brigade was just starting from its original position on the right. Lee, with the two remaining divisions of his corps, was still firmly holding in the Confederate center, though stretched out in a pitifully thin line. Stewart's battered corps had retired to a position roughly parallel to the Granny White Pike, east of that road, with his left near the Bradford house on the pike. Ector's brigade clung to its precarious resting place on the hill (later called Shy's Hill) where General Hood himself had personally placed it when he encountered its members falling back late in the afternoon.

At the close of the fighting Thomas returned to his headquarters in the city and telegraphed Halleck to tell him of the day's success. "I shall attack the enemy again tomorrow, if he stands to fight," said Thomas in closing his message, "and if he retreats during the night will pursue him." Halleck sent him a gracious acknowledgment. Grant, as soon as he heard the news, sent a telegram saying that "I was just on my way to Nashville, but I shall go no farther"; and then went on to urge Thomas to give the enemy no rest "until he is entirely destroyed." President Lincoln the next morning telegraphed "the nation's thanks"; and, taking his cue from Grant, added: "You made a magnificent beginning. A grand consummation is within your easy reach. Do not let it slip."

Possibly the destruction of Hood's army might have seemed "easy" to President Lincoln and to General Grant. But Thomas, on the ground, knew Hood for the determined, tenacious fighter he was, and knew that there was still work to do "if he stands to fight."

Hood, true to his reputation, did stand to fight; but it taxed his military skill and resourcefulness to improvise an adequate defensive line in the face of a victorious enemy. Working throughout the night and the morning of the 16th, however, he and his engineers did patch together a continuous line in which to meet the expected Federal pursuit. Lee's corps, which had engaged in the least actual combat the preceding day, was moved back on the Franklin Pike to high ground about two miles to the rear. Here Hood established the new right wing of the Confederate army, with hastily scratched-out breastworks and gun emplacements on Peach Orchard Hill just east of the Franklin Pike, and his line extending westward across the pike. Stewart was moved back to a position with his left crossing the Granny White Pike, the main part of his force behind a rock wall, behind which a shallow trench was dug, and his right joining with Lee's left. Cheatham's men were to the left of Stewart, constituting the Confederate left. Shy's Hill, inexpertly fortified during the night, was the salient on this flank, with the rifle pits turning sharply southward to a refused position on the next high hills. The distance from Shy's Hill to Peach Orchard Hill is about two and a half miles as the crow flies, but the meandering Confederate line was about a mile longer. The new line was established about midnight, and the men worked the rest of the night feverishly digging out the best defenses possible.

In his official report, General Thomas, after summarizing the events of December 15, states simply: "The whole command bivouacked in line of battle during the night on the ground occupied at dark, whilst preparations were made to renew the battle at an early hour on the morrow."

Thomas does not say just what those preparations were. The net result, however, was that when the Federal forces got into alignment on the morning of the 16th, they had established a continuous line overlapping both Confederate flanks. Schofield was on the right in the position he had taken late in the previous afternoon; to his left was Smith, whose right was opposite the slope of Shy's Hill with his left between the Granny White and Franklin Pikes where it joined the right of Wood, who faced south across the Franklin Pike confronting Lee's position on the Confederate right. Steedman, on the morning of the 16th, after leaving a brigade in his rear to guard the Murfreesboro and Nolensville Pikes, pushed on out the Nolensville Road, eventually taking a position

The State Capitol, designed by William Strickland. The Federals turned it into a veritable fortress that Nashville residents mockingly called Fort Andrew Johnson. (National Archives)

between the pike and the left of Wood's corps. Here he stood until early in the afternoon, when he was instructed by General Thomas to form a junction with the troops of Wood's command and prepare to assault the Confederate right flank.

The morning of the 16th was featured by an exceptionally heavy and continuous bombardment of the whole Confederate line by the superior Federal artillery, particularly severe at Shy's Hill on their left and Peach Orchard Hill on their right. Shy's Hill was subjected to a continuous all-day crossfire from three directions. To reply to this bombardment Bate had only three batteries of smoothbore guns. Lee on the right wing also suffered throughout the day from the guns of Wood's and Steedman's corps, which kept up fire of such intensity that it was considered worthy of special mention in both Federal and Confederate reports.

During the morning and early afternoon the Federals made several feeler attacks on Lee's strong-hold on Peach Orchard Hill, but none was successful. Clayton, describing one of these assaults on his division by Steedman's colored troops, says that the attackers "suffered great slaughter. . . . It was with difficulty that the enthusiasm of the troops could be repressed so as to keep them from going over the works in pursuit of the enemy. Five colorbearers with their colors were shot down within a few steps of the works." Holtzclaw reports a "desperate charge" on his line at 10 a.m. and a "determined charge" at noon, both of which were repulsed. Of the losses suffered by the attacking Federals in their second charge, Holtzclaw says:

I have seen most of the battlefields of the west, but never saw dead men thicker than in front of my two right regiments, the great masses and disorder of the enemy enabling the left to rake them in flank, while the right, with a coolness unexampled, scarcely threw away a shot at their front. The enemy at last broke and fled in wild disorder.

Shortly before noon General Thomas in person joined Wood on the Franklin Pike, approved the disposition of his troops, and told him that he wished Wood and Steedman to cooperate in an effort to carry the Confederate works on Peach Orchard Hill. After conferring with Steedman and looking over the ground, Wood concluded that this could be done, in spite of the strength of the position. After careful preparation the assault, led by Post's brigade, was launched at about 3 p.m. The ardor of the attacking force was not dampened by a cold rain that had begun to fall about noon, and they moved forward with "a cloud of skirmishers" in front to draw the fire of the defending line and annoy its artillerists. Nevertheless the attack was repulsed and heavy casualties inflicted. Post was badly wounded and his brigade hurled back.

While this attack on the Confederate right was being repulsed, however, things were not going so well on Hood's left. Wilson's hard-driving cavalry brigades had gained the rear of the Confederate left and, fighting dismounted, were putting strong pressure on the defensive line that had been bent back into a fishhook extension of the left wing. Even without this pressure from the rear, the Confederate left was none too strong. Shy's Hill was a formidable looking elevation, but when General Thomas Benton Smith's brigade of Bate's division stretched out to fill the place vacated by Ector's brigade when that unit was withdrawn to be placed in reserve, it was discovered that the works established by Ector's men during the night were improperly located. By some engineering blunder, in the darkness and confusion of the preceding evening, the works were placed so far back from the actual brow of the hill as to give the defending force a limited view and range on the front. This fatal weakness was accentuated by the curvature of the hill and the falling away of the entrenched lines from the angle, making it impossible for the defenders to protect the front of the angle by flanking fire. Also, to make a bad matter worse, there was no abatis or other obstruction to impede the approach of an assaulting party. To add to his discomfiture, Bate was told by Cheatham that it would be necessary for him to stretch his thin line still farther to the left to occupy the position vacated by troops that had been withdrawn to protect the extreme left then in process of being turned by Wilson.

Wilson, who had quickly recognized the value of the position he occupied in rear of Hood's raveled-out left wing, set about capitalizing his advantage. Extending eastward from Schofield's right, Wilson's dismounted skirmishers presented a battle-line a mile and a half long, advancing diagonally across the Granny White Pike, inclining toward Nashville and completely in rear of Hood's left. By noon Wilson's 4,000 troopers (almost as many as Cheatham had left in his whole corps) had pressed their way slowly up the wooded hills in a curving line until they were facing Nashville, parallel with (and in rear of) Hood's main line. Here they were looking down on the backs of Bate's and Walthall's men—a lethal weapon aimed directly at Hood's point of greatest weakness.

Punished by the continuing artillery fire, faced in front and flank by two corps of infantry, and seeing the flanking cavalrymen pouring over the hills in their rear, Cheatham's men were in a desperate plight. The jaws of the Federal vise were closing relentlessly on them. In the words of one of the luckless privates caught in this trap: "The Yankee bullets and shells were coming from all directions, passing one another in the air."

Hood's left wing was doomed. After the battle there were rival Federal claims as to just which unit sparked the advance that closed the jaws of the nutcracker on Shy's Hill. Apparently, however, the movement of Smith's men from the south and Schofield's from the flank occurred simultaneously. Bate's report sums up the climactic action:

> About 4 p.m. the enemy with heavy force assaulted the line near the angle, and carried it at that point where Ector's brigade had built the light works; not, however, until the gallant and obstinate Colonel Shy and nearly half of his brave men had fallen, together with the largest part of the three right companies of the 37th Georgia, which regiment constituted my extreme left. When the breach was made, this command—the consolidated fragments of the 2d, 10th, 15th, 20th, 30th and 37th Tennessee Regiments—still contested the ground under Major Lucas; and finally, when overwhelming numbers pressed them back, only 65 of the command escaped. . . .The command was nearly annihilated.

Some of Bate's men did flee to safety, but most of the others who were not killed or wounded stayed resolutely in the line and continued firing until surrounded and captured. Among those taken on the hill were General Thomas Benton Smith and Major Jacob A. Lash, commander of Finley's brigade. General H. R. Jackson, commanding Bate's other brigade, was made a prisoner as he attempted to make his way back from the front line to where his horse had been left.

As the routed forces of Cheatham's corps fled in disorder through the fields and over the hills in their rear toward the Franklin Pike, the contagion of defeat

Thousands of civilians watched the battle on the first day. This photograph was made from the northwest corner of the Capitol grounds, where some of the men seemed more interested in the photographer than in the battle. (National Archives)

spread rapidly down the Confederate line—and the equally contagious exhilaration of victory flashed eastward along the Federal works. The triumphant Federals sweeping eastward from their conquest of Shy's Hill swooped down on Stewart's exposed left flank so swiftly and unexpectedly that he had no time to improvise a defense. In the words of one of the officers in French's division:

> Realizing their almost hopeless situation, they abandoned their line and organizations and retreated in the wildest disorder and confusion. Many remained in the line and surrendered. In a few minutes the organizations of the corps on the left and center of the army had wholly disappeared, and the routed army rushed over the range of hills to the Franklin Pike.

The men in Lee's corps, on the Confederate right, were taken completely by surprise by the collapse and rout of their left and center. They were flushed with the sense of victory, having just successfully repulsed Wood's vigorous assault on their position and, says Lee, were "in fine spirits and confident of success." Lee's corps, of course, was now forced to retreat also; but its withdrawal was in more orderly fashion, making it possible to establish a rearguard along the pike. One of the men in the ranks has left an account of how Lee himself, by personal example, contributed to the prevention of panic in his command:

At the time of the break General Lee was sitting, mounted, in the rear of Clayton's division. Over on the left we could see confusion, and a Federal line advancing from the rear and attacking Johnson's division on the left wing of Lee's corps. Everything else had apparently been swept before it. Clayton's division was divided by the Franklin Pike. General Lee rode across the pike, taking both stone fences, followed by one of his staff and two of his escort. He rode until he reached the rear of Stevenson's division of his corps, and rode right into the midst of fugitives and in the face of the enemy who by this time had reached the rear of Pettus' brigade. General Lee seized a stand of colors from a color bearer and carried it on horseback, appealing to the men to rally. . . .The effect was electrical. Men gathered in little knots of four or five, and he soon had around him three or four other stands of colors. The Federals, meeting this resistance, hesitated and halted. (It was late in the evening and misty.) The rally enabled Clayton's division to form a nucleus and establish a line of battle on one of the Overton Hills to the rear, crossing the Franklin Pike in the woods near Colonel Overton's house. Here he was joined by a few pieces of artillery and a little drummer boy who beat the long roll in perfect time, as Gibson's brigade came up and formed a rear guard.

Lee's corps, in event of disaster, had been entrusted with the responsibility of holding the Franklin Pike until the retreating Confederates could use it as an avenue of escape, and this function was performed most capably. As soon as it became obvious that the day was irretrievably lost and that the Confederates' only hope was to save what they could out of the wreckage of defeat, Lee moved with alacrity and efficiency. Informed by Hood that the Federals were already near Brentwood on the Franklin Pike, Lee quickly abandoned the line he had formed across the pike near the Overton house and hastened everything to the rear. At 10 p.m. a new rearguard line was established at Hollow Tree Gap, beyond Brentwood and seven miles north of Franklin. Wood's pursuit was not particularly energetic, and he bivouacked several miles short of the gap when night fell.

The last combat action of the battle was a spirited cavalry engagement on the Granny White Pike about dark. Chalmers, late in the afternoon, rallied his scattered troopers and moved across from the Hillsboro to the Granny White Pike. He formed a line in front of Brentwood to protect the wagons and ambulances collected there. About 4:30 p.m. he received Hood's frantic message to "Hold the Granny White Pike at all hazards," and the brigade was accordingly placed in position across that road, just north of the lane leading to Brentwood. A stout barricade of logs, brush, and fence rails was built.

In the unusual tactical situation now existing, Chalmers was in rear of Wilson, who was in rear of

Colonel John Overton's house, which served as General Hood's headquarters prior to the Battle of Nashville. Following the battle, the remnants of Hood's shattered army were chased all the way south to the Tennessee River. (Century magazine)

Cheatham's position. Following the collapse of the Confederate left, however, Wilson's victorious and elated troopers had remounted and now came plunging out the pike in pursuit of the fleeing Confederate infantry, through the gathering darkness and the downpour of freezing rain. Only temporarily disconcerted by the unexpected obstacle in their path, the blue-coated riders formed front into line and charged the barricade, thousands against hundreds. Although overwhelmingly outnumbered, the Confederates fought desperately, and what General Wilson later described as "one of the fiercest conflicts that ever took place in the Civil War" ensued.

The battle at the barricade and in the adjoining fields to which it overflowed finally degenerated into a veritable dogfight of individual, hand-to-hand combat, during which Colonel Rucker was wounded, disarmed, and captured. Wilson writes:

> It was a scene of pandemonium, in which flashing carbines, whistling bullets, bursting shells, and the imprecations of struggling men filled the air. . . . Every officer and man did his full duty in the headlong rush which finally drove Chalmers and his gallant horsemen from the field, in hopeless rout and confusion. They had stood their ground bravely, but were overborne at every turn and at every stand by the weight and fury of the Union onset.

Chalmers' last stand had been a desperate and costly one, but it had accomplished its purpose. What was left of his outfit withdrew unpursued to the Franklin Pike, and when the last of the retreating infantry and artillery had passed, the weary troopers camped on the pike with the rearguard for the night. Wilson, his men badly scattered and tired from a full day's fighting, gave orders just before midnight for

each command to bivouac where orders overtook it, and to take up the pursuit the following morning.

The next 10 days were a nightmare of nerve-wracking hardship and struggle for both armies. Alternately marching and fighting, worn down by battle fatigue and sheer physical exhaustion, they somehow managed to carry on an almost continuous running battle from Nashville to the Tennessee River. The weather was abominable—rain, sleet, and snow, with below-freezing temperatures. The wagons and guns quickly churned the roads into seemingly bottomless quagmires which froze into sharp-edged ruts during the cold nights. The heavy rains not only drenched the suffering soldiers but soon flooded the streams and made their passage a serious problem.

Hood's defeat-shocked army was on short rations—mostly parched corn, with an occasional feast of corn pone and fat bacon or perhaps a pilfered pig or pullet. A fortunate few had blankets or overcoats picked up on the battlefield, but most of them had only their threadbare uniforms to protect them from the icy rain that seemed to pierce to the very marrow of their bones. Many had no hats, but it was the scarcity of shoes that presented an especially acute problem. The number of men who were wholly or partially barefooted is almost unbelievable, and Hood's weary veterans left bloody footprints as they stumbled over the frozen ruts.

Thomas' men were well-shod, well-fed, and well-clothed, but they had their share of difficulties. And a steady downpour of freezing rain, with muddy roads and swollen streams, will slow down the progress of the most excellently equipped army.

General Forrest and his men, marching overland from Murfreesboro and driving several hundred head of hogs and cattle, were a welcome addition to Hood's army in Columbia, across Duck River, on the 19th. Here the command of the rearguard was formally assigned to Forrest, and his performance in this capacity was a masterpiece of doing much with little, holding the pursuing Federals at arm's length day after day. On a cold Christmas morning the advance of Hood's weary infantry reached the Tennessee River at Bainbridge, Alabama, near Florence, where the army crossed the river on a pontoon bridge and began the long march to Tupelo, Mississippi, their designated destination. Forrest and the rearguard made a stand at Pulaski on Christmas Day, and on the 26th maneuvered their pursuers into an ambush which, Forrest reported, resulted in their "complete rout" and the capture of one Federal gun. His report concludes: "The enemy was pursued for two miles, but showing no disposition to give battle my troops were ordered back."

That was the last real effort by the Federals to impede the Confederate retreat. Forrest and the last of the rearguard crossed the Tennessee on December 27, and on the 29th Thomas issued general orders declaring the pursuit at an end.

Hood's official report of the battle of Nashville, to General Beauregard, written at Tupelo on January 9, is a masterpiece of half-truths, imparting the news of a disaster in carefully sugarcoated terms. But, sugarcoat it as much as he chose, Hood in his heart knew the bitter truth. His invasion of Tennessee, the last flare-up of aggressive military action by the Southern Confederacy, had ended in disastrous failure. His vision of a victorious Confederate army advancing to the Ohio River was to remain a dream. The Confederate battle-flags would not be seen waving in Cincinnati or Chicago—a possibility Grant had pictured. The Battle of Nashville had decided that, and thereby decided the fate of the Confederate States of America.

It was at Nashville that Hood, wisely or not, had risked all on one cast of the military dice, and lost. For it was by the Battle of Nashville, as one of Thomas' biographers has so well said, that: "One of the two great armies of the Confederacy was eliminated from the final problem, and with the total overthrow of that army, the very cause which it had so long and so gallantly sustained was lost."

Casualties in the Battle

Casualties at Nashville appear to be somewhat light in view of the size and duration of the collision. However, the Federal troops lost many dead and wounded, particularly among colored recruits used in assaulting strong Confederate positions on Rains's Hill on December 15 and on Overton's Peach Orchard Hill on December 16 in diversionary attacks. Confederate reports of killed and wounded are missing, but they are generally believed to be light since they were protected by entrenched positions. The heaviest Confederate loss was in prisoners taken in the swift Federal advance and penetration that surrounded men who were attempting to hold positions to the last in the vicinity of Shy's Hill.

ESTIMATED LOSSES:

Confederate—Total Force 23,000
Engaged 15,000
Casualties (K&W) . . . . Unknown
Captured 4,000
Federal— Total Force 70,000
Engaged 43,000
Casualties (K&W) 3,000
Captured 100

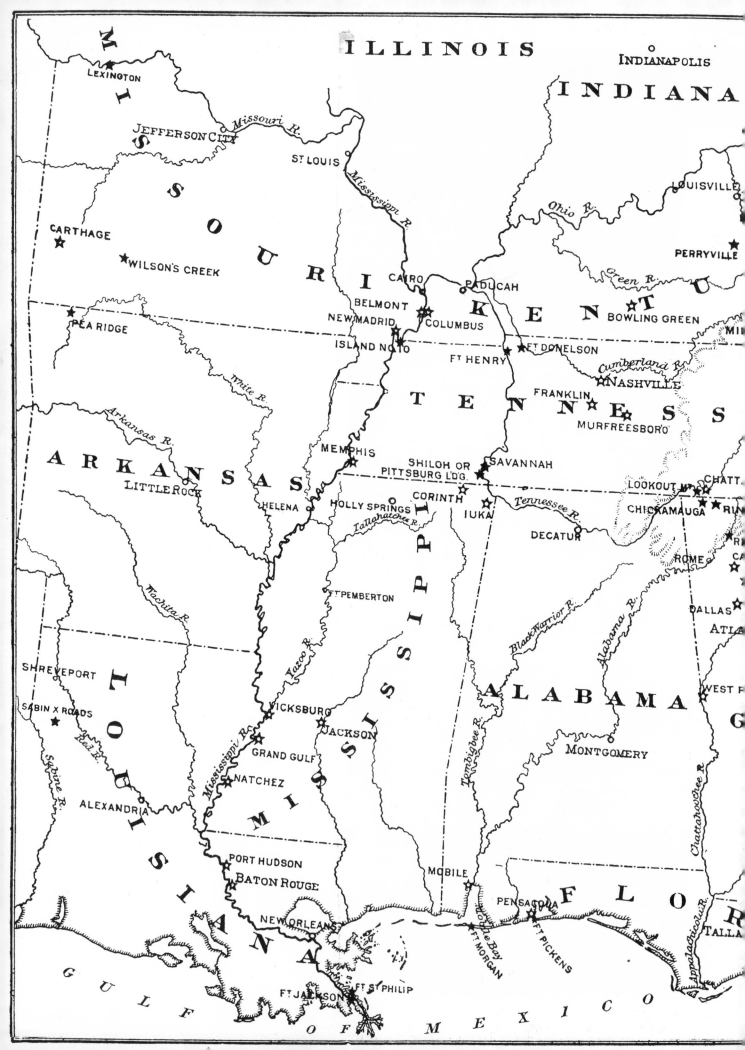